FAITHLESS TO FEARLESS

FAITHLESS TO FEARLESS

THE EVENT THAT CHANGED THE WORLD

DAVID ANDERSEN

Faithless to Fearless

© 2019 New Reformation Publications

All rights reserved. No part of this publication may be reproduced, distributed, or transmitted in any form or by any means, including photocopying, recording, or other electronic or mechanical methods, without the prior written permission of the publisher, except in the case of brief quotations embodied in critical reviews and certain other noncommercial uses permitted by copyright law. For permission requests, write to the publisher at the address below.

Unless otherwise indicated, all Scripture quotations are from The ESV® Bible (The Holy Bible, English Standard Version®), copyright © 2001 by Crossway, a publishing ministry of Good News Publishers. Used by permission. All rights reserved.

Scripture quotations taken from the New American Standard Bible® (NASB), Copyright © 1960, 1962, 1963, 1968, 1971, 1972, 1973, 1975, 1977, 1995 by The Lockman Foundation
Used by permission. www.Lockman.org

[Scripture quotations are from] Revised Standard Version of the Bible, copyright © 1946, 1952, and 1971 National Council of the Churches of Christ in the United States of America. Used by permission. All rights reserved worldwide.

Published by:
1517 Publishing
PO Box 54032
Irvine, CA 92619-4032

Publisher's Cataloging-In-Publication Data
(Prepared by The Donohue Group, Inc.)

Names: Andersen, David, author.
Title: Faithless to fearless : the event that changed the world / David Andersen.
Description: Irvine, CA : 1517 Publishing, [2019] | Includes bibliographical references.
Identifiers: ISBN 9781945978845 (paperback) | ISBN 9781945978852 (ebook)
Subjects: LCSH: Jesus Christ—Resurrection. | Apologetics.
Classification: LCC BT482 .A54 2019 (print) | LCC BT482 (ebook) | DDC 232.5—dc23

Printed in the United States of America

Cover Artist: Brenton Clarke Little

*To my children, Alex, Christian, Katie, Liz, Brayden, and Rowen.
May you know God only in the crucified and risen Jesus.
And to my incredible wife, Jeana, without whose encouragement this
book would never have been written.*

Contents

Foreword ix

Introduction 1

1. Where I'm Coming From 13
2. Natural Human Obstacles 27
3. Tethering Thinking to Reality 37
4. Textual Reliability of the New Testament 53
5. Kodak, Blockbuster, and Jesus' Disciples 63
6. The Crucifixion: Jesus as Messiah? 75
7. Jesus as *Kyrios* 91
8. Transmission of Jesus' Words and Deeds 111
9. How We Are Wired: Memories, Biology, and Social Influence 127
10. What Are the Gospels, and Who Stands behind Them? . . . 147
11. The Conversion of Paul the Persecutor 167

12. Alternative Theories and a Response 185

Conclusion 203

Postscript: On Happiness 209

Bibliography 229

Foreword

The existence of Christianity is a bit of a miracle. It should not have survived the ancient world. It enjoyed no power or privilege. Its leader was brutally tortured and executed on a cross. Many of his closest friends and followers were killed for their confession that Jesus was the Christ, the son of the living God.

And yet they persisted. Christianity grew by leaps and bounds in the face of tremendous adversity and extreme violence. Beheadings, crucifixions, flaying alive, being set ablaze, thrown before wild animals, and many more forms of torture and execution were used to deter the early Christian church. What motivated them to remain steadfast in the faith?

In short, it was Jesus. They were convinced that Jesus was God and Lord, Messiah and Savior, who had died for their sins and rose for their justification. But not only theirs. No. He had died for the sins of the whole world (1 John 2:2). This is the good news, the gospel.

Christians contend that this is not just good news though. It is news that is also true. The New Testament insists that the story of Jesus was not a cleverly devised myth (2 Pet. 1:16). The first generation of Christians were convinced of this and felt compelled to share it.

What made them so sure? What lead them from being hopeless after having their faith crushed when Jesus was crucified to fearless preachers and defenders of the faith? The evidence is clear; it was Jesus' resurrection.

This is the central theme of this book. Arguing from what is often called a minimal facts approach to apologetics, David Andersen leaves no stone unturned in this rigorous argument for Jesus' resurrection. Starting from commonly accepted historical facts and avoiding specious reasoning, Andersen explores the evidence and, on this basis alone, draws the only conclusion that accounts for all the data—that Jesus did, in fact, rise from the dead.

Had he not, Christianity would not exist. Or, at the very least, it should not exist. Paul said as much in 1 Corinthians 15:14-17:

> If Christ has not been raised, then our preaching is in vain and your faith is in vain. We are even found to be misrepresenting God, because we testified about God that he raised Christ, whom he did not raise if it is true that the dead are not raised. For if the dead are not raised, not even Christ has been raised. And if Christ has not been raised, your faith is futile and you are still in your sins.

It is for this reason that Jesus' resurrection is essential to the Christian faith and the apologetic task.

This book is an example of apologetics at its best. It is positive in its approach, careful in its method, and exhaustive in its consideration and explanation of the evidence. Regardless of its reader's disposition to religion in general or Christianity in particular the argument of *Faithless to Fearless* needs to be taken seriously by anyone interested in the veracity of the claim that Jesus rose from the dead.

Adam S. Francisco

Introduction

For a good portion of my adult life, I wanted to live as an academic teaching philosophy and theology—an aspiration I was able to realize while I earned a PhD and for some time after. As it became clear that my student loan debt could not be serviced by a professor's salary (at least not in the humanities), I made the choice to cofound and run a small business. Because of that, I have had the fortune of seeing things from completely different perspectives, which I hope will make this book somewhat unique. Based on my multidisciplinary background, my intention is to give an updated summary of the best New Testament research as well some of the fascinating conclusions suggested by other fields. I'm hoping the synthesis will be intriguing and provide a fresh perspective from someone whose interests have had to remain broad.

As a bit more context, my views over the last fifteen years have been shaped by research from many fields, including data from psychology, neurology, and the social sciences, particularly on how people make decisions. Among the more interesting findings that will be referenced is that we are only aware of our judgments and not the sophisticated processing that produces them.[1] That makes our judgments about issues and people, as well as the resulting decisions, a bit of a mystery since what goes on underneath still isn't well understood. Bottom line is that we are complicated, and our wiring reflects it, which neurological studies are showing in no uncertain terms. In today's business world, there is a growing need to have a basic grasp of findings like this, especially relating to the biases people exhibit

---

[1] Gerald Zaltman, *How Customers Think: Essential Insights into the Mind of the Market* (Boston: 2003), 67.

when faced with change. If you're a leader in an organization, you know firsthand how difficult change can be. It is as if we all have a default setting against new things.

While my interest in such matters has been business focused, it is clear they have broad implications for the case I'm making for Jesus' resurrection. Human nature being the common denominator, current data helps illuminate some of the perplexing facts surrounding the Easter event. Specifically applicable will be how human beings are wired, our natural reactions to change, and the ways we are influenced by culture and the groups we identify with. Though this research plays a more minor role in this book than that of New Testament studies, its effects won't go unnoticed. It will help to explain things like why the disciples reacted the way they did and why we'd expect them to remember certain details with sufficient accuracy to warrant serious consideration of their claims.

Saying all this, I recognize how emotionally charged this topic can be. People don't generally come to religious questions with a blank slate but have preexisting biases and beliefs about what is possible and what is not. Because of that, our task has added complexity in that prior beliefs can skew facts—what experts call confirmation bias. We will talk more about this as the book proceeds, but research shows that we have to be aware of the tendency if we hope to unpack what actually happened on Easter morning. Given its prevalence, let's preview some of the biggest pitfalls.

Pitfalls to Avoid

Thinking through possibilities is a natural human process. We are really good at creating multiple combinations of different scenarios and then running through them one by one. Academics are often charged, fairly or unfairly, with ivory tower thinking, which is a form of possibility thinking. In some cases, to be sure, it can be helpful. But taken too far, it can wreak havoc on decision making as it tends toward analysis paralysis and obsesses over improbable scenarios. If you struggle with anxiety, you know this one firsthand. It is something cognitive therapy tries to address by focusing the patient on what is realistic, not what is possible.

The penchant to think in possibilities is no less a problem in the business world. Today's managers struggle to base decisions on realistic outcomes and are often pulled down the rabbit hole of the possible. It is clearly a human problem. Remaining focused on probabilities is difficult, even for the most disciplined. It surfaces as a big enough problem to highlight, and Ray Dalio makes it a point in his best-selling management book, *Principles*:

> **Don't mistake possibilities for probabilities**. Anything is possible. It is the probabilities that matter. Everything must be weighed in terms of its likelihood and prioritized. People who can accurately sort probabilities from possibilities are generally strong at "practical thinking"; they're the opposite of the "philosopher" types who tend to get lost in the clouds of possibilities.[2]

We all recognize that anything is possible, but making decisions in the real world, which is often messy, requires the distinction between possibilities and probabilities. Dalio's point is that decisions are hampered if a person is ruled by what is possible. It is too easy to get caught in the possibility rut, and anyone who's spent much time in an organization knows how debilitating the tendency can be.

Beyond the possibility trap, Dalio highlights three other pitfalls that merit attention. The first is our ego, which always wants the last word and defends its ideas to the death. Ego is our subliminal defense mechanism that makes it difficult to accept mistakes and weaknesses.[3] Because it operates under the covers, we are unaware of its tendency to oversimplify and react instinctively. Second, we all have blind spots that prevent us from seeing things accurately. Each of us views things in our own way, and oftentimes we can't see important facts that are obvious to others. Any manager can attest to this. If you're a detailed person, it is likely you have a blind spot with the big picture and vice versa. Complicating the matter, we don't like to see ourselves as having blind spots. They betray weaknesses, and we shy away from admitting personal flaws. The trouble is that

---

[2] Ray Dalio, *Principles* (New York: 2017), 254.
[3] Dalio, *Principles*, 183–87, 236.

they create closed-mindedness and presumption, both of which come at a high cost. The third pitfall is harmful emotions, which isn't to denigrate emotions; after all, who'd want to live in a world without them? The fact is they can be good or bad. When they are bad, however, they can subvert the rational thinking process and cause us to skew our judgments in the wrong direction, resulting in poor decisions.

In pointing these out, Dalio certainly isn't the only one to have sounded the alarm; but unlike others, he tackles them within the messy context of the real world, where making good decisions with imperfect information is important. Having built one of the largest investment management firms, he brings a fresh perspective to how natural human weaknesses interact in the decision-making process. And for the most part, his conclusions mesh with research streaming in from neuroscience. Because good decisions are the end game, Dalio emphasizes that you need to acquire enough information about a subject that what you know paints a "true and rich picture of the realities that will affect your decision."[4] That means sifting and triangulating what we think we already know against other well-known facts.

Why does it matter here? Because I can't think of a more relevant subject to review biases and unwarranted presuppositions than the purported resurrection of Jesus. Due to its implications for the idea of God and the value of life, it is as emotionally charged as any subject gets. As we proceed, it is essential to keep our biases in check and follow the facts where they lead, no matter what opinion one has over whether it is possible or not for dead men to rise again. The question will be, does the evidence warrant the conclusion that Jesus rose from the dead? I believe it does, but keeping our judgments free of bias will be vital as we look at the data.

In her best-selling book, *Thinking in Bets*, Annie Duke contends that our decisions are always bets based on probability. Dalio makes the same point.[5] We routinely decide among alternatives and assess the likelihood of different outcomes. Every decision commits

---

[4] Dalio, *Principles*, 236.

[5] Dalio, *Principles*, 253.

us to a different course of action and thereby involves trade-offs, meaning that each eliminates taking action on some alternative. Not placing a bet is itself a bet. As the saying goes, if you don't choose, someone or something will choose for you. In most life decisions, we are betting against future versions of ourselves. Since bets reflect our beliefs about the world, the trick is to become a better "belief calibrator," using experience and information to update our beliefs to more accurately represent the world. "The more accurate our beliefs, the better the foundation of the bets we make."[6]

Coming down on the side of probability isn't easy, even for the most seasoned. There is a reason Dalio and Duke have to spell it out even after hundreds of management books have been produced in the last two centuries. Faulty thinking resulting from bias, emotion, and blind spots make reasoning around the probabilities especially difficult. Following the crowd and preferring answers that confirm previous biases is human. But as we look at the evidence surrounding the disciples' claim to have seen the risen Jesus, it will be important to consider the theory with the highest probabilities.

Moreover, because there are a plethora of counter-theories to Jesus' resurrection, we need to keep in mind that possibilities are just that, but no more. It is possible that aliens from Mars deceived the disciples into thinking Jesus had been raised (of course, no one seriously believes this), but the probabilities are stacked heavily against such a notion. The alternative theories we will discuss at the end of the book are possible explanations for the appearances. But they're not the most probable ones and fail to account for other generally well-attested facts. I'll argue that the probabilities heavily favor Jesus' physical resurrection from the dead, and because of that, and despite any preexisting biases to the contrary, one makes a better bet accepting it as the best explanation for the appearances.

Before setting our course, a comment is warranted about my intended audience. Even though you'll encounter some of the best academic thinking available, I'm not writing to the academic. I'm writing rather to the man in the arena (as Theodore Roosevelt might

---

[6] Annie Duke, *Thinking in Bets: Making Smarter Decisions When You Don't Have All the Facts* (New York: 2018), 44, 48.

say), to the person "whose face is marred by dust and sweat and blood."[7] I'm writing to those in the trenches, to those who (as Brené Brown might say) muster the courage to be vulnerable and open to a new perspective—to those who are curious about whether such a life-altering event could have really occurred in human history. In the end, it isn't the critic who counts. We each have to make the best judgment we can about the disciples' claim to have seen the risen Jesus, but make it we do, even if we don't.

What I'll Argue

This book's argument is simple: Jesus' physical resurrection from the dead best accounts for the evidence virtually every scholar accepts, no matter what their religious conviction. As we will see shortly, there are a core group of universally accepted facts that require some sort of historical explanation. I'll argue that the claim of the disciples and Paul to have seen the risen Jesus has greater explanatory power than the alternative naturalistic theories we will examine. Very briefly, here is what you'll see in the pages that follow.

Having been unable to extricate themselves from their cultural ideas of who Israel's Messiah was supposed to be, Jesus' disciples were lost and dejected after his sudden and unexpected crucifixion. Fearing for their lives, they fled at Jesus' arrest and remained hidden, unable to process the contradiction between their expectations and what actually occurred. Jesus had been laid in a tomb, which meant they had been mistaken in believing he was Israel's long-awaited deliverer.

On the road to Emmaus, Cleopas (one of the disciples) was representative of the group as he explained to the stranger that they had hoped Jesus was the one to deliver Israel—a hope extinguished now that he'd been executed as a state criminal and Messianic pretender. Expectations built from a lifetime of Jewish upbringing had set the stage for a Messiah who'd come with sword in hand, deliver Israel from Roman pagan oppression, and initiate a new sociopolitical order

---

[7] Theodore Roosevelt's "Citizen in a Republic" speech at the Sorbonne in Paris, April 23, 1910.

in which Jews would be freed to worship in the Jerusalem temple. As Jesus rode triumphantly into Jerusalem on Palm Sunday not long before his arrest, this was the belief that was sustaining the cheering crowd. All of it was despite what Jesus plainly told them throughout his ministry about his impending death and resurrection.

Nevertheless, the disciples persisted in their long-held beliefs in a triumphant political Messiah, which explains why they fled in fear at Jesus' arrest and abandoned him at his time of need. All but Peter, that is—and only until he denied Jesus by swearing an oath that he did not know the man. The women alone remained, along with John. As the women approached the tomb to anoint Jesus' body according to custom, they were stunned to see the stone already rolled away. After Jesus' appearance to the women, they reported what they had seen to the disciples. No doubt skeptical of a woman's testimony, a few of them went to see for themselves. One by one and in group settings, the disciples claimed to have had encounters with the risen Jesus and proclaimed their message in Jerusalem, the very city where Jesus had been crucified a short time before.

One to three years later, Saul of Tarsus (Paul)—a highly trained Pharisee—was commissioned by Jewish authorities to arrest any Christian he could and was complicit in the death of Stephen (the first Christian martyr) and probably others. Breathing threats of persecution, he rode to Damascus to capture Christians who fled from Jerusalem and was stopped in his tracks by what he described as an encounter with the risen Jesus—the very one he was persecuting. In the blink of an eye, this formidable persecutor of Christianity became its most famous defender and suffered innumerable punishments and eventual death for his about-face.

That neither the disciples nor Paul expected to see a risen Jesus is well attested. Also well attested is that no one in this period would have made the connection between crucifixion and Messiah, Messiah and resurrection before the end of time, and Messiah and *kyrios* (Israel's God, YHWH). Yet, all of them spontaneously exploded like a big bang among the earliest Christians. From an historical standpoint, it is perplexing since there is nothing that served as the evolutionary starting point for any one of these, let alone all of them combined and at the same time. I'll argue that none of the naturalistic counter-theories do justice to the general weight of the evidence and that Jesus' physical resurrection from the dead best explains the data. It alone fits the facts like a key does a lock.

What to Expect

To avoid controversial assumptions, I'm going to follow the minimal facts approach of Gary Habermas—and expanded by Michael Licona—which takes bedrock facts accepted by virtually every scholar and argues that the resurrection of Jesus best accounts for the Easter claims. Deserving emphasis is that these core facts are accepted across the board by atheist, agnostic, and Christian scholars, so we can't be charged with using questionable data.

Briefly, they're as follows: (1) Jesus died by crucifixion and his body was buried.[8] After his execution, the disciples were crestfallen because they had expected him to redeem Israel, and they fled in fear. (2) Shortly afterward, the disciples had experiences they believed were appearances of the risen Jesus, and they occurred in private and communal settings over an extended period of time. Convinced that Jesus was alive, they were transformed from being hopeless and faithless to fearless proclaimers of Jesus' resurrection, even to the point of martyrdom. Not only this, but they preached the message in Jerusalem, the very city where Jesus had been crucified and buried only a short time before. (3) One to three years later, Saul of Tarsus (Paul) claimed to have had an encounter with the risen Jesus on the road to Damascus. Having been commissioned by the Jews to arrest Christians, Paul was a persecutor of early believers and had been complicit in the stoning of Stephen (and probably others). Breathing threats against Christians, he rode into Damascus and was stopped in his tracks by what he described as a sudden encounter with the risen Jesus. (4) The belief in Jesus' resurrection is attested in the earliest example of a Christian creed in 1 Corinthians 15:3–8 (and elsewhere). Scholars agree that it is to be dated no later than just a few

---

[8] Gary R. Habermas, "Jesus' Resurrection and Contemporary Criticism: An Apologetic," *Criswell Theological Review*, Part 1, 4/1 (Fall 1989). Available online at http://www.garyhabermas.com/articles/criswell_theol_review/1989-fall_jesusresandcontempcrit_pt1.htm, p. 2.

years after the crucifixion, meaning that belief in Jesus' resurrection erupted suddenly with a big bang. Further, Jesus' resurrection was *the* central Christian message from the beginning. (5) In addition to these, I'm including the sudden eruption of the early belief that Jesus is fully divine—that he is actually YHWH, Israel's God. I do so because there is no evidence of any evolutionary development of the idea, and it appears to have originated alongside belief in Jesus' resurrection.

To reiterate, these are considered bedrock facts that virtually every scholar recognizes, and they're beyond reasonable doubt. Any theory explaining the appearances, atheist or Christian, must account for them or it does not meet the prerequisites of a good theory. I'll argue that the physical resurrection of Jesus best accounts for both the individual and combined facts better than rival theories. More specifically, I'll argue that in light of the core facts, it is highly probable Jesus rose from the dead, appeared to his disciples, and then appeared to Paul the persecutor on the road to Damascus.

To do so, the chapters will proceed as follows. So that my approach is completely transparent, the first chapter will highlight my Mormon upbringing, with chapters 2 and 3 discussing how we come to know things and how theories contribute to our judgments. I have included chapter 1 to make it clear where I'm coming from. Too often writers veil their assumptions under the guise of conclusions based on hard data. To avoid that I'll discuss briefly what drove me to adopt the approach I'm using and why I focus on the questions I do. A word of caution is in order, though. Because misaligned expectations are the mother of disappointment, I should point out that this isn't a book about me or my transformation from Mormon to Christian. Anyone hoping to read about Mormon history and how it compares to Christianity will be disappointed. My aim is rather simple: to provide an updated case for the historicity of Jesus' resurrection in light of a broad range of recent research—including contributions from New Testament scholarship and research from psychology, neurology, and the social sciences.

How we come to know things and the process we use to make judgments will consume chapters 2 and 3. How we know things and how we *think* we know things are two different things. I'll point out that while truth can be known, including the cause of the appearances, our theories have to be sifted and checked against other things we know to be true. Human beings have an automatic default for jumping to conclusions from sparse data, from which we create theories (or narratives) in the blink of an eye and then use them to make judgments about causes and effects. Because this is hard-wired in the human brain, we will look at what attributes a good theory should have. Serving as a baseline, we will be in a position to examine the merits of the case for Jesus' resurrection.

One of the questions I'll begin with that concerned me as a Mormon was whether the New Testament had been corrupted in its long transmission process. In other words, since it was copied by hand over many centuries, has it been completely corrupted through accidental and willful scribal errors? It is a legitimate question, because if the text we have bears little or no relation to the original, then any case for Jesus' resurrection might be on shaky ground. Chapter 4 will examine this important question. The rest of the book will deal with the question of Christianity's origins. Chapter 5 will start by asking what the disciples believed about Jesus during his ministry and how they took his sudden crucifixion. Because the evidence shows that they weren't expecting his resurrection, their Easter claims are perplexing. The fact that Jesus was crucified under Roman law as a criminal and Messianic pretender makes it even more confusing. We will see in chapter 6 that no one in this period would have connected crucifixion with Israel's long-awaited Messiah (or deliverer). Neither, as we will see in chapter 7, would anyone have connected Israel's God, YHWH, with a crucified man. This is precisely what the evidence suggests as the early believers confessed Jesus as *kyrios*, or YHWH himself. To state it succinctly, no one in this period would have made the connection between crucifixion and Messiah, Messiah and resurrection before the end of time, and Messiah and *kyrios*—yet this belief spontaneously exploded like a big bang among the earliest believers.

Next, since the earliest Christian writings start to appear in the 50s (AD), some twenty years after Jesus' crucifixion, chapter 8 will ask how traditions about Jesus were transmitted until they were fixed in written form. We will look at how oral tradition—meaning important information passed down from mouth to mouth—was handled in the first century and how accurately the first Christians preserved it. Because memory obviously plays a central role in the process, chapter 9 will deal with memory accuracy. We will interact with research on what things create long-lasting and accurate memories and then see if they can be seen in the Jesus tradition. Chapter 10 will then cover the important issue of eyewitness testimony. Do we see traces of it in the New Testament, and if so, where and how do we know? Paul's unlikely conversion to the Christian movement will conclude our study in chapter 11. With the evidence in mind, chapter 12 will consider naturalistic counter-theories to Jesus' resurrection. Finally, interacting with the flood of recent research on the topic, the book will end with a postscript on human happiness.

CHAPTER 1

Where I'm Coming From

Psychologists tell us that our family of origin, meaning the family we are born and raised in, plays an enormous role in who we become. While we might think our upbringing concerns mainly our childhood, it is becoming more evident that its impact isn't restricted to childhood, but it also partly determines how we presently see ourselves, others, and the world. The views we develop in childhood, some say already by age four or five, stay with us throughout life. Though at some point most of us leave our families and spread our wings, we rarely leave them emotionally.[1] As Ronald Richardson puts it, "Even if you put an ocean between you and your family of origin... you will continue to re-enact the dynamics of your original family in any new family you establish."[2] This is true despite the fact that so many of us swear we won't act like our parents or siblings.

Experts say it is hard to gain emotional independence from our family environment and then not repeat or react against it as adults. The idea of reacting seems counterintuitive because most of us assume that family effects show up in what we do like about our family, not in what we don't. But research tells us that being the opposite is itself conditioned by our family. There are all sorts of ways we do this, including showing how our parents failed, being emotionally

---

[1] Roberta M. Gilbert, *The Eight Concepts of Bowen Theory: A New Way of Thinking About The Individual and the Group* (Lake Frederick, VA: 2004), 51–52.

[2] Ronald W. Richardson, *Family Ties That Bind: A Self-Help Guide to Change Through Family of Origin Therapy* (Vancouver, BC: 2002), 1–2.

distant, or simply taking opposite positions. But no matter what, they all bear testimony to the powerful hold our families retain on our emotional and intellectual lives.

An example will help. Roberta Gilbert reports that anxiety is often placed onto the child by parents. "That worried focus, or 'projection' of anxiety is how anxiety gets off-loaded to offspring. If one worries excessively about one's child . . . one transmits—or projects—that anxiety directly onto the child."[3] This family projection process is normally automatic and completely beyond the parent's awareness and stretches back to their own connectedness to previous generations. They too received parental anxiety, as did their parents before them. Blame would be misplaced because the family projection process extends too far back for any one person to be responsible. To a greater or lesser extent, this stands true for every family, although how children deal with the fusion to parents differs based on their level of differentiation from them. If you think about your own family, it is likely that some siblings achieved more independence from the family unit than others. The bottom line is that our families retain a huge influence on who we are now and how we behave, including even how we see the world (whether we repeat or react).

Bestselling author and research professor Brené Brown gives us a vivid picture of this as she describes being raised in a "dry emotional well."[4] In her family, feelings and vulnerability weren't discussed. Emotions don't fix problems, it was thought; they make things worse. Because of that, she did not learn about emotions until her teens when her mother started going to therapy. Relevant here is her realization that if you were raised in an environment where emotion was downplayed and seen as weakness, then exploring feelings later in life is a challenge. Much of the power behind her books is due to how she has interacted with and embraced her past.

While perhaps the rest us don't deal with exactly the same issues, we are all in the same boat of having to sort through our

---

[3] Gilbert, *Eight Concepts*, 58, 62.

[4] Brené Brown, *Rising Strong: How the Ability to Reset Transforms the Way We Live, Love, Parent, and Lead* (New York: 2017), 57, 69.

own family of origin. I'm certainly no exception. To the extent that mine has influenced how I'm approaching core religious beliefs, it is important to state where I came from and uncover some of my underlying assumptions. Although I have been thinking about these issues for over thirty-five years, my family of origin and the culture I grew up in maintains an influence on both the questions I have asked and the conclusions I have drawn. So rather than leaving them as half-acknowledged assumptions, I'd rather state overtly what led me to ask the questions in this book.

Particularly prominent will be the contrast I make between subjective experience and the role of objective reality. Yet it is a contrast that would not make as much sense if I did not relate it to my religious upbringing. It also partially explains my reaction to perfectionism, which I was immersed in as far back as I can remember. In many ways, I'm still confined by how I was raised, and like so many others I still viscerally react against particular things negatively associated with my upbringing.

In *Rising Strong*, Brown persuasively argues that, without wholeheartedly integrating who we are with all of our baggage, we end up fractured, unable to understand the stories we carry, and alienated from ourselves.[5] This is an attempt to provide a wholehearted account of my story that I hope can in some way resonate with yours.

Mormon Heritage

I was fortunate enough to be born into a loving home, and my mother and father genuinely gave everything for their six children. My childhood years were happy, and my memories are full of those things that make a stable home. My mother was very affectionate, and we all knew how much we were loved. Her laugh was contagious, and even now I hear old neighbors talk about how much they miss her. While my dad was more reserved, we never doubted his love. Everything he worked so hard for was dedicated to the family. And his love for my mother was obvious.

---

[5] Brown, *Rising Strong*, 41–43.

In many ways it was a charmed home. Holidays were abuzz with activity, and Christmases still stand out as my most hallowed memories. That line from the movie *A Christmas Story*—that the entire kid year revolves around Christmas—described me exactly. Even now I have strong emotions around my reminiscences. It is surprising just how powerful family of origin is. In so many ways, my childhood stands out as blessed, and I'll be forever grateful for the huge role my parents and family played.

Yet life is more complicated than sentimental childhood memories. Religiously I did not fare as well. I was born and raised in a staunch Mormon family in Salt Lake City. My family had deep ties to the LDS community, and we were in church every Sunday and also attended activities throughout the week. I was raised with a certainty that Mormonism was true and everything else false. From a very young age, I sat through Sunday school classes that constantly reinforced the moralism that marks Mormon culture.

Lessons abounded in how to be a faithful churchgoer, child, father, mother, and the like. In Sunday school classes we used to regularly see videos that were made by the church on various topics, and one that is still burned in my memory was about a father manning a train switch station. As I remember it, the scene showed happy families approaching the little station when suddenly the man in charge of the switching the tracks noticed his son, who was running in his direction in the distance, but on the very track the train was on. Immediately we all knew what his choices were: run out to save his son, leaving his post and letting the people on the track perish, or let his son perish and save the families on the train. In a heartwrenching scene, he chooses the latter. The film is illustrative of what I was taught throughout my childhood: that our actions and works determine our standing before humanity, the church, and God himself. It was all on us and how we choose to live. I remember how excited I was when I received my Choose The Right (CTR) ring, a visible reminder and pledge given to young Mormons that further drives home the idea that actions determine worth. For impressionable children, such things leave their marks.

Constant progress to greater and greater perfection was at the core of our religious beliefs, and my sense of self-worth was inextricably tied to it. It is why we went to church, why we participated in activities throughout the week, and why we were so connected to Mormon culture and practice. As early as I can remember, I had the belief that someday I was supposed to attain perfection and be a god myself, ruling over my own world just as God does this one. But to get there, to be connected with my own family, I had to keep up the works, and my mind had to be clean.

Regular appointments with a Mormon bishop were part of my life, as it was for every other Mormon. We were asked very pointed questions about whether we masturbated, whether we'd fornicated with the opposite sex (both of which were considered wrong), and generally if we were living the "gospel principles"—which in reality were a series of works and religious regulations—laid out by the Mormon leaders. We were expected to attend every Sunday worship meeting, participate in all the weekly activities, and even be in Boy Scouts (which is why I was an Eagle scout). Those who did not fulfill their duties were looked down upon and even disciplined by church leadership.

Unpacking what that did to me as a child reveals a boy with intense religious beliefs, but also a boy with an equally intense religious anxiety that was perhaps unusual for someone of my young age. To this day, I vividly remember sitting on the floor of our bathroom in tears because I knew that, despite the perfectionism I was working toward, I was far from perfect and deeply feared being separated from my family in the next life. I was only seven or eight at the time, but even then I knew I was broken, especially against the standards of my religion.

Even so, I mustered on, pushing my anxiety to the back burner as I attempted to grow in my beliefs. We were always taught that religious truth is known by a "burning in the bosom," that as we read the Mormon scriptures, we'd feel the spirit's presence testifying directly of its truth. The justifications for our beliefs were at heart subjective and completely dependent on the testimony we developed from within. No external verification was possible or necessary because the spirit would make the truth known directly within our hearts, which would be self-authenticating and undeniable. These testimonies were the linchpin of our faith, and an entire church meeting every month was devoted to random members standing up to "bear their testimonies." By all measures, as a young man I was growing strong in my own testimony and was zealous for Mormon traditions. More than most people my age, I engaged friends who weren't members in discussions about my faith, zealously trying to convert them. As far back as I can remember, my goal was to go on a mission for the church at age nineteen.

When I was sixteen, I got a job at a local ice cream store and met someone who became a best friend. He got me interested in studying martial arts, and I started under the direction of his then stepdad. Concurrently, I began reading as much as I could on the Eastern mysticism often associated with martial arts, as well as works in the occult. I became fascinated with the unseen forces of witchcraft and the thought of being able to tap into powers outside normal experience. Interestingly, this wasn't out of order with many Mormons, as they were constantly circulating stories of seeing dead relatives and other so-called miraculous events that bolstered their faith in the church. My mind was always on the topic, absorbed with the belief that I could progress in my knowledge and manipulation of occultic practices—until it all came crashing down on me.

At the time my bedroom was downstairs, and my window was adjacent to the front porch, which always seemed to bring light in from the outside, especially since my drapes were thin. I woke up one night, as I often did (and still do because of a small bladder), to see a black form standing between my window and my bed. Terror swept over me, and I could not move. Then I felt my bed (which was a single waterbed) depress as though someone put the weight of their knee on it to climb in. I felt as though something dark was enveloping me, and in my fear all I could think about was what my martial arts instructor used to tell me, to "shrink to my center." While that advice was useful when sparring (making yourself a smaller target), it was a ridiculous thought given the circumstance, but it is what popped into my mind. The next thing I remember was waking up a little later and having to turn the light on out of fear of what had just happened. I left the light on at night for at least the next two weeks. Looking back now, there was irony in my martial arts teacher's advice, which was to read a psalm every night before going to bed. We were both Mormons, but the Bible was never really the cornerstone of a Mormon's faith so the advice seemed strange. Needless to say, I was terrified for a long time.

Challenge to My Faith

At no point during this period did I question my Mormon faith. I knew a lot of churchgoers who studied Eastern mysticism and occultic works, so it wasn't anything that challenged my faith. So much of Mormon thinking is mystical anyway that it wasn't a stretch. But things changed when I started studying kung fu under an instructor who was a Christian. Through many conversations he challenged me to take an honest look at the history of Mormonism, as well as the evidence for the resurrection of Jesus and the transmissional accuracy of the New Testament documents.

Excruciating does not begin to express how I felt as I read about the Mormon founders and how strange their beliefs really were. Discovering that Joseph Smith's family was known for their tall tales and how deceptive official Mormon records are about important historical details threw me into a tailspin. My entire life had been predicated on the truth of Mormon claims, one of which was that if Mormonism isn't right then nothing is. It left me feeling alone, empty, and scared. But the evidence was all there. Facts are stubborn things. Worse, my entire religious upbringing was based on a completely unverifiable, subjective experience that could not be backed up by any evidence. I can't overstate the conflict. It was like waking up one day and finding out that your father, a longtime faithful public servant and a high government official, was actually a spy for a hostile foreign government—and that his treasonous acts resulted in the murder of US citizens. Sounds dramatic, I know, but from a spiritual perspective, it is not far from the truth.

For a long time, I kept my questioning to myself. But when it finally came out, I discovered just how alone a person can be in his own home. My parents were devastated, and we spent countless evenings arguing until the wee hours of the morning. Disappointment in my choice pervaded their comments from then on. Our relationship never recovered to its original state. I think my mom took it the hardest, though I know my dad struggled as well. On my eighth birthday, my mom took me out to lunch (as she did on every birthday) and said that before she was pregnant with me, she'd heard a voice telling her to have another child (these experiences are common among Mormons). She really believed I was born to be an important person in the Mormon church, so my exit from the faith left her despondent. Although I know she loved me, I also know that she died feeling bitter disappointment in my decision. From her perspective, not only did I leave the one true religion, but I also did the unthinkable and enrolled in a traditional Christian university for theological studies.

To understand why this was so hard for my parents, one has to look at what the Mormon prophets, and particularly Joseph Smith, said about traditional Christianity. To them it was especially misguided, with the crucifix being the symbolic height of error because of its focus on the death of Jesus. The concept of salvation by grace and the doctrine of the Trinity were vigorously rejected. On top of that was the fact that many Mormons believed that the people relegated to outer darkness (their version of hell) are especially those who were once Mormon and then rejected it.

Throughout my college years, my dad wrote letters to me arguing for the Mormon faith and why traditional Christianity was wrong. Of course, he believed he was doing the right thing and was motivated by love and concern. But still, it was hard. And though I know he loved me, our relationship was always strained.

Most Pivotal Years

It wasn't long after I enrolled at Concordia University Irvine that I met Dr. Rod Rosenbladt. His influence would prove immense. Because of my upbringing in Mormonism and its focus on spiritual and emotional experience over the rational, my mind struggled with exactly how to understand the relationship between reason and faith (which for perhaps the majority of religious people is based on pure emotion). It was providential that I landed at a college with professors who had a healthy understanding of and appreciation for science and the history of philosophy.

Though my major was biblical languages (Hebrew and Greek), my minor was philosophy, and I was privileged to do upper division seminars on the great works, theology, and the philosophy of science. I threw myself into my studies. Looking back, I know my dad was always in the back of my mind. I felt that to defend the rationality of my religious switch, I had to learn the biblical languages and understand the development of early Christian thought. Growing up I was taught that the Bible had been completely corrupted through thousands of years of scribal errors. Joseph Smith once said that hardly a sentence had survived in its original form. It was hammered in my head from the earliest days from teachers who illustrated it with the telephone game. After arranging us in a semicircle, the teacher would whisper something in the first person's ear and they had to pass it along to the rest of us through a chain of people. By the end—and this was their rather superficial demonstration of the Bible's untrustworthiness—the words had changed from the first person to the last. Therefore, the Bible must have likewise changed, setting up the need for new Mormon scriptures and prophets.

Because my dad's beliefs hinged on the supposed untrustworthiness of the Bible (which Mormonism takes as a given), I felt I had to do a deep dive into the transmission of the New Testament to understand what the issues really were. Being able to read the original languages myself and understanding the textual transmission of the ancient texts became extremely important. So I learned to read ancient Koine and classical Greek as well as ancient Hebrew. Not exactly marketable skills, but I felt the need to be educated on these critical details.

While the original languages were my academic major, my real love turned out to be philosophy, theology, and the philosophy of science. The reason was that these subjects started to address my longtime struggles over the relationship of reason and faith, or of the intellect and emotional and spiritual experience. I'd already learned to distrust subjective experience, but I also knew, even in my early Christian days, that many Christians relied heavily on subjective experience. So I struggled with how to make sense of it all in my early Christian life.

As a preview of the next chapter, it turns out that my struggle had to be redefined. The opposite of faith shouldn't be reason or intellect, because our reason as much as our emotions tend to be flawed. What often seems like common sense and intuitive truth isn't. Over the past three hundred years, science has systematically dismantled many of our common-sense beliefs. So if my time at Concordia taught me anything, it is that human reason, as much as human emotion and so-called spiritual illumination, all need to be restrained. As Francis

Bacon said long ago, our imagination shouldn't be given wings for flight but harnessed with lead weights to keep it grounded firmly in the real world. Recent research has amassed a tremendous amount of data indicating that our minds, our emotions, and our spiritual feelings all tend to take flight without any firm grounding in reality.

It has always interested me that people take more time to examine financial investments than they do religious beliefs. Somehow it is important to look at the brutal truths when money is on the line, but similar care isn't taken for the soul. Can you imagine someone making an investment purely on emotion? Surely this does happen, but luckily there is a natural corrective against irrational behavior when the market eats the investment. Learning comes from these types of failures. Yet when dealing with religious beliefs, emotions seem to rule the day. My time in Irvine gave me a healthy skepticism of what people feel or believe they know from otherworldly "spiritual" or emotional experience. And it is a skepticism, partially in response to my childhood religion, that drives the questions in this book.

Marks of the Past

In *The Lord of the Rings*, the main character, Frodo (a hobbit and the least of creatures), has the ominous task of delivering a ring forged by the Dark Lord Sauron back to the pits of Mount Doom to save Middle Earth from destruction. On his thirteen-month journey, Frodo and his companions encounter unbelievable odds and hardship, narrowly escaping death on countless occasions. It becomes clear in the three-part series that Frodo will forever bear the scars of having to carry the ring, with all its dark powers, back to where it was forged and the only place it can be destroyed. There is a powerful scene in *The Return of the King* (the last of the series), where Frodo realizes he has been forever changed and that he can never return to innocence. As the scene unfolds, Frodo is alone in his home walking through his narrow hallway, and we hear him narrate, "How do you pick up the threads of an old life? How do you go on, when in your heart you begin to understand, there is no going back? There are some things that time cannot mend, some hurts that go too deep, that have taken hold."

In her research about how we fall and rise again, Brené Brown, though not referring to this scene, echoes some of Frodo's sentiments. She says that though we often wish we could go back in time to before the hard things came our way, we can't, and that we need to move forward with those ugly stories and wholeheartedly integrate them into who we now are.[6] I believe she is right, and that like Frodo, we are all forever changed by our own stories, by our struggles and pain. Some experiences can't be mended, and rarely can we go back to our naive selves. While our struggles may not be as dramatic as fighting the Dark Lord Sauron, to us they're still as real. We can't dismiss them as though they didn't happen or as if they don't have a huge impact on who we are. To move forward we need to own our stories, integrating them fully into who we are and how we think. With our family of origin, they also matter and can't be ignored.

All of us come with a completely unique set of experiences, good and bad, that make us the complex people we have become. And like most people, my stories shaped me, and I have realized that in many ways I can't go back, that there are some things that go too deep and can't be reversed. My spiritual struggles have left their mark. They've changed how I think about everything, and not just about religion.

Not the least of which is that my religious struggles have changed my attitude about human emotion and reason. I was raised believing I could trust my feelings and thoughts and that I could recognize truth with the immediacy a person has when flinching in the face of danger. It was a comforting notion. It resonated when people stood up in "fast and testimony" meetings bearing their souls, often weeping as they told the congregation they know the church is true and that they've felt the spirit validate their beliefs so powerfully that it can't be denied any more than their love for their own family.

That I can feel my way to the truth and trust my thinking simply because I feel it so deeply is a romantic notion. I felt it, and I get its appeal. I, too, read the Mormon scriptures and felt that "burning in the bosom," and I believed I knew the truth like other Mormons. To say there isn't a certain comfort and security in that would be to misunderstand the Mormon experience. It works because it

---

[6] Brown, *Rising Strong*, 39–43.

validates itself. It needs no external verification. While I had painful realizations about how flawed I really was compared to Mormon perfectionism, I'd be remiss if I did not also acknowledge the peace and comfort I felt as a Mormon within a tight-knit community that echoed my beliefs. I understand the attraction of the system.

This all throws into relief my struggles as they crystalized around that idea of being able to rely on self-authenticating truths—around the notion that just because I feel and think something so deeply that it must be true. That is what I have struggled with ever since. Our thoughts and feelings are so immediate and so real that they're difficult to dispute. But that is the problem. They're not all true, and they don't all reflect an accurate picture of the world. They're often biased and self-serving, and they cause us to make faulty judgments. For now I only wish to make clear that this realization left its mark on me. I'm forever a skeptic in many ways. I will always question the idea that people know and feel truth directly, without any confirming external evidence. But I'm also a Christian. And while that may sound paradoxical, my skepticism forced me also to acknowledge and believe that Jesus rose from the dead three days after his crucifixion. But more on that later.

Perfectionism: Living Upside Down

Brené Brown makes the point that the value we place on emotions depends on how we were raised.[7] Thinking this through has made me realize just how right she is. Growing up as a Mormon I was taught to overvalue emotions, in one sense, and devalue them, in another. On the one hand, we were taught to overvalue their ability to deliver truth and were constantly told to trust, without question, the feelings—the "burning in the bosom"—we got when reading Mormon scriptures. On the other hand, all emotions that betrayed our inability to fulfill Mormon perfectionism were relegated to the dust bin; they were undervalued and then stomped down.

I realized early on that my thoughts and feelings did not come close to church perfectionism. That much I knew, because I knew then

---

[7] Brown, *Rising Strong*, 69.

as I know now my own thoughts. Like most human beings, I know when I'm jealous; I know when I covet; I know pride; and I know when I harbor hatred. I know all this as much as I know anything because I have, as do all normal human beings, direct access to my own thinking and feelings—a fact that makes them so compelling.

As a result, I developed two distinct visceral reactions. I now feel immediately skeptical about truth claims generally, especially religious ones, but even about mundane claims that typically occur in the business world. The other reaction is just as visceral, though different. Because I had to suppress the truth about my own thoughts and emotions to comply with Mormon perfectionism, I now reel in horror at any form of perfectionism, whether found in Joseph Smith or John Wesley. Reflecting on this, I have concluded that it is because Mormons, and other like-minded people, have it the wrong way around. What should have been provisional and dependent on verification was wrongly made to be self-authenticating truth, while the things we should have been certain about were wrongly pushed down and devalued. The whole system is topsy-turvy. All the research shows that I can't accurately intuit objective truth without deferring to evidence. If I don't look outside of myself, my mind takes flight with ever more fanciful notions. On the other hand, it does not take much to look at the brutal truth inside—that is, if one is willing. And doing so dooms all forms of perfectionism, which I knew even as a child.

As a system, Mormonism teaches members to believe that emotions are good and self-authenticating when it comes to its truth claims, but it delegitimizes the truth of what we actually *know* we think and feel. Thus, what we should verify—its truth claims—we don't; and what we know to be true about ourselves, we deny in the service of perfectionism. It is completely upside down. What we need when someone makes a truth claim is evidence and good reasons. On the other hand, we shouldn't ignore the brutal facts within ourselves, which is exactly what is required in every form of perfectionism.

While this is all true of Mormonism, it is also true about all religious systems, with the lone exception of historic Christianity. They all focus on achieving some form of holiness or perfection, and every one of them also tells members to accept their truth claims solely on faith. No evidence other than their subjective experience is necessary. Because of this, a dual problem is created. First, emotions are given a power they don't actually have. Unaided by outside evidence and reason, emotions can't tell us whether someone's claim is true. Second, we are alienated from ourselves—from reckoning with our ugly truths and coming to terms with the stories we tell ourselves. Ironically, at the same time perfectionism tells us to improve, it is preventing our forward progress by conveniently stepping over our most blaring obstacles. Anyone in the business world knows you can't make progress until you've reckoned with major obstacles. All forms of perfectionism are inherently wrong as they keep us forever alienated from our true selves; they separate us from our own ugly truths and imprison our minds in an anxiety-filled dungeon.

But exactly what are the ugly truths? Why should we be troubled with our minds' intuitions and self-made stories? And how do our emotions figure into this complex calculation? It is to that we now turn.

CHAPTER 2

Natural Human Obstacles

In college and throughout my time as a PhD student, I was intensely curious about how human beings see the world and form judgments. My doctoral thesis touched on the topic, but I approached it from the perspective of Martin Luther, who was the subject of my research. Through that process I became aware of some of the potential pitfalls of human reason and how we come to conclusions. Luther argued that reason is often busy thinking religious (and nonreligious) thoughts and drawing conclusions based on weak evidence, or none at all. He argued that the human mind, for whatever reason (which he attributed to sin), is never idle and rushes to conclusions without even stopping to consider whether those conclusions are justified by evidence. It is a precarious situation that is made more so by the frequent irrationality of human emotions, which in truth operates with reason as a partner. It is an interesting observation from someone in the sixteenth century, but at the time I did not delve into whether it was supported by modern research. Little did I realize how much recent work on the subject confirms what Luther observed five hundred years ago.

How we actually think through things, as opposed to how we *think* we think through things, is important because it raises questions about the quality of our judgments. As you'll see, it is not that we can't process information and come to truth but rather that we can do so best by understanding our natural obstacles. And this isn't just for religious matters, but it also includes everything else we have to make decisions about—finance, business, and even interpersonal issues. We have all developed theories about the world and how it works regardless of whether we are aware of it or not. How we develop our theories matters if we are going to make progress in understanding how the world really is in comparison to how we want it to be. There can be a big difference. So, before I proceed on why I believe the resurrection happened, I think it is important to first take the covers off of how our judgments normally work so we can examine judgments on the question of Jesus of Nazareth. Whatever theory is used to explain it all, it has to meet a bare minimum of conditions or it shouldn't be seriously considered. So rather than assume we don't have roadblocks as we look through these often emotionally charged issues, I'd rather examine them head-on and up front.

Our Natural Disregard for Truth

In his recent bestseller, *Thinking Fast and Slow*, Daniel Kahneman distinguishes between what he calls System 1 and System 2 thinking.[1] The former operates automatically and quickly and requires little to no effort, while the latter involves all that effortful mental activity included in complex calculations.

System 1 is gullible, is biased to believe, forms causal connections that are not backed by evidence, and isn't prone to doubt its quick conclusions. Not only does it fail to keep track of alternatives it rejects, but it also does not acknowledge that there even were alternatives. Because of its tendency to create causal connections, it constructs coherent stories (even when there are none) and suppresses ambiguity. And unless it is immediately challenged, the stories can spread as if they were true. While System 2 is in charge of doubt, it is often busy and lazy.

Annie Duke reports similar research, noting that we form our beliefs in a rather haphazard way, accepting all sorts of things based on what we hear but have not actually verified.[2] She summarizes the problem as follows:

This is how *we think* we form beliefs:

---

[1] Daniel Kahneman, *Thinking Fast and Slow* (New York: 2011), 19–49.

[2] Duke, *Thinking in Bets*, 50–51.

(1) We hear something.
(2) We think about it and vet it, determining whether it is true or false. Only after that:
(3) We form our belief.

But this is how we *actually* form beliefs:

(1) We hear something.
(2) We believe it to be true.
(3) Only sometimes, and later, if we have time or the desire, do we think about it and vet it, determining whether it is true or false.

Citing Harvard professor Daniel Gilbert, she points out that people naturally find it easy to believe and very difficult to doubt. Believing is so easy that it is more like involuntary comprehension than rational assessment. Gilbert demonstrated that our default setting is to believe as true what we hear and read. And even when the information is clearly presented as false, we are still likely to process it as true.

This was demonstrated in a 1994 study in which subjects read messages about a warehouse fire. Some of them read that the fire started near a closet containing paint cans and pressurized gas cylinders, which predictably caused them to infer a connection. Five messages later, however, the same subjects received a correction that the closet was actually empty, yet they still blamed burning paint for toxic fumes and cited negligence for keeping flammable objects nearby. Thus, while we think we are capable of easily updating our beliefs based on new information, numerous studies like this prove otherwise. Duke puts it best: "Instead of altering our beliefs to fit new information, we do the opposite, altering our interpretation of that information to fit our beliefs."[3]

Making matters more precarious is that human rationality inclines dangerously to pride, in the sense that all I know is all that

---

[3] Duke, *Thinking in Bets*, 55–56.

needs to be known. Jordan Peterson observes that pride falls in love with its own creations and tries to make them absolute.[4] Rationality is therefore subject to the single worst temptation: to raise what it knows now to the status of an absolute. This does not mean that rationality is in itself doomed because it can and does produce clarity, but it shows that it has the capacity to deceive, falsify, mislead, deny, omit, rationalize, bias, and exaggerate.

The cause? Reason falls in love with itself—a point Luther made many years ago but that Peterson drives home with surprising force. It falls in love with its own productions, elevates them, and worships them as absolutes. He puts it this way:

> To say it again: it is the greatest temptation of the rational faculty to glorify its own capacity and its own productions and to claim that in the face of its theories nothing transcendent or outside its domain need exist. This means that all important facts have been discovered. This means that nothing important remains unknown.

We will see this surface again and again in this book.

Why is all this important? Because it shows that we are wired for gullibility and for preferring nicely stated conclusions over reasoning, based on probabilities and facts. We also seem to be stubbornly attached to the first things we read and hear, which serve as anchors for future beliefs. It also shows that we have the dangerous tendency to fall in love with our own ideas and, in an almost idolatrous way, to worship them. The point isn't that we can't have evidence-based reasoning, but that, in light of our natural tendencies, it has to be carefully cultivated. The short of it is that it takes discipline to get at truth, and this is as true in academics and business as it is in religious matters.

So far, though, we have only dealt with how our reason operates, but what happens when you throw emotions into the mix? Some interesting research throws light on this.

---

[4] Jordan B. Peterson, *12 Rules for Life: An Antidote to Chaos* (New York: 2018), 210, 217–18.

Emotions: Ups and Downs

Professor of Neuroscience Antonio Damasio says that emotions are enmeshed with the proper function of reason, for good and bad.[5] On the positive side, emotions provide a critical tool for people with normal brain function. For example, when we are presented with a choice, emotions spare us an endless cost/benefit analysis of the vast array of options when a bad outcome comes to mind and we experience an unpleasant gut feeling (a somatic marker, *soma* being the Greek word for body). Sounding the alarm, the marker puts an image in our mind, and we reject the option immediately, thereby narrowing down the possibilities. Markers operate whether we are aware of them or not, and most of the time we are not. As you can see, they're indispensable for our ability to choose among what might be an otherwise overwhelming number of possibilities.

Yet while emotions can be positive, they can derail quality decisions by creating a bias against objective facts, something that happens too quickly to be recognized. In addition, they can steer us into irrational behavior and impair sound decision making by: (1) causing us to skew the probabilities of things outside our control, (2) causing us to think our actions are more effective than they are, or (3) creating the tendency to jump to conclusions and act immediately, even if we have nothing to lose by waiting to find out more.[6] In sum, emotions can subvert rationality by their disregard for consequences and lack of concern for more information.

The question is, why? One finding provides a clue. Brain research reveals that the connections from the cortical areas (higher-level thinking) to the amygdala (the emotional center) are far weaker than the connections from the amygdala to the cortex, which is why it is so easy for emotions to invade our conscious thoughts but so hard for us to gain control of our emotions.[7] Connections from the

---

[5] Antonio Damasio, *Descartes' Error: Emotion, Reason, and the Human Brain* (New York: 1994), xvi–xix, 172–74, 179, 185, 193–94.

[6] Jon Elster, *Alchemies of the Mind: Rationality and the Emotions* (Cambridge: 1999), 285–87, 298.

[7] Joseph LeDoux, *The Emotional Brain: The Mysterious Underpinnings of Emotional Life* (New York: 1996), 265.

emotional systems to the cognitive systems are much stronger than the connections from the cognitive systems to the emotional systems. Emotions can easily bump mundane things out of our awareness, but non-emotional events (like thoughts) don't easily displace emotions from the mental spotlight; simply telling yourself you shouldn't feel depressed or anxious isn't helpful. The takeaway? We have little direct control over our emotional reactions, which means that emotional arousal can easily dominate and control our thinking.

All in the Way We Are Built

Consider another point. Emotions are regulated by the lower levels of our brain. The lower levels in turn maintain a direct connection with our bodily organs and are constantly scanning the landscape of the body. Because there is a direct connection between the lower levels and the highest reaches of our brain, emotions and biological regulation all play a role in human reason; they all work together. Nature has built the apparatus of rationality not just on top of our biological regulation, but also *from* it and *with* it such that rationality results from their joint activity.[8]

But because emotions are tied to body states, much of emotion occurs without our awareness. The background sensing of our body is continuous, although we hardly even notice it since it represents everything rather than just a specific part of anything in the body. Emotions offer a glimpse of what goes on in our flesh and modify our understanding of situations. Damasio tells us that feelings thus have a privileged status, and they retain a primacy that subtly pervades our mental life. Feelings are winners among equals because of the way we are built.[9]

Here is the point in all this. While this body-based mechanism is advantageous in many ways, it can also impair the quality of our reasoning. One example concerns the fear most people have about flying compared to driving, despite the fact that statistically we are far more likely to survive a flight from one city to another than a

---

[8] Damasio, *Descartes' Error*, 147, 192.

[9] Damasio, *Descartes' Error*, 159–60.

car ride between the same cities. Perhaps the most dangerous part of the journey is the car ride to the airport. Yet still most people feel safer driving than flying. Why? Because the image we have of a plane crash, with all of its emotional drama, dominates our reasoning and generates a negative bias against the correct choice.

The same problem afflicts how we evaluate many other decisions, such as investment and business decisions where probabilistic reasoning delivers better outcomes. Studies abound showing how our emotions and attitudes are activated automatically, but the real kicker is that their influence isn't even questioned by our conscious mind. This would explain phenomena like the Halo Effect, which, among other things, causes us to attribute good outcomes to our own efforts (thus pumping our egos) while we blame outside causes for the bad ones. Bottom line is that we are often mistaken about the internal causes of our actions and beliefs, meaning that our own understanding of why we do what we do isn't knowable to our conscious self.[10] Much of our mental life occurs outside of conscious awareness, as our emotions are more easily influenced when we are not aware it is happening.

Our Reality

What research reveals is how precarious our judgments can be. So much of our thinking happens *to us* rather than us cognitively choosing our thoughts. Not only do we tend to form judgments in the blink of an eye, developing stories around them in split seconds, but our emotional system helps to drive the process and all without our conscious awareness. Think about how many times you're anxious about something and you can't pinpoint why. Thoughts flood our minds of the worst possible outcomes and then spread like wildfire, much of the time in contradiction to reality. We don't question our own thoughts because they come from us. This sheds light on the challenge if our goal is to know the truth of things, even if mundane.

---

[10] LeDoux, *The Emotional Brain*, 32–3; Elster, *Alchemies of the Mind*, 269–70.

Does this mean we can't know objective facts? Can we not make sound judgments or tie our thinking more to the way things really are? I believe we can, but recognizing our obstacles in life is critical if we are going to make headway. If we are in counseling, it is obvious we can't make progress without admitting what our issues and weaknesses are. The same holds true in most things. To get at truth, we have to come to terms with things as they are in all of their (often) brutal reality. To begin, we need to recognize that we are prone to accept our thoughts, emotions, and intuitions as absolute truth. And all because they originate inside us with a speed too fast to be easily disputed by logic. Originating from ourselves, our feelings and thoughts feel better because our brains fire much faster with the familiar than they do when challenged.

One of my favorite people in history is George Washington. It is not just that I'm a fan of the system of government the founding fathers developed, though that is true, but also because of his uncommon character. He was made by his times and was the perfect man to turn the tide of the Revolutionary War. Not a flamboyant character, he was rarely perturbed and did not often lash out in anger or with harmful emotions that might have inflamed an already flammable situation. His recent biographers agree that one of his greatest strengths was his uncanny ability to see the world the way it was, not the way he wanted it to be. That is no small thing. As general of the continental army and at a severe disadvantage against the better trained and equipped (in fact professional) British army, he refused to get caught up in wishful thinking about his chances for victory. He understood the brutal reality he was up against and because of that came to understand that victory could only be achieved by extreme patience. Because of this grounding he was able to achieve an unlikely victory for the American colonies.

That ability to see the world as it actually is might be rare, but it is critical if we are going to achieve much. Facing up to our obstacles, to the things that stand in our way, forces us to recognize our weaknesses and devise strategies around them. In fact, research shows that the purveyors of visualization techniques have been wrong in telling people to simply visualize what they want (implying it will make it reality). While having a goal is important, without identifying obstacles and devising ways around them, people were hardly any more likely to achieve goals than if they had done no visualization at all. But the people who did identify obstacles were significantly more likely to achieve desired results. This makes complete sense. We need to recognize where and how we get derailed in order to put workarounds in place. This was Washington's genius.

The same trait was illustrated nicely in the best-selling business book *Good to Great*, in which Jim Collins relates an interview he did with Admiral Jim Stockdale—the highest-ranking US military officer in the "Hanoi Hilton" prisoner-of-war camp during the height of the Vietnam War.[11] He was tortured over twenty times during his eight-year imprisonment, and Stockdale lived out the war without any prisoner's rights, no set release date, and uncertain whether he'd ever see his family again. Collins relates the interview and asks about those who did and did not make it out:

> "I never lost faith in the end of the story," he [Stockdale] said, when I asked him. "I never doubted not only that I would get out, but also that I would prevail in the end and turn the experience into the defining event of my life, which, in retrospect, I would not trade."
>
> I didn't say anything for many minutes, and we continued the slow walk toward the faculty club, Stockdale limping and arc-swinging his stiff leg that had never fully recovered from repeated torture. Finally, after about a hundred meters of silence, I asked, "Who didn't make it out?"
>
> "Oh, that's easy," he said. "The optimists."
>
> "The optimists? I don't understand," I said, now completely confused, given what he'd said a hundred meters earlier.
>
> "The optimists. Oh, they were the ones who said, 'We're going to be out by Christmas.' And Christmas would come, and Christmas would go. Then they'd say, 'We're going to be out by Easter.' And Easter would come, and Easter would go. And then Thanksgiving, and then it would be Christmas again. And they died of a broken heart."
>
> Another long pause, and more walking. Then he turned to me and said, "This is a very important lesson. You must never confuse

---

[11] Jim Collins, *Good to Great: Why Some Companies Make the Leap . . . and Others Don't* (New York: 2001), 85.

faith that you will prevail in the end—which you can never afford to lose—with the discipline to confront the most brutal facts of your current reality, whatever they might be."

Conclusion

My aim in highlighting the problems in the way we know things isn't to argue that understanding truth is impossible, such as the postmodernists tell us. We clearly have the ability to know things and prove it every day. This isn't an either/or but a both/and situation. Had Washington or Stockdale not been brutally honest about their circumstances, things would have turned out very differently. Thankfully neither took an either/or approach. Truth can be known, but the things we think we know have to be sifted, evaluated, and checked against other things we know to be true. This includes our theories, including those about the resurrection appearances.

In the next chapter we will talk about how theories best operate and what to look for. What we will see is that not all theories are created equal because not all of them pass the stress test of dealing with the various facets of reality. They can as easily lead us in the wrong direction as well as point us to true north. Because of this, it is important to have a basic understanding of their role, especially as we explore the beginnings of Christianity.

CHAPTER 3

Tethering Thinking to Reality

In a fascinating study that measured how people jump to conclusions from limited information, research participants were given one-sided evidence of a disagreement between a union representative and a manager that led to the representative's arrest. Not only was the evidence one-sided, but participants were also fully aware of it. The conclusions they jumped to were telling because based on how the information was presented, the participants could have easily generated the arguments for the other side. Despite that, the one-sided information skewed their judgments in favor of the side presented. Further, the evidence made the participants more confident in their judgments than another group exposed to both sides. Daniel Kahneman, who reports the study, says that this is what you'd expect if the confidence people have is determined by the coherence of the story they construct from available information. "It is the consistency of the information that matters for a good story, not its completeness. Indeed, you will often find that knowing little makes it easier to fit everything you know into a coherent pattern."[1]

Kahneman calls this tendency "what you see is all there is." Information that isn't retrieved or present might as well not exist. You may remember from last chapter that this is a symptom of System 1 thinking, which excels at constructing the best story from currently activated ideas—without allowing for information it does not have. System 1 measures success by a story's coherence, with the

---

[1] Kahneman, *Thinking Fast and Slow*, 85–88.

amount and quality of the data it is based on being largely irrelevant. Despite the fact that information is commonly scarce, it operates as a machine for jumping to conclusions. But lack of information does not affect our confidence in our judgments, as that depends mostly on the quality of the story we can tell about what we see, even if it is very little. In other words, we often settle on a coherent pattern and suppress doubt and ambiguity.

The human preference for cognitive ease explains much of this. Something being easy is a sign that things are going well, meaning no threats, no major news, and no need to mobilize our logical mind, which is the purview of System 2. You might recall that System 2 is lazy, however, and that mental effort is aversive. The bottom line is that predictable illusions occur if a judgment is based on cognitive ease or strain. Anything that makes it easier for our brain's machinery to run smoothly tends to bias beliefs. In fact, something politicians know well is that a reliable way to make people believe in falsehoods is frequent repetition because familiarity isn't easily distinguished from truth. Many studies have demonstrated this. In one of them, people who were repeatedly exposed to the phrase "the body temperature of a chicken" were more likely to accept the statement "the body temperature of a chicken is 144 degrees" as true (or any other arbitrary number). The familiarity of one phrase made the whole statement feel familiar and therefore true in the person's mind. "If you cannot remember the source of a statement, and have no way to relate it to other things you know, you have no option but to go with the sense of cognitive ease."[2]

Moreover, if a statement is linked to other beliefs or preferences you hold, or comes from a source you trust and like, you'll feel a sense of cognitive ease. Here is the trouble, though. There may be other causes for your feeling of ease, but you have no simple way of tracing the feelings to their source. Kahneman notes that people can with some difficulty overcome some of these problems when motivated, but on most occasions System 2 is lazy and will adopt the suggestions of System 1 and march on.

---

[2] Kahneman, *Thinking Fast and Slow*, 59, 62, 64.

Along the same lines, Brené Brown cites her own research that we naturally form stories about people and situations that tend to be untrue.[3] She points out that our brains are wired to love tight stories with simple conclusions, which our bodies encourage through dopamine hits.[4] Acting on our stories, we not only fail to engage with what is real and what is not, but our behavior often damages those involved, including ourselves. Because of this she talks about the need to "rumble" with the stories we tell ourselves and ask the tough questions about truth. Seeing what she calls the delta (or difference) between our stories and the truth allows us to develop a healthier outlook.[5]

This idea of rumbling with the truth and tethering thinking to reality is a good way to describe the present chapter. Because jumping to false conclusions is so natural, you can see why we'd want to check our thinking against the facts; forming half-baked judgments and then acting on them isn't something any of us would be proud of. It is interesting in light of recent research that even better-run companies are addressing these issues in a way never imagined years ago.[6] But it is equally important to do so here as we negotiate the terrain of the early Christian claims that Jesus rose from the dead. Not only do they raise the potential for emotional bias based on one's view of the world, but we also have additional biases that need to be corrected before objective judgments can be made. In this chapter, we are going to examine some of the things we will have to consider and then discuss what facts need to be explained by any theory on the resurrection appearances.

Theories in the Loose Sense

Kahneman and Brown both talk about our tendency to create stories from limited information and then act on them as though we had

---

[3] Brown, *Rising Strong*, 77–82.

[4] R. A. Burton, *On Being Certain: Believing You Are Right Even When You're Not* (New York: 2008), 98–99.

[5] Brown, *Rising Strong*, 94–97.

[6] Dalio, *Principles*, 183–84, 219–20.

all the facts. For our purposes, we can view our stories loosely as theories (though not of course in the technical scientific sense) of how the world works and our relationship to it. What is clear from the research is that our theories about the world have a huge impact on how we think and behave. Consider the hypothetical example of an employee working his way through college selling shoes and who believes his boss is trying to get him fired. Because the employee thinks he is the most valuable person on the team, he has developed a theory that his boss' insecurities are the only explanation for the constant criticism.

His thinking might break down like this: the boss is a jerk, and he is intimidated by my competence, which brings his own insecurities to the surface; and causes him to lash out at me unfairly. As a theory, it does explain some facts (at least the facts the employee admits). Insecurity often causes people to lash out unfairly. We have all seen it happen. But if he were to "rumble with the truth," as Brown might say, then he might have to do the vulnerable and brave work of taking a hard look at his own insecurities and consider that some of his boss' critiques could be accurate. Doing so would yield a truer theory of what is happening and account for a lot more data, such as his own failings, overconfidence, and work habits. Casting a wider net around the evidence would better explain how he operates under certain conditions and could even predict how he'd behave in the future under similar conditions. The point is this. We all form loose theories about the world—about ourselves, other people, and a vast array of circumstances. Yet time and again we fail to hold them up to reality to see if they're actually true.

At least one problem with our theory-making appetite is that we are rarely stumped. We have intuitions and feelings about almost everything. We like or dislike people way before we get to know them; we trust or distrust strangers without knowing why; we feel that an organization will succeed without analyzing it.[7] Bottom line is that we often have answers to questions we don't completely understand and rely on evidence we can't explain or defend. Kahneman suggests that we generate intuitive opinions on complex matters

---

[7] Kahneman, *Thinking Fast and Slow*, 97–98.

by substituting an easier question for a harder one. In other words, if an answer to a hard question isn't found quickly, then System 1 finds an easier related question and answers that instead. For instance, in place of the more difficult question, "How happy are you with your life these days?" we answer instead the easier "What is my mood right now?" Or for the hard question, "How popular will the president be six months from now?" we substitute the easier "How popular is the president right now?" Because System 2 often follows the path of least effort, it quickly endorses the answer without much scrutiny. "You will not be stumped, you will not have to work very hard, and you may not even notice that you did not answer the question you were asked."[8]

This is important because we also develop theories about religion and spirituality. It does not matter what end of the spectrum you're on, whether atheist, agnostic, or Christian, your theories can determine what and how you think. In fact, they can bias what evidence you deem worthy of consideration. We find the same biases in academic studies on Jesus by professional historians. In his extensive study, Michael Licona points out that every historian comes with certain preunderstandings that determine how Jesus is evaluated. He calls these the historian's horizon. "It is how historians view things as a result of their knowledge, experience, beliefs, education, cultural conditioning, preferences, presuppositions and worldview."[9]

Theories in the More Technical Sense

Given the importance of theories, let's consider them in the more technical scientific sense, since in science theories are handled with some rigor. The famous twentieth-century philosopher Ludwig Wittgenstein gave us a useful definition for theories when he said that they're nets that catch what we call the world. They help us explain, rationalize, categorize, and master it. As we develop a theory

---

[8] Kahneman, *Thinking Fast and Slow*, 99.

[9] Michael R. Licona, *The Resurrection of Jesus: A New Historiographical Approach* (Downers Grove, IL: 2010), 38–39.

over time, we endeavor to make the net's mesh finer and finer so it explains the evidence without letting facts slip through the cracks. We gauge the theory's truth by whether it fits all the important data. Does it explain, for example, the facts in a way that makes them explicable as a matter of course? Does it provide a "keystone idea" that makes the various physical, chemical, biological, or even historical characteristics intelligible?[10]

In the sixteenth century, Nicolaus Copernicus was able to explain the movement of the planets with greater effectiveness than rival theories with his keystone idea of heliocentrism, which says that the planets all revolve around the sun at the center of the solar system. Part of its effectiveness was that it had fewer assumptions (it was the simplest explanation of the data) than the competing theory. By theorizing that the planets all revolved around the sun—rather than then-current thinking that the planets and sun revolve around the earth—he was able to explain a vast amount of data more simply than the rival theory. Even today, explaining more data and doing it with greater simplicity (involving the fewest assumptions) are considered hallmarks of a good theory.

But simplicity and explanatory power are not the only things that characterize good theories. Because they don't create reality but rather explain it, theories should always correctly mirror the world. Yet successfully mirroring the world happens on a sliding scale, meaning that over time they can get closer and closer to the truth without ever capturing the whole of reality. This means that their truth is based on probability, so our confidence depends on how weak or strong the evidence is.

We can go further and point out that every statement we make about the world is based on probability. Consider the statement, "The sun will rise tomorrow." While it might sound strange to say the sun will *probably* rise tomorrow, it is all we can really say. As probable as it is, there is no guarantee it will do so tomorrow. There is always the possibility, no matter how small, that something

---

[10] John Warwick Montgomery, "The Theologian's Craft: A Discussion of Theory Formation and Theory Testing in Theology," in *The Suicide of Christian Theology* (Irvine: 2015), 272–73, 275–76.

unforeseen could occur preventing it from rising. Nature has an uncanny way of invalidating our assumptions about it. Any certainty about the sun rising comes from our observation of it doing so time after time. Nevertheless, even though we think we "know" it will rise, that knowledge is based on probability, albeit high.

Now take the statement, "Jesus rose from the dead three days after his crucifixion." It too is a statement about the real world because it postulates an event that occurred within human history, and it is therefore, like all other such statements, more or less probably true or false. While that may sound odd, there is no getting around it. Like every other statement about the world, it has its own probability and can be falsified, at least in principle. When St. Paul said that "if Christ has not been raised, your faith is worthless" (1 Cor. 15:17), he was self-consciously acknowledging that "Jesus rose from the dead" is a falsifiable claim. It is no different in principle from statements about atoms, molecules, or any others open to falsification. One way we could falsify Christian belief is to uncover the bones of Jesus. In one fell swoop we'd see that the disciples' claims were false or, more truthfully, a downright lie. But the flip side is true as well: of all the world's religions, Christianity is alone in its claim about a foundational event that happened in time and space, one that can be verified—shown to be probably true—or falsified. In my opinion, that makes Christianity the only religion worthy of consideration.

Why Do We Need Theories at All?

We have seen how we form loose theories about the world. We can't help but to create our own about how the world operates, how and why people do what they do, and how we fit into the grand scheme of things. We have also seen how science uses theory in a more technical sense to organize and broaden our understanding of the same things. The difference between the two lies in the fact that science formalizes a method around how its theories are tested, including a built-in feedback loop and a process for constant improvement. But you might be wondering why we need them at all. Can't we just dispense with them altogether and gain knowledge through particular observations? And why are they relevant to our present discussion about the Christian faith?

Stated plainly, without theories there would not be any learning. This is true in every area, not just science. It includes our personal lives as well as our businesses. I know this sounds overstated, but here is why it is true. Let's say we could move through life with only individual observations, seeing and thinking about one thing here, and one there, in a long sequence leading up to old age. Say further we documented our observations and then donated the vast collection to science. Though impressive, would anyone be interested? Nope. The reason is that worthwhile knowledge and learning consist in seeing relationships between things, perceiving causes and effects, and understanding how things work at a deeper level. Merely documenting our observations would be useless because it would not uncover *why* things work the way they do. For that we have to go beyond the surface and interrogate nature about underlying causes. Theories alone give us the means to do this: they provide a roadmap of where to look, what to test, and how to organize our work. As strange as it sounds, no business today could operate successfully without theories that predict how people—customers and employees alike—behave under certain circumstances.

Yet theories without a practical way to test for accuracy would be similarly worthless. All of us have the ability to come up with grand theories about a whole host of things, but divorced from a method of testing to see if they're true, we are no better than the man who gazes at his navel for truth. So we need a balance of theory and practical application, because each mutually informs the other in a dynamic process that ends with continuous improvement over time. One wonders if once-great organizations like Kodak or Blockbuster had institutionalized this important balance, would they still be around? I suspect they would, and I also suspect that present great businesses like Netflix would not.

Now to why this is relevant to my belief in Jesus' resurrection. Like anything else, Christianity is chock full of data points. Everyone brings their own theories to the table when talking about Christianity, religion or spirituality. Some presuppose that miracles are impossible, others that we don't have reliable information about Jesus, while others theorize that God does not exist at all. I have many friends whose theories about the universe exclude God's very possibility, and therefore Jesus' resurrection as a matter of course. Most of us have unvetted theories—ones we assume are true but that have not been methodically tested. Because of this, and because they determine our thinking, it is best that we address them directly rather than leaving them unexamined. Unacknowledged assumptions are always dangerous. Any doubts about that will be dispelled the minute you work for a business that operates under unstated and unvetted assumptions; get ready for downsizing because it is inevitable. Think Kodak and Blockbuster.

Whatever theories or assumptions people have about Jesus of Nazareth and his purported resurrection from the dead, they have to account for a few well-attested facts. In other words, it is not enough that a person can come up with a home-brew theory; regardless of where it comes from, the theory still has to account for the things we are highly confident actually occurred. If a person's theory about Jesus does not account for those basic facts then it is obviously wrong. It does not matter what your personal beliefs are—whether you're Christian, agnostic or atheist—facts are stubborn things and have to be explained.

In the introduction, I referred to Annie Duke's idea of thinking in bets. She says rightly that part of the skill in life is learning to be a better belief calibrator (given that beliefs determine what we bet on), using experience and information to update our beliefs to more accurately represent the world. Since all decisions are bets, meaning we decide between alternatives (even when we don't), it follows that the more accurate our beliefs the better bets we make.[11] To make a more informed "bet" about Jesus' resurrection from the dead, we have to consider a few facts granted by the vast majority of scholars, whatever their horizon.

Method and Bedrock Facts

We have made the case that it is critical to minimize the human tendency of jumping to conclusions from limited information. This is a problem in every field of research. So how can we minimize their

---

[11] Duke, *Thinking in Bets*, 44, 48.

corrupting effects? Licona proposes some helpful suggestions, but I'll mention two.[12] First, a person's method should be stated explicitly. The way he views and weighs facts and theories (and counter-theories) should be clearly outlined, which should highlight any biases at work. Those who are and are not open to the supernatural should make that clear, because one's conclusions can be determined beforehand on that presupposition alone. Second, any theory worthy of consideration should account for the relevant historical bedrock. These are facts so strongly accepted by historians of all horizons that they're virtually indisputable. As Licona correctly points out, if a theory fails to explain all the historical bedrock, it is time to relegate it to the trash bin.

So what are the core facts? Following the extensive research of Gary Habermas,[13] Licona documents three historical bedrock facts that the vast majority of scholars accept no matter what their horizon and two additional ones that are arguably established facts, too.[14] They're as follows:

(1) Jesus died by crucifixion, a common form of execution the Romans employed to punish members of the lower class, slaves, the violently rebellious, and those accused of treason. It was usually preceded by brutally torturing the victim. We have four reasons for believing that Jesus died by crucifixion. First, the crucifixion is multiply attested (meaning we have multiple sources documenting the event) by Christian and non-Christian sources. Josephus, Tacitus, Lucian, and Mara bar Serapion are all aware of the event, with Lucian adding that Jesus' crucifixion took place in Palestine. Further, all four Gospels report Jesus' death by crucifixion, as do numerous other books and letters of the New Testament. Second, reports of the crucifixion are early, with Paul mentioning it no later than AD 55 and within twenty-one years of Jesus' crucifixion. Third, the passion narratives (the New Testament narratives describing the suffering and

---

[12] Licona, *The Resurrection of Jesus*, 52ff.

[13] Gary Habermas, "The Minimal Facts Approach to the Resurrection of Jesus: The Role of Methodology as a Crucial Component in Establishing Historicity," *Southeastern Theological Review* 3/1 (Summer 2012), 21.

[14] Licona, *The Resurrection of Jesus*, 302ff.

death of Jesus) appear credible because they satisfy something scholars call the criterion of embarrassment, which includes embarrassing material the church would not have made up about its founder or first leaders. We have a number of reports of Jewish martyrs who supposedly acted bravely—which was certainly exaggerated—under extreme torture and execution. Everyone would have been aware of these accounts, so reports of a weaker Jesus at his arrest and crucifixion would have caused embarrassment in contrast.

Fourth, it is highly unlikely that Jesus would have survived crucifixion. Roman execution teams knew their business, and every bit of evidence we have (which is plentiful) attests to his brutal torture and subsequent death on the cross. In fact, we only have one account of someone surviving crucifixion. Josephus reports seeing three of his friends crucified. After he quickly pleaded with a friend who happened to be the Roman commander, they were removed immediately and given the best medical attention Rome could offer. In spite of this, two of the three still died. We will have much more to say on crucifixion in a later chapter.

(2) Shortly after Jesus' death, the disciples claimed he had returned to life and appeared to them in both individual and group settings. The sources are clear that it was the literal resurrection of Jesus' corpse. In Luke 24:1–12, Jesus' tomb is empty on Easter morning and the grave clothes he was wrapped in now contain nothing. Jesus has flesh and bones and eats with the disciples (Luke 24:36–43), and his body is said not to have decayed as King David's did but was instead raised up (Acts 2:30–32; 13:35–37).

We have many reasons to believe the disciples made these claims. First, although we will talk about it in more detail later, Paul's letter to the Corinthians (1 Corinthians 15:3–8) contains an extremely early formula that predates the letter itself. Here is what that portion says:

> For I delivered to you as of first importance what I also received, that Christ died for our sins according to the Scriptures, and that he was buried, and that he was raised on the third day according to the Scriptures, and that he appeared to Cephas, then to the twelve. Then he appeared to more than five hundred brothers at one time, most of whom are still alive, though some have fallen asleep; then he appeared to James, then to all the apostles. (ESV)

Scholars agree that this section reaches back to the first five years after Jesus' crucifixion. Its early date is universally recognized. What is important is that it is highly likely the formula was used by Jesus' disciples, and its sequence—Jesus died, was buried, was raised on the third day and appeared to individuals and to the disciples—is multiply attested. Further, most of the appearances listed in the formula are multiply attested. The appearance to Peter in verse 5 may be alluded to in Mark 16:7 and is specifically mentioned in Luke 24:34. Regarding the latter, Luke indicates his use of different sources within the same chapter, because he uses the name Peter in 24:12 and then Simon (also referring to Peter, Simon Peter) in 24:34. Also, the appearance to the disciples in 1 Corinthians 15:5 is mentioned by Luke and John. Licona concludes that the "tradition in 1 Corinthians 15:3–7 is quite early, very probably based on eyewitness testimony, and is multiply attested in terms of a general outline of the sequence of events. Also, many of the events themselves are multiply attested."[15]

A second reason for accepting that the disciples made appearance claims is that all four Gospels report that the women saw one or two angels at Jesus' tomb, who then told them Jesus had risen. In two of the accounts (Matthew and John), Jesus appears to the women after their angelic encounter. Historians generally think these encounters are based in history because the early Christians would not have invented the stories given the low status of women in the first century. Their testimony would have raised credibility problems since they did not have the legal status to serve as witnesses. Men in the Greco-Roman world thought of women as gullible in religious matters and especially prone to superstitious fantasy. First-century historian Josephus says that from "women let no evidence be accepted, because of the levity and temerity of their sex."[16] While it is regrettable, one can't change the fact that it was the norm in the ancient world. The debate between Origen and Celsus illustrates how critics of Christianity would have seized on the story of the women in order to mock the faith.

---

[15] Licona, *The Resurrection of Jesus*, 323.

[16] N. T. Wright, *The Resurrection of the Son of God* (Minneapolis, MN: 2003), 607.

Thus, the case for historicity of the appearance to the women is extremely compelling; it would have been an embarrassment to the early church, and they would not have perpetuated the tradition if it weren't true. As Licona states, "Why fabricate a report of Jesus' resurrection that already would have been difficult for many to believe and compound that difficulty by adding women as the first witnesses?"[17] This is important. If the gospel writers were going to make something up, then they would have made one of the men, someone with status like Joseph of Arimathea who was member of the Sanhedrin, the first to see Jesus alive, not women. Their inclusion was an embarrassment, and the way Acts 1:14 refers to them as an unspecified group as well as Paul's silence in 1 Corinthians 15:5–7 are signs of that.[18] Think about it—if you're trying to get a message across, the last thing you want to do is include something that causes unnecessary offense. No doubt some of the reports tried to negotiate this sticky situation. The inclusion of the women as the first witnesses is plausible only if the tradition was grounded in history and so well known that the Gospel writers had no choice. Many of these witnesses were still living and could be asked. It is that simple.

Third, the disciples endured persecution, and a number of them were martyred for their claims that Jesus had risen from the dead. Liars don't make good martyrs. Tradition tells us that Jesus' statement to Peter, "when you grow old, you will stretch out your hands and someone else will gird you, and bring you where you do not wish to go" (John 21:18), meant that he too would die by crucifixion.[19] Jesus' statement to James and John that they'd drink the cup he drinks indicates they would both be martyred (Mark 10:35–40), which is supported by Acts 12:2, where James the brother of John was martyred.

Clement independently reports the continual sufferings of Peter and Paul and probably refers to their martyrdoms, which are attested in other sources. There were also women who were martyred and

---

[17] Licona, *The Resurrection of Jesus*, 350–51.

[18] Samuel Byrskog, *Story as History—History as Story: The Gospel Tradition in the Context of Ancient Oral History* (Boston: 2002), 196.

[19] Licona, *The Resurrection of Jesus*, 366–71.

probably raped beforehand. In addition, Polycarp reports the fate of some early Christians, including Paul. What we know with certainty is that, by AD 100 in the case of Polycarp and AD 97 in the case of Clement, there were strong traditions that Peter and Paul suffered martyrdom. Licona points out that, "The disciples' willingness to suffer and die for their beliefs *indicates that they certainly regarded those beliefs as true.* The case is strong that they did not willfully lie about the appearances of the risen Jesus. Liars make poor martyrs."

Two final observations deserve mention. First, while it is true that others have willingly died for their faith, they've done so out of their trust in beliefs passed onto them by others. The disciples died for their own testimony that they had *personally* seen the risen Jesus. "Contemporary martyrs die for what they *believe* to be true. The disciples of Jesus suffered and were willing to die for what they *knew* to be either true or false."[20] Second, there are no hints that any of the disciples recanted or walked away from the Christian community. If any did, the Christian faith would have been dealt a severe blow, and it no doubt would have been widely known. We have plenty of derogatory commentary on the early Christian movement but none suggesting the disciples ever recanted their testimony.

(3) Paul, known early on as Saul of Tarsus, zealously persecuted early Christians and then claimed to have experienced an appearance of the risen Jesus on the road to Damascus. This was a shocking reversal of his earlier views. We know he studied Jewish tradition under the best of his day. Also, he was extremely zealous in persecuting the early Christians and at least partially responsible for the death of Stephen and probably others. While still breathing threats of violence and on his way to inflict more punishment on the early believers, he claims to have had a sudden encounter with the risen Jesus on the Damascus road. That claim, together with his about-face and defense of the Christian movement, demands historical explanation.

Further, as in the case of the disciples, Paul faced endless suffering for his conversion. In 2 Corinthians 11:23–28, he reports being imprisoned and beaten so many times he can't count them. He lived

---

[20] Licona, *The Resurrection of Jesus*, 370–71.

in danger of death and received thirty-nine lashes five times from the Jews, who would have been all too eager to punish him in light of his betrayal. He was beaten with rods three times, stoned once, shipwrecked three times, and endured hunger, cold, and exposure.[21] Acts 14:19 reports that he was stoned, dragged outside the city, and left for dead. In Acts 16:19–24, Paul and Silas are flogged, thrown into prison, and have their feet fastened in stocks. In Acts 17:5, Paul and Silas are hunted by a mob, while in 18:12–13 the Jews arrest him and bring him before a Roman proconsul. In Acts 21:27–36, a Jewish crowd drags Paul from the temple and tries to kill him. Thus we can conclude that Paul, like the disciples, genuinely believed he'd seen the risen Jesus and was willing to die for that belief if necessary.

It is important to note again that the majority of modern scholars grant that the disciples and Paul had experiences they were convinced were appearances of the risen Jesus. No fact is more widely recognized by scholarship across the board, critical or otherwise.

(4) Gary Habermas includes an additional item he regards as an historical bedrock, and because I think that any theory about the rise of Christianity has to account for it, I'm including it as well.[22] It concerns the early dating of the appearances found particularly in 1 Corinthians 15:3–8. We mentioned it above, but this resurrection formula is extremely early and shows that the early Christian belief in Jesus' resurrection erupted suddenly and seemingly out of nowhere. This is a fact that needs to be explained as much as anything because we see no evidence of any evolutionary development of the idea, only a big bang explosion.

(5) Along with the early dating of the appearances, I'm also going to include the extremely early conviction among believers of Jesus as divine. Like the appearance traditions, the idea that Jesus is YHWH—the God of Israel—in human flesh erupted with a suddenness that requires explanation, and again we can find no traces of an evolutionary development. In neither case of the resurrection nor the divinity of Jesus was there any precursor or expectation on the

---

[21] Licona, *The Resurrection of Jesus*, 397–99.

[22] Habermas, "The Minimal Facts Approach," 25.

part of the Jews generally or the disciples in particular. We will see plenty of evidence for this as we proceed.

Whatever theory a person has, it must account for *at least* these bedrock facts in a way that does justice to their individual and combined force. We will refer to various attempts to explain the facts, but my opinion is that the keystone idea that best explains all the relevant data is the historic resurrection of Jesus shortly after his crucifixion. Accounting for more evidence than other theories, and involving fewer strange assumptions, the resurrection has much greater explanatory power and makes better sense of the other evidence we will discuss.

However, there is one thing that needs to be settled before proceeding. As I stated at the beginning, my Mormon upbringing instilled the idea that the New Testament documents had been so corrupted over the last two thousand years that they can no longer be trusted. If that is true, then little of what we say otherwise makes a whole lot of difference. We have to possess at least as secure a source of information as we do of other famous people in history—such as Socrates, Aristotle, or Plato. Any details about their lives presuppose this fact. This is no less true for Jesus of Nazareth than for any other important person.

CHAPTER 4

Textual Reliability of the New Testament

Among the more important questions needing to be answered in my argument, is how reliable the textual transmission of the New Testament actually was. After all, texts were manually copied by countless scribes over a long period of time, so it is legitimate to ask if the text we have now accurately represents the originals. Listening to my Mormon teachers, you'd think the New Testament texts were irreversibly corrupted by the transmission process. I believed it my whole life—that is, up until I decided to absorb the scholarly literature on the topic. What I found astounded me. It turned out that one of those truths that seemed so intuitive at the time wasn't true at all.

For the transmission of the New Testament, we need to address the following questions: Of the manuscripts we possess, how far removed are our earliest copies from when the originals were written? How many copies do we have, and how does the New Testament evidence compare with that of classical authors such as Aristotle or Plato? Finally, because there were certainly errors in the transmission process, what types of errors do we actually find?

Dating Manuscripts: How Do They Compare?

There seems to be no better way of addressing the issues around the dates of the manuscripts than to start with comments from an undisputed expert whose authority was second to none. They come from Sir Frederic Kenyon—formerly director and principal librarian of the British Museum. After a lifetime of scholarly work on the New Testament, here is what he has to say:

> In no other case is the interval of time between the composition of the book and the date of the earliest extant manuscript so short as in that of the New Testament. The books of the New Testament were written in the latter part of the first century; the earliest extant manuscripts (trifling scraps excepted) are of the fourth century—say, from 250 to 300 years later. This may sound a considerable interval, but it is nothing to that which parts most of the great classical authors from their earliest manuscripts. We believe that we have in all essentials an accurate text of the seven extant plays of Sophocles; yet the earliest substantial manuscript upon which it is based was written more than 1400 years after the poet's death. Aeschylus, Aristophanes, and Thucydides are in the same state; while with Euripides the interval is increased to 1600 years. For Plato it may be put at 1300 years, for Demosthenes as low as 1200.[1]

Kenyon's remarks provide important perspective, yet after he made this statement, numerous portions of the New Testament were discovered going back to the end of the first century, thus bridging the gap of 250 to 300 years of which Kenyon spoke. With these in mind, Kenyon concluded shortly before his death:

> The interval then between the dates of original composition and the earliest extant evidence becomes so small as to be in fact negligible, and the last foundation for any doubt that the Scriptures have come down to us substantially as they were written has now been removed. Both the *authenticity* and the *general integrity* of the books of the New Testament may be regarded as finally established.

To expand our context, consider the following information on classical authors.[2]

---

[1] John Warwick Montgomery, *Where Is History Going? A Christian Response to Secular Philosophies of History* (Minneapolis, MN: 1969), 44–45.

[2] Adapted from J. P. Moreland, *Scaling the Secular City: A Defense of Christianity* (Grand Rapids, MI: 1987), 135.

Author	When Written	Earliest Copy	Time Span	No. of Copies
Plato	427–347 BC	AD 900	1,200 yrs.	7
Tacitus	AD 100	AD 1100	1,000 yrs.	20
Pliny the Younger	AD 61–113	AD 850	750 yrs.	7
Thucydides	460–400 BC	AD 900	1,300 yrs.	8
Suetonius	AD 75–160	AD 950	800 yrs.	8
Herodotus	480–425 BC	AD 900	1,300 yrs.	8
Sophocles	496–406 BC	AD 1000	1,400 yrs.	100
Euripides	480–406 BC	AD 1100	1,500 yrs.	9
Aristotle	384–322 BC	AD 1100	1,400 yrs.	5

F. F. Bruce points out that no classical scholar would argue, for example, that the authenticity of Herodotus or Thucydides is questionable because the earliest manuscripts we have of their works are thirteen hundred years later than the originals, or that we should be especially skeptical because we have fewer than ten manuscripts. Further, Caesar's *Gallic War* was originally composed around 50 BC, and our earliest manuscripts date from nine hundred years later than Caesar's day—and we only have ten of them as well.[3] But again, scholars don't question that we substantially have texts accurately representing the original. As you can see from the above table, the situation is roughly equivalent for all classical authors, yet we have every reason to believe that we possess accurate accounts of their works.

Now consider the manuscript evidence for the New Testament. We have around 5,000 Greek manuscripts containing all or part of the New Testament, 8,000 manuscript copies of the Vulgate (a Latin translation of the Bible), and more than 350 copies of Syriac (Christian Arabic) versions of the New Testament.[4] We can also

---

[3] F. F. Bruce, *The New Testament Documents: Are They Reliable?* 5th ed. (Grand Rapids, MI: 1988), 16–17.

[4] Moreland, *Scaling the Secular City*, 35–136.

reconstruct virtually all the New Testament from the quotations found in the writings of the early church fathers.[5]

Another interesting source comes from official church lectionaries. Designed to follow the custom of the synagogue in which portions of the Law and Prophets were read at the divine service each Sabbath, lectionaries were developed as a similar system of lessons from the New Testament to be read according to fixed Sundays and other holy days. If you've ever attended a liturgical church service, you'll recognize the lectionary system. According to Metzger, these are valuable because they often preserve a much older text than the age of the lectionary manuscript itself.[6] An astounding 2,135 lectionaries of the Greek New Testament have been catalogued.

Taken as a whole, our evidence for the New Testament is impressive, to say the least. In contrast with classical authors, Metzger says that the New Testament scholar should almost be embarrassed by the wealth of his evidence. While the works of many ancient authors have been preserved in manuscripts dating from the Middle Ages and far removed from their originals, the time between composition of the New Testament and the earliest extant copies is brief. In fact, we have several papyrus manuscripts of portions of the New Testament that were copied within a century or so after they were actually written.[7] One striking example is the John Rylands fragment containing a few verses from St. John's Gospel, which is dated at the latest around AD 130.

Think about that for a moment. John's Gospel was written around AD 90. Yet we have a fragment dating only a few decades after John's original was written. Classical scholars would give their left arm for such evidence, and this is just one of many pieces of evidence we have for the integrity of the New Testament. One other thing stands out. The John Rylands fragment was found in Egypt, far removed from where it was written in Ephesus in Asia Minor. That means John's Gospel was widely circulated very early, as it traveled

---

[5] Bruce M. Metzger, *The Text of the New Testament: Its Transmission, Corruption, and Restoration*, 2nd ed. (New York: 1968), 86.

[6] Metzger, *The Text of the New Testament*, 30–31, 33.

[7] Metzger, *The Text of the New Testament*, 34–35, 39.

rapidly and over a great distance to end up in Egypt. Metzger notes that although the fragment is slight, in some respects it has as much evidential value as a complete manuscript. And again this is just one example of many similar discoveries.

Methods for Ensuring Accuracy

From the fourth century, it became usual for commercial book manufacturers—called scriptoria—to have specific processes in place to ensure accuracy when copying from one manuscript to another.[8] When manuscripts were completed, they were checked over by a corrector who was specially trained to rectify copying mistakes. In fact, we can still detect corrections today because of the difference in style and tint of ink. Another form of quality control came in AD 301 when the Emperor Diocletian set the wages for scribes for each copied line (called stochiometric reckoning). Because scribes were paid per line, every one would be counted, which provided the added benefit of further guaranteeing the accuracy of the copy in that any manuscript falling short of its original was obviously defective.

Later on, books were copied by monks, a sort of monastic scriptoria, and certain rules were developed and enforced. Metzger provides us an interesting example from AD 800 of rather severe punishments for monks who weren't careful. A diet of bread and water was the penalty of a scribe who became so interested in what he was copying that he neglected his responsibilities. If monks failed to keep their parchment leaves (their copying pages) neat and clean, they would incur a penalty of 130 penances. If anyone made more glue than he could use at one time, the penalty was 50 penances. If a scribe broke his pen out of anger, it was 30 penances.

Though being a scribe would have been difficult (many said as much), it was also considered one of the greatest honors to copy the Scriptures. Metzger cites an interesting example from Cassiodorus:

> By reading the divine Scriptures [the scribe] wholesomely instructs his own mind, and by copying the precepts of the Lord he spreads

---

[8] Metzger, *The Text of the New Testament*, 14ff.

them far and wide. What happy application, what praiseworthy industry, to preach unto men by means of the hand, to untie the tongue by means of the fingers, to bring quiet salvation to mortals, and to fight the Devil's insidious wiles with pen and ink! For every word of the Lord written by the scribe is a wound inflicted on Satan. And so, though seated in one spot, the scribe traverses diverse lands through the dissemination of what he has written ... Man multiplies the heavenly words, and in a certain metaphorical sense, if I may dare so to speak, three fingers are made to express the utterances of the Holy Trinity. O sight glorious to those who contemplate it carefully! The fast-travelling reed-pen writes down the holy words and thus avenges the malice of the Wicked One, who caused a reed to be used to smite the head of the Lord during his Passion.[9]

The point here is that scribal responsibilities were taken with all seriousness, which no doubt is one of the reasons we have such incredible accuracy in the New Testament textual tradition—something that classical scholars could only wish for with other ancient authors. Scribal attention to detail was remarkable relative to other ancient authors, even down to maintaining a consistent font size throughout a large manuscript. It was considered their duty to God to ensure accuracy, which also explains why they often included variant readings that they weren't sure what to do with.

Variant Readings and Types of Errors

With such a long and tedious transmission process, there were sure to be errors that would creep into the manuscripts. Considering that, we need to ask how serious those were and if they affected any doctrinal or historical details. F. F. Bruce notes that while the number of manuscripts increases the number of scribal errors—which you'd expect—it also proportionally increases the means of correcting the errors because we can detect how and when they originated. So the process of recovering the exact wording in any given book or letter in the New Testament is much easier than you might imagine. In fact, we can go further by saying that the variant readings

---

[9] Metzger, *The Text of the New Testament*, 18.

about which any doubt remains among textual scholars of the New Testament "affect no material questions of historic fact or of Christian faith and practice."[10] That is incredible and speaks volumes about the sheer amount of evidence we have.

So what types of errors do we actually find? Let's pull the covers back a bit on the transmission process and see what we are dealing with. Scholars classify transmission errors under two categories: unintentional and intentional changes.[11]

Unintentional and Intentional Changes

These are interesting. Unintentional errors have various causes and include things like faulty eyesight. A scribe who had astigmatism sometimes found it difficult to distinguish between Greek letters that resemble each other. An example of this occurs in Romans 6:5, where most manuscripts have "but" while a few have "together." Here two letters were written too close together, which made it appear as an entirely different letter in the Greek alphabet. Another type of error we see is when two lines in the manuscript from which he was copying happened to end with the same word(s). His eye sometimes wandered from the first, which is what he was supposed to be copying, right to the second, thus causing him to omit the sentences in between. Its opposite occurred as well. Sometimes the scribe's eye would return to the sentence or phrase he just copied and copy it again. In a show of human solidarity, we find these same types of errors even today in modern spreadsheets.

Errors arising from faulty hearing is another common type. When scribes made copies from dictation, whether reading aloud to himself or having someone else read, confusion sometimes happened with words having the same sound but different spellings. English words such as "there" and "their" are an example. It would be easy to

---

[10] Bruce, *The New Testament Documents*, 19–20.

[11] Metzger, *The Text of the New Testament*, 186–206; Kurt Aland and Barbara Aland, *The Text of the New Testament: An Introduction to the Critical Editions and to the Theory and Practice of Modern Textual Criticism*, trans. Erroll F. Rhodes (Grand Rapids, MI: 1995), 282–97.

make a mistake on hearing alone. One other unintentional error is when a scribe would hold a phrase in his mind after glancing at the original and then inadvertently copy a phrase also in his memory from a parallel passage found elsewhere in the New Testament. So, for example, more than once in the Epistles of Colossians and Ephesians scribes introduced words or phrases really belonging to the parallel passage in the other Epistle.

Intentional changes, on the other hand, were usually by well-intentioned scribes who thought they were correcting an error that previously crept into the manuscript. We find some of these in the manuscripts of the Book of Revelation, due to its fairly rough style. (It reads as if John was writing as quickly as he could just to get it down, which might not be far from the truth.) Because of this, scribes had the tendency to smooth out the spelling and grammar, which we can see clearly in some of the manuscripts. Another type of change results from the fact that monks usually knew extensive portions of the New Testament by heart, so they could be tempted to harmonize parallel passages. So, for instance, the words from John 19:30, "It was written in Hebrew, in Latin, and in Greek," were introduced into the parallel text of Luke 23:38, which lacks it. In another instance, the shorter form of the Lord's Prayer in Luke 11:2–4 was assimilated at times to include the longer version in Matthew 6:9–13.

Sometimes scribes made minor additions to sentences they felt were incomplete, such as in Matthew 9:13, "For I came not to call the righteous, but sinners," with the added words "unto repentance." Or they would add "the scribes" to a passage that simply read "the chief priests." Also when scribes had two manuscripts in front of them that had two different readings of the same passage, they would often conflate the two and include both. This happened in one manuscript in which the scribe (in the Gospel of Luke) had the statements that the disciples "were continually in the temple blessing God" and "were continually in the temple praising God." Instead of choosing between them he combined them, "were continually in the temple praising and blessing God."

Although we find minor variants like these, one of the characteristics of the New Testament textual tradition is its tenacity, or what eminent scholars Kurt and Barbara Aland refer to as its stubborn resistance to change.[12] In fact, as they point out, the very existence of different readings can be explained only by the tenacity of the textual tradition. Some 10 to 20 percent of the Greek manuscripts have faithfully preserved such variants, which is part of what makes it possible to retrace the original text of the New Testament through its wide range of manuscripts.

Conclusion

What is remarkable about all this is how minor the issues are. On the whole, scribes were faithful in copying even the most incidental details, which is why F. F. Bruce can say that none of the errors that occurred impact any element of the Christian faith and practice.[13] From the standpoint of the average person, the errors were rather boring.

I began the chapter by noting how I'd been raised to think that the text of the New Testament had been brutalized over the years by scribes with seemingly little care for its transmission. But nothing could be further from the truth. Once again facts are stubborn things, and we can say with a high degree of certainty that we have accurate texts to work with in our reconstruction of the events surrounding the death and resurrection of Jesus.

---

[12] K. and B. Aland, *The Text of the New Testament*, 69–70.

[13] Bruce, *The New Testament Documents*, 19–20.

CHAPTER 5
Kodak, Blockbuster, and Jesus' Disciples

From the title of this chapter, you may be wondering what two modern companies have to do with Jesus' first-century disciples. It is a strange comparison. How could there be any resemblance between people so far removed and a cultural setting so different than our own? No doubt we have to tread carefully. But insofar as we can glean lessons of human behavior that transcend culture and time, we may be able to better appreciate what the disciples were up against as they experienced the unique events surrounding Jesus of Nazareth.

As we mentioned in the last chapter, whatever theory we use to explain the appearances has to, at minimum, account for the bedrock facts. One fact widely accepted by scholars of all stripes is the odd behavior of the disciples. Far from the heroes in novels, the disciples are consistently painted as weak, fearful, impetuous, and stubborn. In other words, they're surprisingly portrayed like the rest of us: flawed and deeply influenced by social groups and cultural norms. Scholars largely regard the accounts as historical because they conform to something they call the criterion of embarrassment, which simply means that it is unlikely the church would have made up unflattering stories about its first leaders.[1] As you'll see, the disciples misunderstood Jesus time and again and never really understood him. But what is interesting is that, based on recent research about how people behave in groups, their reactions were predictable.

---

[1] Craig S. Keener, *The Historical Jesus of the Gospels* (Grand Rapids, MI: 2009), 156, 170.

The modern company happens to be one type of group we have quite a bit of data on. To see what we can learn, let's take a quick look at how individuals react under the influence of group thinking.

A Tale of Two Companies

Kodak

Matched only by its once-dominant market position is Kodak's stunning downfall when it filed for bankruptcy protection in 2012. When I grew up, it was a household name, and everyone knew what it meant to have a "Kodak moment." It was one of those rare instances in which a company name became synonymous with an entire category of products, like when we "Google" something today even though we might use a competitive browser. Given Kodak's meteoric rise to the top, how could it so quickly become yesterday's news?

To explain what happened, let's look deeper. Kodak started in 1880 and quickly became a household name, reaching $1 billion in sales in 1962 and an astounding $10 billion in 1981. Very early it developed the belief that its revenue came from consumables, like film, and not hardware, like cameras. While it sold cameras, it did so at low cost and only to drive its core business of selling film. A Kodak executive once commented that no "matter what they said, they were a film company. Equipment was ok as long as it drove consumables."[2] Between 1921 and 1963, the company spent over $120 million developing color film and became the industry standard in photo finishing. By 1976, Kodak controlled 90 percent of the film market and 85 percent of camera sales in the United States. To maintain its leadership, it developed procedures and processes to protect the status quo, which meant that risk taking and innovation were minimized. Preserving its position was so important that the company even hired similar CEOs.

But then disruptive changes ripped through the industry with the emergence of the digital age. Becoming ever more obvious was the fact that consumers wanted pictures digitally rather than

---

[2] Giovanni Gavetti, Rebecca Henderson, and Simona Giorgi, "Kodak and the Digital Revolution (A)," *Harvard Business School*, vol. (2005), 2.

on paper. Kodak's competitor, Sony, got the message and in 1981 announced a filmless digital camera that would display pictures on a TV screen. Describing the reaction around Kodak, one manager said that it "sent fear through the company," and the response was "my goodness, photography is dead." Tragically, it was Kodak's entrenched culture that proved to be its downfall. In other words, the very culture erected to protect its status as leader became the cause of its stunning collapse.

Making this more unbelievable, experts agree that industry leaders like Kodak are actually the ones best positioned to take advantage of emerging technology. So why didn't Kodak do that? Why does it look like they were blindsided by the digital disruption? The answer goes to the heart of something we will see again and again in this book. It is not that digital technology caught Kodak by surprise because of its myopic focus on film. The first prototype of a digital camera was created in 1975 by Steve Sasson, an engineer working for Kodak.[3] In fact, the company's research and development went much further. In 1983, Kodak created a division to explore new technologies such as digital imaging, and in 1986 it introduced the world's first electronic image sensor—the heart of the camera. Then in 1987 it established an electronic photography division. Thus in no way was the technology a surprise: Kodak actually invented the most important components and had spent $5 billion on digital research by 1993.

Adding to the mystery, that same year the company appointed George Fisher as CEO, who immediately pushed Kodak to attack the digital market with new products, including new models of the digital camera. Fisher believed the company could be successful in the equipment business because it had the capabilities to "do much more than make film."[4] However, despite the orders, Kodak insiders resisted Fisher's initiatives. One industry executive commented that while Fisher was able to change the culture at the very top, he wasn't

---

[3] Scott D. Anthony, "Kodak's Downfall Wasn't About Technology," *Harvard Business Review* vol. (July 15, 2016), 2.

[4] Gavetti, Henderson, and Giorgi, "Kodak and the Digital Revolution (A)," 4–6.

able to change the huge mass of middle managers. Harvard Business School researchers, Giovanni Gavetti et al., remark that the "culture in Kodak was so deeply ingrained that even disposable cameras had been considered almost sacrilegious."

Blockbuster

Blockbuster also seemed unbeatable, and at its peak the company operated ten thousand stores. In 2002, it had a market value of $5 billion, but by 2010 the once-unstoppable company declared bankruptcy.[5] The reasons for its demise are very similar to Kodak, but here is the short version. Like Kodak, huge success at their core business ironically laid the groundwork for their downfall. Blockbuster dominated the video rental industry and had millions of customers, massive marketing budgets, and efficient operations.[6] Then in 2000, Reed Hastings—founder of a new company called Netflix—flew to Dallas to propose a partnership with Blockbuster. Because of Blockbuster's industry dominance, Hastings was laughed out of the room. As we know, the rest is history. Blockbuster is bankrupt, and Netflix is now many times larger than the former ever was.

But like Kodak, there is an interesting backstory. When Blockbuster CEO John Antioco realized that Netflix was a threat, he discontinued late fees for rentals and heavily invested in a digital platform. Although he convinced the board to back his plan, one of his key executives worked behind his back and sabotaged his orders. Eventually he lost the board's confidence and was fired in 2005. Blockbuster went bankrupt five years later. Resembling so many once-great companies, Blockbuster failed because it had a well-built operational machine and could execute with extreme efficiency. However—and this is a point we will see again and again—its

---

[5] Larry Downes and Paul Nunes, "Blockbuster Becomes a Casualty of Big Bang Disruption," *Harvard Business Review* (November 7, 2013).

[6] Greg Satell, "A Look Back at Why Blockbuster Really Failed And Why It Did not Have To" *Forbes* (2014): 1, 5–6. Available at https://www.forbes.com/sites/gregsatell/2014/09/05/a-look-back-at-why-blockbuster-really-failed-and-why-it-didnt-have-to/#708adc8d1d64.

tight-knit culture tended to reject new information that did not fit with current ideas.

Summary of the Data

If there is one thing we have learned over the years, it is that when in groups people are extremely resistant to change. Because beliefs are built and fortified by both individual and group history, defending the status quo becomes the unstated goal of most organizations. This is what management consultant Peter Drucker meant when he famously said, "Culture eats strategy for breakfast." To prove Drucker's point, even when Kodak's CEO tried to save the company, people en masse rose up in opposition. While we will talk about the reasons later, it is enough to point out that people are highly susceptible to surroundings, a finding that has been verified by modern research many times over.

But let's ask again, what do Kodak and Blockbuster have to do with something as remote as Jesus' disciples? The answer is this: because humans are profoundly influenced by culture, it is extremely difficult to process fundamental change. Although in retrospect the behavior of the disciples seems odd, it is actually understandable in light of modern research. The same change-resistance we find in modern organizations also explains the data we have in the Gospels. Human expectations, formed by years of social influence, are difficult to manage and often impervious to revision. Even with in-your-face evidence to the contrary, we can easily still miss important clues.

A Word of Caution

Generally speaking, the Gospels don't portray a flattering picture of the disciples. Rather they show a group of fallible and failing people who often embarrass themselves and display a surprising lack of understanding. Looking back, it is easy to feel embarrassed for their inept responses and obliviousness to the obvious. It is easy to think that if we were in their shoes, we would have known better. But some interesting research tells a different story. Let's illustrate with a couple of questions. How well do you understand what you believed about the 2008 financial crisis before it happened or how the 2016 election would turn out months or even days before voting took place? That we need to take extra steps to keep the disciples within their first-century context is shown by data suggesting that we are all vulnerable to something called "hindsight bias." It is the tendency to think that whatever happens was inevitable, and because it was, we knew the outcome all along, which in turn causes us to retroactively change our past attitude to fit a more flattering self-narrative.

This "I-knew-it-all-along" bias was demonstrated by researchers Baruch Fischhoff and Ruth Beyth. Conducting a survey before Richard Nixon visited China and Russia in 1972, they asked people to assign probabilities to fifteen possible outcomes of Nixon's diplomatic initiatives. After Nixon's return, the researchers asked the same people to recall the probability they had originally assigned to each of the fifteen outcomes. The results were clear. If an event actually occurred, people exaggerated the probability they had assigned to it earlier. If the event hadn't occurred, the participants erroneously recalled that they had always considered it unlikely.[7] Hindsight bias also causes people to exaggerate the predictions made by others.

Closely related to this is "outcomes bias," which leads people to assess the quality of a decision not by whether the process used to make it was sound but by whether its outcome was good or bad. Think about a low-risk surgical procedure where an unpredictable event occurred, causing the patient's death. After the fact, juries will be prone to believe the operation was risky and that the doctor should have known better. This bias makes it difficult to evaluate a decision in the present that was reasonable when it was made. One area we see outcome bias being especially harsh is on decision makers. The Swedish-Swiss industrial company ABB serves as an example. While the company was successful, people said that CEO Percy Barnevik had a clear vision, excellent communication skills, impressive charm, and self-confidence. When ABB's fortunes turned, Percy was demonized as arrogant, too controlling, and abrasive.[8]

---

[7] Kahneman, *Thinking Fast and Slow*, 202–04.

[8] Phil Rosenzweig, *The Halo Effect . . . and the Eight Other Business Delusions That Deceive Managers* (New York: 2007), 57–58.

Interestingly, no one argued Percy had changed. Assessments of him were completely biased on outcomes.

Obviously similar, these biases skew our memory and judgment based on outcomes. The reason I bring them up is twofold. First, it is too easy for us lose the context within which the disciples lived. Outcome bias causes us to retroactively inject current thinking into the past; and while alluring, it is misleading and skews the probabilities of past actions. To compensate for the bias, we have to situate people in their original setting and make our judgments only on what would have been probable at the time. Any theory attempting to account for the resurrection appearances therefore has to place the disciples, with all of the brutal truths, within their first-century context. Second, in the case of the disciples, the Gospels display little or no evidence of these biases. Instead of making the disciples look like they knew Jesus would rise all along—presenting them more favorably—our accounts are brutally honest about what they actually thought and did. In fact, embarrassingly so. Given that, the picture below should be considered historically trustworthy and given priority in any theory about Jesus' appearances.

Very Human Disciples

A few things stand out about the disciples, and they span the entirety of Jesus' ministry: first, no matter how bluntly Jesus puts things, they consistently fail to understand; second, they fail to see how Jesus' death could be related to their engrained Jewish ideas of the Messiah, so the idea of a crucified Messiah is inconceivable; third, after Jesus' crucifixion, their disappointment that he wasn't the Messiah enters center stage; finally, they fail to make the connection between a crucified Messiah and Israel's God, YHWH. Here is some of the data in no particular order.

In Mark 4:35–41, Jesus gets in a boat with the disciples and as they cross to the other side, a fierce wind springs up, causing waves to pour in the boat. Having fallen asleep, the disciples wake Jesus and ask, "Teacher, do You not care that we are perishing?" Jesus then gets up and rebukes the storm, and it becomes perfectly calm: "'Why are you afraid? Do you still have no faith?' They became very much afraid and said to one another, 'Who then is this, that even the wind and sea obey Him?'" Something similar occurs two chapters later (6:45–52). Here Jesus sends the disciples on a boat without him while he disperses a crowd. As they struggle against the wind, he approaches them, walking on water. Seeing it, they're terrified and think they see a ghost. Calming their fears, he says, "'Take courage; it is I, do not be afraid.' Then He got into the boat with them, and the wind stopped; and they were utterly astonished, for they had not gained any insight from the incident of the loaves, but their heart was hardened."

The loaves incident refers to Jesus' prior feeding of the five thousand from just five loaves and two fish (Mark 6:33ff.). Only two chapters later (8:14–21), again, Jesus chides them for not understanding:

> "Why do you discuss the fact that you have no bread? Do you not yet see or understand? Do you have a hardened heart? . . . And do you not remember, when I broke the five loaves for the five thousand, how many baskets full of broken pieces you picked up?" They said to Him, "Twelve." "When I broke the seven for the four thousand [referring to yet another incident], how many large baskets full of broken pieces did you pick up?" And they said to Him, "Seven." And He was saying to them, "Do you not yet understand?"

Adding to the embarrassment, in Mark 10:35–45 James and John foolishly ask Jesus for the best seats in heaven, after which the remaining ten disciples are "indignant." And typifying the other disciples, Peter is front and center with his inept suggestion of building three tabernacles in Mark 9:5–6 at Jesus' transfiguration. None of them understand and have no idea what to do, and the account says that "they became terrified." Separately, John the Baptist, after confessing of Jesus, "Behold, the Lamb of God who takes away the sin of the world!" then asks Jesus through his disciples if he should be looking for someone else, revealing his own fear and doubt (John 1:29; Matt. 11:2–6).

Time and again the disciples fail to understand Jesus' prediction about his impending death (Mark 8:32–33; 9:32; 10:32–41). When Jesus predicts they'll all flee and that Peter will deny him (Mark 14:27–31; Matt. 26:31–35), Peter protests that his loyalty to

Jesus is greater than the others—who nevertheless all join Peter in determining to die rather than deny Jesus.[9] Further, in Mark 8 Jesus asks the disciples, "But who do you say that I am?" to which Peter responds, "You are the Christ." Jesus then bluntly tells them that he'll suffer, be killed, and then rise again (Mark 8:29–33). Peter immediately rebukes him and protests, after which Jesus in turn rebukes Peter, "Get behind Me, Satan." Even though Mark singles out Peter, it is clear that he is a representative of the group of disciples because Jesus' rebuke is to all the disciples "turning and looking at his disciples."

Painfully obvious is that Peter could not process Jesus' prediction because of what none of them could then fathom: the crucifixion and resurrection of Israel's God—an understanding that would not emerge until the shocking confrontation of the risen Jesus. All of them desert Jesus as he is taken into custody (Mark 14:50; Matt. 26:56): "Then all the disciples left Him and fled." Soon after, Peter completely denies him (Mark 14:37–50, 66–72; Matt. 26:69–75). In his third denial "he began to curse and swear, 'I do not know this man you are talking about!'" The extreme nature of Peter's denial (Mark 14:71) implies that he invoked a curse on Jesus. His repudiation reached such an intensity he was willing to take an oath he did not know Jesus,[10] the tragedy of which is starkly contrasted with his prior confession of Jesus as Messiah.

After the crucifixion, the disciples are terrified. Jesus was executed as a criminal and Messianic pretender, and they know that any association with him puts them in danger. Their hopes in him have been crushed. So they flee. Later on the road to Emmaus, Cleopas and another disciple lament, "But we were hoping that it was He who was going to redeem Israel," betraying their fixation on traditional Jewish Messianic expectations at the heart of their early education (Luke 24:13–42). Soon after this, Jesus appears in the midst of the disciples and the Gospels describe them as "startled and frightened,"

---

[9] Richard Bauckham, *Jesus and the Eyewitnesses: The Gospels as Eyewitness Testimony* (Grand Rapids, MI: 2006), 169ff.

[10] Raymond E. Brown, *The Death of the Messiah: From Gethsemane to the Grave, vol. 1* (New York: 1994), 604–05, 622.

resulting in Jesus' acknowledgment of their fear and doubt. Even after he shows them his hands and feet, they still don't believe "because of their joy and amazement." Separately, John reports the disciples shut in a room with closed doors "for fear of the Jews" (John 20:19). Thomas, after being told by the others that Jesus had risen, refuses to believe: "Unless I see in His hands the imprint of the nails, and put my finger into the place of the nails, and put my hands into His side, I will not believe" (John 20:24–25). Finally, Matthew reports that after Jesus had been raised the remaining eleven disciples went to Galilee and, "When they saw Him, they worshipped Him; but some were doubtful" (28:16). Such doubt in the face of overwhelming physical evidence is explicable only if they had no expectation of a risen Jesus, which is exactly what the data suggest.

We can summarize by saying that their constant misunderstanding, fear, and inept questioning and their flight from Gethsemane demonstrate how removed Jesus was from their long-held expectations. Even Jesus' own family "went out to take custody of him; for they were saying, 'He has lost His senses'" (Mark 3:21ff.). New Testament scholar Raymond Brown remarks that without the strengthening made possible through Jesus' victory over crucifixion, even those closest to Jesus failed. It is only with the resurrection that they were brought back.[11]

What the Disciples Knew

We have seen how people in Kodak and Blockbuster resisted change to the way they did business. Because they existed in a tight-knit culture, they resisted new thinking, and the hard part is that they had good reasons not to change. What they were doing worked—it had made them successful. They knew what to do and who they were because of their cultural habits; altering things seemed inconceivable. Change feels threatening, so they resisted. As we will see throughout this book, this is a fundamentally human characteristic not confined to any particular culture or period. It can be demonstrated at virtually any point. In this respect Jesus' disciples were no

---

[11] Brown, *The Death of the Messiah*, 49–50.

different. Living in a deeply ingrained first-century Jewish belief system, they were no less resistant to change. Evidence for this is abundant. Despite everything Jesus said or did, they continued, even days after the crucifixion, to interpret him *within the constructs* of their long-held Jewish beliefs. They too knew what to do and who they were. One thing they understood was that the Messiah would be victorious over foreign rule and deliver Israel and its temple from pagan corruption. No one believed he'd fail, let alone be executed as a blasphemer and enemy of the state. They knew all men would rise from the dead at the end of time. No one believed that one man would be raised from the dead before all were raised. And there is no hint of any expectation that the Messiah would be Israel's God in human flesh. According to the standards of the time, the disciples could not pick a poorer and more offensive candidate for Messiahship, let alone deification.

Based on what we have now seen, what requires explanation is how the disciples connected three concepts that were virtually impossible to link at the time: crucifixion and Messiah, Messiah and one man's resurrection from the dead, resurrected Messiah and his direct identification with Israel's God, YHWH. Whatever theory is used to explain the appearances, it must account for the failure of the disciples and their big bang fusion of these separate concepts. It is too easy to *say* that they made the appearances up, or that they hallucinated en masse seeing Jesus eat and talk with groups over different periods. A good theory has to account for what we know of the disciples themselves and their cultural background. What we see in the record is what we'd expect after the horrifying crucifixion of their master. It is not pretty, but it shows that in no way did they expect to see the risen Jesus.[12]

Conclusion

The disciples behaved in just the way we would have expected. Because Jesus did not fit their tight-knit preconceptions of what Israel's Messiah would be, they continued to interpret his words and

---

[12] Licona, *The Resurrection of Jesus*, 354.

deeds through the prism of first-century Jewish thinking. It is not only that the evidence is clear on this but also that humans show strong tendencies of clinging to status quo beliefs even when faced with disconfirming evidence. We will see more evidence of this as we go on. For now it is enough to highlight what their mindset actually was and not confuse it with what we think it should have been. They were devastated at Jesus' crucifixion, plain and simple. They fled, and in no way were they expecting to see Jesus risen three days later. As we proceed, this will be critical to keep in mind.

My contention is that the only thing explaining the appearances is the physical resurrection of Jesus from the dead. Only with a cataclysmic event can we explain not only the disciples' radical about-face, but also the sudden connection of the ideas of crucifixion and Messiah, Messiah and one man's resurrection from the dead, and resurrected Messiah and YHWH. Without such an event, none of this makes historical sense. And as we will see, it is the best explanation of the sudden and unprecedented eruption of Jesus worship. "The story of devotion to Jesus in earliest Christianity shows that the struggle erupted, volcano-like, at an amazingly early point."[13] The big bang explosion of Jesus worship is something we will talk about in some detail later, but I think it could only have come about if Jesus actually rose from the dead, especially since neither the disciples nor anyone else expected a resurrection.[14] Faking one would have gotten them nowhere. On the contrary, the Gospels betray hurried, puzzled accounts of those who saw with their own eyes something that took them totally by surprise and that they have not yet come to terms with.[15] The disciples were in no psychological state to have concocted an elaborate hoax, and any suggestion to the contrary disregards one of the historical bedrocks the majority of scholars accept.

---

[13] Larry W. Hurtado, *Lord Jesus Christ: Devotion to Jesus in Earliest Christianity* (Grand Rapids, MI: 2003), 650–53.

[14] Keener, *The Historical Jesus*, 341–42.

[15] Wright, *The Resurrection*, 612.

CHAPTER 6

The Crucifixion

Jesus as Messiah?

Imagine a financial advisor trying to get you to invest your life savings in the latest scheme promising an unparalleled return on your money. Now imagine him adding that the portfolio is being handled by someone formerly convicted of financial fraud and sentenced to twenty years in prison. He is out now and ready to make you rich. Do you do it? Highly unlikely, at least one would hope. Not only would it seem foolish to trust your money with a criminal convicted of financial crimes, but it would also smear your reputation as a wise investor. It is one thing to get swindled by someone you did not know was deceitful but another entirely if you knew beforehand he was a convicted criminal. Bad would not begin to describe your judgment.

Ratchet that scenario up ten notches and you'll understand the absurdity of preaching Jesus as Israel's Messiah (or deliverer). The problem was threefold: first, Jesus wasn't anything like what first-century Jews expected of their Messiah, throwing a major obstacle in the way of him being eligible for the role; second, the early Christian claim that Jesus had been raised from the dead met with stiff opposition due to what Jews believed about *the when* of resurrection; third and most decisively, Jesus was crucified by the Romans as a criminal of the state and Messianic pretender. We will talk about each but begin with the idea of crucifixion because its stigma is lost on us today. There was a reason St. Paul deliberately pointed out that in the eyes of those who are perishing the "word of the cross" is "folly" (1 Cor. 1:18). The crucified Christ, he insisted, is a "stumbling block" for the Jews and "folly" for the Gentiles. What we will see is that Jesus was a poor candidate for deification or the foundation of a religion. Criminal and pretender, yes, but creator and ruler of the universe, an emphatic no. Thus when Paul used the strong language of folly and stumbling block, he explicitly acknowledged the absurdity of claiming Jesus as Messiah. Let's see why.

Crucifixion in History

Crucifixion was a common form of execution by the Romans to punish the lower class, slaves, the violently rebellious, and those accused of treason.[1] It was reserved for the worst of society, and because of its public nature, it represented the victim's uttermost humiliation. Normally it was preceded by brutal torture. We have multiple reports of people being tortured with whips and fire, and Josephus tells of a man who, before the destruction of Jerusalem in AD 70, was whipped to the bone by Pilate's successor. He also reports that a group was whipped until their intestines were exposed. If you can imagine what the victim looked like before crucifixion, you can only imagine what he would have looked like after being nailed to a cross.

After being tortured, victims were often followed by crowds while being escorted outside the city walls, where they were nailed to a cross. Not uncommonly, there were particularly brutal treatments exacted on victims. Two examples will suffice. In the latter part of the first century, Martial describes a theatrical performance in which a condemned man was substituted for the actor and crucified in the theater, after which a bear was let loose that tore him to pieces while still alive. Josephus also reports of a group of men that, after being whipped with rods, were crucified, and that while they were alive, their wives and sons were killed—and their now-dead infant sons were then hung around their necks. It is not hard to see why Cicero referred to crucifixion as "that most cruel and disgusting penalty," "the worst extremes of tortures," and "the terror of the cross."

To die by crucifixion meant that the victim was considered a criminal of the worst sort, such that the entire ancient world would

---

[1] Licona, *The Resurrection of Jesus*, 303–18.

have considered Jesus' death highly offensive. Martin Hengel tells us that the younger Pliny—who was a magistrate of ancient Rome and lived from AD 61–AD 113—reported that Christians sang hymns to Christ their Lord "as to a god." For Pliny, it would have been particularly offensive that the one who was honored "as a god" had been nailed to a cross by Roman authorities as a state criminal. His friend, Tacitus, also speaks harshly of the "pernicious superstition" and relates the shameful fate of Jesus: "Christus, from whom the name had its origin, suffered the extreme penalty during the reign of Tiberius at the hands of the procurator Pontius Pilate."

The disdain the ancient world felt about worshiping a man executed as a criminal on a cross is summed up in the dialogue *Octavius*. Caecilius, who acts as the pagan spokesman in the document, insists that Christians have "sick delusions" and a "senseless and crazy superstition," which leads to an "old-womanly superstition" and the destruction of all true religion. The worst of their monstrosities is that they worship one who was crucified: "To say that their ceremonies center on a man put to death for his crime and on the fatal wood of the cross is to assign to these abandoned wretches sanctuaries which are appropriate to them and the kind of worship they deserve."

Octavius, a Christian, does not find the charge easy to counter, and because he can't deny the shamefulness of the cross, he is deliberately silent about Jesus' death. While he tries to go on the counter-attack, he avoids the real problem: that the Son of God died a criminal's death on the tree of shame. His evasion illustrates the dilemma that often led educated Christians to downplay Jesus' human nature. Such a move would have been natural for people of this time because Platonic thought—which did not think much of the body—held enormous clout, especially among the educated.

But it also illustrates exactly what the real problem was with Christians trying to pass off a crucified man as God. The one whom Christians claim as their God is a "dead God," a contradiction. Further, Jesus had been justly condemned as a criminal by the Roman state to the worst form of death: he had to endure being placed on a cross with iron nails. When Suetonius said that Christianity is a "new and pernicious superstition," he simply voiced the contempt the ancient world had for the Christian message. Jesus' disciples would had to have had their heads under a rock not to know that their preaching would breed universal contempt.

Christianity ran counter not only to Roman political thinking but also to the whole ethos of religion in ancient times and in particular to the ideas of God held by educated people. Hengel remarks that "to believe that the one pre-existent Son of the one true God, the mediator at creation and the redeemer of the world, had appeared in very recent times in out-of-the-way Galilee as a member of the obscure people, the Jews, and even worse, had died the death of a common criminal on the cross, could only be regarded as a sign of madness." Thus, St. Paul's audience would not have been open to "the word of the cross," not to mention the Jews, who saw crosses erected in Palestine and fully aware of the curse in Deuteronomy 21:23 laid upon anyone hanged on a tree. To every single ancient group, Jesus was cursed, cast out both politically and religiously. A crucified God would have been a contradiction to anyone, Jew, Greek, Roman, or barbarian; if asked to believe such an absurd claim, each of them would have thought it offensive and foolish.[2]

Why does this matter? Because for St. Paul and his contemporaries, the cross was highly offensive and imposed a huge burden on the earliest Christians and their missionary preaching. We already see evidence in the young community in Corinth as it sought to escape the crucified Christ in an enthusiastic life of the spirit with heavenly revelations and less-offensive mysteries. In his letter, Paul has to remind them that the crucified Messiah is a "stumbling block" for the Jews and "madness" to the Greeks, which he knew probably better than anyone with twenty years of missionary experience.[3]

Historically, these facts throw serious doubt on the idea that the disciples manufactured the appearances. Even if they had stolen the body, unlikely as that is, it still would have benefitted them little given that making the criminal and crucified Jesus a God would have smacked as repugnant to the entire Jewish and Gentile world. And that is of course not taking into account that the disciples themselves were crushed and scattered by the horrid scene. Their Master

---

[2] Martin Hengel, *Crucifixion* (Philadelphia: 1977), 3–7, 10.

[3] Hengel, *Crucifixion*, 18–19.

was proven a fraud, even if their sentiments for him remained. He was dead, and in the most inhumane and degrading way.

Psychology of Crucifixion

In addition to cultural objections, there is a fundamentally human revulsion against the idea of a crucified God. Jürgen Moltmann makes the case that the idea of God being revealed in the abandonment of Jesus by God on the cross is far from attractive. "What interest can the religious ... have in the crucifixion of its God, and his powerlessness and abandonment in absolute death?" The cross is really the *irreligious* thing in Christian faith that helps explain why Paul acknowledges its folly. Rather than gloss it over, he admits how offensive the claim is that it is the suffering of God in Christ that forms the basis of true faith. Faith in a "crucified God" was, and still is, a contradiction of everything humans think by the term "God."

The ancients would have seen in Jesus' crucifixion the triumph of death and the Roman state at the hands of the soldiers. Even the disciples fled from the cross.[4] For them, his shameful death was the ultimate rejection of his claim to be the Son of God. It is profoundly unsound to suggest that the cross confirmed their hopes in him; the cross destroyed their hopes. As we will see, they had no concept of a dying Messiah or a bringer of salvation condemned by the law as a blasphemer. Considering their flight, there can be no suggestion that they maintained their faith. Jesus' death was the ultimate negation of their belief in him, and they ran.

Making things worse, consider this. As Jesus hangs on the cross in agony, having been whipped and humiliated by the soldiers, taunted by bystanders, and insulted by the religious class, he utters, "My God, My God, why have you forsaken me?" It is not enough that the crucifixion proves Jesus' failure as a would-be Messiah, but he betrays the fact that he too feels abandoned by God. It matters because on top of proclaiming a dead Messiah, early Christians shook

---

[4] Jürgen Moltmann, *The Crucified God: The Cross of Christ as the Foundation and Criticism of Christian Theology* (Minneapolis, MN: 1993), 36–38, 132–33.

the ancient world by a revolution in the very idea of the term "God." No small thing, and another reason the Christian message would have fallen flat on its face. Throughout his earthly ministry Jesus talked of his oneness with the Father—implying that his rejection on the cross expressed in his dying cry was something that took place between Jesus and his Father, or something that took place between God and God. In other words, his abandonment by the Father took place within God himself. But the idea of God in the crucified Jesus, being abandoned *by God*, required a revolution in the very concept of God.[5] No one in the ancient world would have dreamed such a thing. Yet from the beginning Christians claimed that in Jesus, God himself took the fate of sinful humanity—a revolution that would have struck Jew and Gentile alike as absurd.

The challenge for the disciples, however, went further. Jesus' crucifixion happened outside the gates of Jerusalem with its temple, and thus outside the boundary of Israel, in a desolate place called Golgotha.[6] In fact it happened on the boundary of human society, where it does not matter if a person is Jew, Gentile, Greek or barbarian, master or servant, man or woman.

The implications were clear: Jesus' death destroyed the things that distinguished people as educated or uneducated, rich or poor, free or enslaved, black or white, pious or godless. None of these matter because confronted with the cross, all men "are sinners and fall short of the glory of God" (Rom. 3:23). This is the scandal of the "word of the cross." It is this that made Christian preaching even less palatable to the ancient ear as equally as it does today. The distinctions forming the backbone of the ancient world (and modern world alike) were eliminated, making the word of the cross then and now a scandal. It demands recognition that we are all under the power of corruption and sinners in solidarity with all others. The cross says that we will be made righteous without any merit on our part, solely by the grace that has come to pass in Jesus Christ. The God of freedom is therefore not recognized by his power and glory

---

[5] Moltmann, *The Crucified God*, 151–52, 193.
[6] Moltmann, *The Crucified God*, 194–96.

in the world but through his helplessness and death in the scandal of Golgotha.

Pause and think about that. None of this flatters the self-aggrandizing human ego that always wants the last word—that always wants praise from others for its self-sufficiency. The cross reduces the ego to ashes, forcing it to acknowledge its helplessness in the helplessness of the crucified Jesus and acknowledge its solidarity with the sin and weakness of others. Try selling that to a species full of itself and its accomplishments. Definitely not a prescription for success, and surely not something anyone would make up if his aim was to deceive for personal gain. Give people something they can relate to, something flattering to the ego, and you'll have a successful religion. But reduce human effort to ashes and make your God an executed criminal and one would be right in calling you mad, especially in the ancient world. Even now the cross is a scandal, not just for the unbeliever, but also for much of the Christian world when understood in all its radicalness.

To sum it up, we'd do well to remember that Jesus was crucified as a rebel, and proclaiming him as Messiah would have had dangerous consequences. According to the social values of the first century, crucifixion was dishonor and shame. And consider this: if the crucified Jesus was raised from the dead and exalted to the right hand of God as Christians claimed, then what public opinion held (and still holds) to be lowliest, what the state determined to be disgraceful, is changed into what is supreme. "In that case, the glory of God does not shine on the crowns of the mighty, but on the face of the crucified Christ. The authority of God is then no longer represented directly by those in high positions, the powerful and the rich, but by the outcast Son of Man, who died between two wretches."[7] That is a tough sell in any culture, and I don't see any reason to think it would have occurred to the disciples as an attractive narrative had they not been forced into it themselves.

---

[7] Moltmann, *The Crucified God*, 326–27.

Who Was the Messiah Supposed to Be?

First, what does the term *Messiah* mean? Generally it simply means deliverer. Specifically, from a first-century perspective and the viewpoint of Jesus' disciples, the Messiah was supposed to win a decisive military victory over the pagans, which meant overthrowing Roman rule and restoring Jewish national interests. Expectations of the Messiah were sociopolitical and ethnically tied to the Jewish nation. He was supposed to fulfill a Jewish version of the imperial dream of Rome. We can't overemphasize that this is what the disciples expected throughout Jesus' ministry, especially as he entered Jerusalem on Palm Sunday. What no one expected was the Messiah's death at the hands of pagans. Neither would they have expected him to symbolically attack the temple and warn of imminent judgment. "The crucifixion of Jesus, understood from the point of view of any onlooker, whether sympathetic or not, was bound to have appeared as the complete destruction of any messianic pretensions or possibilities he or his followers might have hinted at." Jesus' violent execution would have said in irresistibly powerful terms that he wasn't the Messiah and that God's kingdom had not been established on earth.[8]

N. T. Wright vividly illustrates the difficulty of the Christian claim using another situation. Consider the would-be Messiah Simon bar-Giora, who revolted in AD 66–70 and was then killed by the Romans at the climax of Vespasian's triumph. Imagine Simon's supporters a few days later still insisting he was the Messiah because of a vision they had of him after his death. And moreover, that they should launch a movement preaching his lordship and declare that YHWH's anointed is in their midst establishing his kingdom—even though Caesar's kingdom is more firmly established than ever—and that Simon is the king of the Jews and lord of creation. Everyone, Wright points out, Jew and Gentile alike, would have considered the claim madness.[9]

---

[8] Wright, *The Resurrection*, 557–58, 562–63.

[9] Wright, *The Resurrection*, 558–59.

How Then Is Jesus Messiah?

Why early Christians preached Jesus as Messiah when, in the eyes of the ancient world, he obviously wasn't requires an explanation. Worse than Simon's fate, Jesus was tortured and executed under Roman law as a criminal and further condemned under Jewish law as a Messianic pretender and blasphemer. Wright puts it best when he says that "anybody who knew anything about messiahs knew that a messiah who had been crucified by the pagans was a failed messiah, a sham."[10] No Jew of the first century would have seriously considered worshiping a Messianic failure, including Jesus' disciples, unless forced by something unexpected. Without that we can predict with high likelihood what they would have done after Jesus' crucifixion. Following the death of their would-be Messiah, they would have run for their lives (which is exactly what they did) and escaped back home, thankful they weren't executed with him. We know of cases where this is exactly what happened: the followers relinquished dreams of revolution and found a different way to be loyal to Israel's God.

There was still one other alternative, however: his followers would find another Messiah. It happened with several first-century movements where a sequence of leaders emerged from a single family, ending with the infamous final stand on Masada. Since Jesus' brother James emerged as an undisputed leader of the Jerusalem church, this would have been a natural direction for the movement. James was highly regarded by the Jerusalem church as well as devout Jews, so the early Jesus movement by all accounts should have followed suit. James was a prime candidate for Messianic consideration. Yet no one ever dreamed of saying he was the Messiah. All he was known as was the brother of Jesus. That is it, which is really odd since given the spirit of the times we'd have expected the title to transfer to James. It is found nowhere, not even a hint.[11] As Wright explains, from a purely historical standpoint, we have to account for the fact that a group of first-century Jews claimed that, after Jesus' death, he really was the Messiah—despite crushing evidence to the contrary.

---

[10] Wright, *The Resurrection*, 243–44, 373–74.

[11] Wright, *The Resurrection*, 561–62.

Jewish Idea of Messiah Transformed

How Jesus' disciples completely transformed the idea of Messiah is perplexing. From the first moments after the appearances, they had a shockingly different view of who the Messiah was and what his role and rule was. While for any first-century Jew the Messiah belonged specifically to the Jewish nation, Christians believed that Jesus is the *world's* one and only Lord. Instead of fighting a military battle for Israel's national restoration, Jesus the Messiah confronts evil itself. Rather than a physical focus on a temple in Jerusalem, the true temple is now in the heart of Jesus' followers. Instead of the local restoration of Israel, Jesus pours out renewal on the whole creation.[12] And whereas the Jews expected the Messiah to appear as the judge of sinners, Jesus turns toward sinners and the lost in forgiveness and unconditional acceptance.

Here is one of the big problems with the transformed view. From a first-century perspective, Jesus' actions abandoned the Messianic hope that the righteous would be exalted and the godless put to shame. Rejecting this, Jesus preached the gospel as the justification of all by grace. Not only did he preach it, but he also acted it out through his identification with sinners and tax collectors (the lowest of society).[13] To Jesus' fellow Jews, his behavior would have contradicted the law and blasphemed God, not to mention the insult it inflicted on first-century social mores. So again, the notion of Jesus fulfilling the Messianic role would have seemed absurd, as he was more apt to offend than be followed.

No Resurrection before the End Time

We have seen a number of instances in which the disciples failed to understand Jesus. Particularly stubborn was their resistance to prophecies around his impending death and resurrection. Mark relates one of the more memorable moments in which Jesus is transfigured in the presence of Peter, James, and John, "and His garments

---

[12] Wright, *The Resurrection*, 562–63.

[13] Moltmann, *The Crucified God*, 129.

became radiant and exceedingly white, as no launderer on earth can whiten them" (9:2ff.). Elijah and Moses suddenly appear and start talking to Jesus, after which Peter makes an embarrassing suggestion to construct tabernacles for each of them. Mark then relates that as "they were coming down from the mountain, He gave them orders not to relate to anyone what they had seen, until the Son of Man rose from the dead. They seized upon that statement, discussing with one another what rising from the dead meant."

If you look closely at the text, you can see where they get tripped up. As Jesus tells them not to talk about his transfiguration, he implies that they *will* talk about it within their lifetime—which they fail to understand because he also says that they won't do so "until the Son of Man rose from the dead." Their confusion was predictable because they had been taught their whole lives that no one would be raised until all are raised at the end of time. How could they talk about Jesus' transfiguration during their lifetime if they had to wait until the Son of Man was raised at history's end? What they could not understand was that the resurrection has split in two, with Jesus' coming first and right in the middle of history.[14] Let's explain this in a bit more depth so you can understand why they had such a mental block.

There were two meanings of resurrection in the first century. One was metaphorical and referred to the social and political restoration of the nation of Israel from pagan oppression, while the other involved the reembodiment of the human body after death. Both concepts were intertwined and would have been thought as occurring together. The "making alive of the dead" wasn't simply about life after death. It was about a new embodied life *after* life after death. No one supposed that the great patriarchs like Moses, Abraham, Isaac, and Jacob had yet been resurrected from the dead.[15] Their thinking rather involved a two-age and two-stage process. The two-age process consisted of the present age (the here and now) and the age to come; the two-stage personal process concerned the souls of the righteous after death, which were believed to live in heaven with

---

[14] Wright, *The Resurrection*, 414–15.

[15] Wright, *The Resurrection*, 180, 199, 201.

Israel's God until, in the age to come, they receive a new resurrected body.

Stated concisely, the dead are those who at present are souls held in that state by the creative power of YHWH. As to where, they're in the hand of the Creator God, or paradise. However, they're not yet reembodied because God hasn't completed his purposes for the world or for Israel. Ultimately they'll be reembodied by YHWH's power. But it is still now the "present age"; the "age to come" hasn't yet begun.[16] The great event of the resurrection, it was believed, would not be accomplished until the very end of the present age, and it would inaugurate the age to come. The literal sense of resurrection about the raising of the body and the metaphorical one about the nation of Israel were thus united, being two sides of the same coin.[17]

But here is the important point in all this. Nobody imagined that any *individual(s)* had already been raised from the dead, or would be raised before that great last day, the age to come. Equally important, there were no traditions about a Messiah being raised to life from the dead.[18] This explains the persistent mental block of the disciples throughout Jesus' ministry. Nothing in their mental furniture would have suggested anything else. More likely they would have believed a belief that Jesus was with God as all the other great prophets were, in paradise, which would have been widely understood and accepted. The claim that Jesus, a would-be Messianic pretender, rose from the dead before the end of time would only have hardened resistance to the early Christian movement.

Despite this, the early believers saw in the appearances the shocking fulfillment of Israel's hope, which inaugurated a new and unexpected breaking in of the kingdom of God in the here and now. The "age to come" has broken into the "present age": "God the Father ... raised [Jesus] from the dead" (Gal. 1:1). The divine rescue operation through Jesus' death and resurrection is for all people, delivering Jew and Gentile from the present evil age.[19] As Wright points out, the

---

[16] Wright, *The Resurrection*, 203.

[17] Wright, *The Resurrection*, 204–05.

[18] Wright, *The Resurrection*, 205.

[19] Wright, *The Resurrection*, 218–20, 686.

Christian mutation within Jewish resurrection belief rules out any possibility that their understanding could have spontaneously originated from its Jewish context. Something more violent is necessary to explain the radical Christian innovation around these core Jewish concepts. I believe the combination of the empty tomb and Jesus' resurrection from the dead is the most plausible explanation.

What about Visions?

Since there were people who claimed to have visions of the dead, these phenomena were already a known category. Because of that, visions could not have, by themselves, given rise to the belief that Jesus had been raised from the dead. Ancients as well as moderns knew the difference between visions and real-world events and were no more gullible than we are today. If the disciples encountered Jesus in a vision, there was already a known way to explain it. The important point is that ancient people had a rich way to explain post-mortem disembodied states; however, none of those included resurrection. "Resurrection" meant the same thing for Jew and pagan alike: embodiment. Many other Jewish leaders, heroes, and would-be Messiahs died in this environment, but in no case did anyone suggest that they had been raised from the dead.

Thus a visionary experience is an insufficient explanation of the early Christian belief. First-century people—as well as modern—understood visions to mean that the person was dead, not alive.[20] And in fact, this is what we would have expected as the most natural course for the disciples to take, since in Judaism the pious ones and martyrs were exalted to God and closely associated with angels.[21] Such a belief would have been easier to sell and would never have caused trouble with their fellow Jews or the Roman state. But this isn't what we find in the disciples' testimony, centered as it was on the empty tomb and physical appearances of Jesus. We can make a pretty safe bet that if Jesus' body had still been in the tomb, then friends and foes alike would have quickly corrected the oversight.

---

[20] Wright, *The Resurrection*, 690–91, 694–95.

[21] Martin Hengel, *Studies in Early Christology* (London: 2004), 221.

We'd hardly even know of Christianity's rise, and it would have been relegated to a mere footnote in history.

No Veneration of Jesus' Tomb

We know that Jews and some of the early Christians of the period venerated the tombs of prophets and martyrs.[22] After the person's burial, friends and family would meet at the tomb regularly to pray and have commemorative meals in honor of the deceased. But there is no evidence that Jesus' tomb was ever venerated, which is inconceivable given his status as a great prophet among his followers.

Adding to the puzzle, we also have evidence that Christians continued the first-century Jewish practice of secondary burial in caves and catacombs. It was customary to collect the bones of the deceased after the flesh decomposed and place them in careful order in an ossuary (or container), which was then stored in a special compartment in a cave or tomb. Reflecting the belief that the bones of the deceased continued to matter, the practice affirmed continued hope of the resurrection. There were pragmatic reasons as well for the custom, in that tomb space was limited and had to be consolidated for future family members. Nobody who owned a burial cave would leave it with only one body, which would have included Joseph of Arimathea, who laid Jesus' body in his own tomb.

Wright points out that Jesus' burial, which is so carefully described in the Gospels, was intended to be the first stage of a two-stage burial. The body was wrapped in grave-cloths with significant amounts of spices to offset the smell of decomposition, all on the usual assumption that other shelves in the cave would be required by the same family or group. After six months to two years, the body would be completely decomposed, with only the bare skeleton remaining. It would then be collected and reverently folded according to traditional pattern and placed in an ossuary, which would be stored in either the same cave or another location nearby. Joseph of Arimathea would have expected this with the bones of Jesus.

---

[22] Wright, *The Resurrection*, 579, 707–08.

But what is striking is that not even a trace of evidence suggests either that Jesus' tomb was venerated or that his bones were collected and placed in an ossuary, further corroborating the multiply attested New Testament claims that the tomb was empty. What is more is that this would have occurred at the same time Jesus' followers were busily proclaiming him as the Messiah on the grounds that he'd been raised from the dead. One of the early accounts of Christian preaching comes from the book of Acts (2:22ff.), where Peter very specifically asserts that Jesus' body did not undergo decay because God raised him from the dead. This was easily refutable. All one had to do was point out the tomb where Jesus' body laid, but no one did. Also during the same period, Saul of Tarsus, persecutor of the early Christians, made an about-face on the grounds that he'd been confronted by the risen Jesus. All this evidence points in one direction: the tomb was empty and Jesus had been raised from the dead, as he'd predicted.

Conclusion

We started this chapter with a thought experiment about a financial advisor asking you to put your life savings in an investment fund operated by a convicted criminal. You likely reeled in horror at the thought. What we have now seen is that the disciples would have done the same at the sight of Jesus' arrest, torture, and crucifixion. Predictably, the record shows that they ran and found solace in privacy, fearing what might happen next as the state sought out those who followed Jesus to Gethsemane. We can now see why they fled. Everything they had been taught from childhood was contradicted by both Jesus himself and the events surrounding his trial and crucifixion. Not only were they dumbfounded at Jesus' predictions of his impending death and resurrection before the end of time, but the entire ancient world was also repulsed at the thought of crucifixion and its association of criminality and treason. Making a Messiah out of Jesus would have been the last thing on anyone's mind.

The radical innovation of the earliest believers around the ideas of crucifixion, Messiah, and resurrection have no evolutionary predecessors. It is highly unlikely that without something dramatic they would have been able to make those ideas connect the way they did. A crucified Jesus meant the end of his ministry and proof that he was nothing more than a would-be and failed Messiah. The disciples' sudden about-face when they claimed to have been shockingly confronted by the risen Jesus requires explanation. The same goes for Paul's radical transformation from Christian persecutor to defender.

I have contended that the keystone idea that makes the best sense of the data is the actual resurrection of Jesus soon after his crucifixion. The combination of the empty tomb and physical appearances of Jesus are the only things that account for the radical innovation and sudden commitment of the disciples to preach Jesus' resurrection even to martyrdom. And as we will see shortly, it best explains Paul's sudden conversion on the road to Damascus soon thereafter.

CHAPTER 7

Jesus as *Kyrios*

So far we have seen strong evidence that the disciples were in no position—culturally, emotionally, intellectually, or religiously—to think that Jesus was Israel's long-awaited Messiah. My contention has been that against every impulse, they were forced into confessing Jesus as Messiah by his shocking appearances shortly after his crucifixion. Confronted by the risen Jesus, they had to realign everything they had believed around the unexpected Easter event. Nothing in their Jewish background prepared them for what happened. The idea of a crucified Lord had been preposterous, such that connecting it with Israel's Messiah would never have occurred to them or anyone else without the shock of seeing the risen Jesus.

Adding to our case, and the subject of this chapter, is a fact I mentioned earlier, namely, the sudden eruption of the disciples' belief that Jesus is YHWH (YHWH being the sacred name of God in the Old Testament). As much as anything we have talked about, an explanation is required for how a dejected band of disciples came to believe that Jesus is YHWH. That they did is beyond dispute. Here is how we know. When the original Hebrew Bible was translated into Greek, the word used to translate the sacred Old Testament name of God, YHWH, was the Greek word *kyrios*. It is perplexing that from the earliest times, Christians applied *kyrios* to Jesus without reservation. We need to unpack how they came to understand Jesus as *kyrios*, because not only did it appear blasphemous but it also occurred instantaneously and without precedent. Two of the questions we will address concern when the belief originated and what evidence we have, and then where the belief originated. The reason they're important is because we need to make sure the idea of Jesus as *kyrios* can be traced to the disciples themselves and not to a later group of people who weren't eyewitnesses.

First-Century YHWH Belief

First of all, for Jews of this period the God of Israel was known through his acts in Israel's history and from the revelation of his character (Exod. 34:6). Second, he'd revealed to Israel his name, YHWH, which was important because it revealed his unique identity; in other words, it revealed who he is. Third, YHWH is the only creator of all things and the sole ruler of all things, which clearly distinguishes him from all other reality. God alone created all things, and God alone rules supreme over all things. Fourth, only the God of Israel is worthy of worship because he is the sole creator and ruler of all things. Worship of anything or anyone else was considered idolatry. This is the essence of Jewish monotheism: the belief in only one God and the insistence that only that one God be worshipped. As we proceed, it is important for us to remember that Jesus' disciples lived as strict Jewish monotheists within a pagan environment that believed in many gods (called polytheism).

What we are going to see is that the early Christians consciously used this Jewish framework to create what New Testament scholar Richard Bauckham calls "christological monotheism"—which simply means that they included Jesus in the unique identity of the one God of Israel. In other words, they included Jesus in *who God is*. To know and worship God is to know and worship Jesus. We will see that not only was Jesus worshipped, but he was also included in God's unique identity of being sole creator of all things and sole ruler. We can't overstate the radicalness of the Christian transformation of God's identity. The disciples were mostly Jews who believed it was idolatrous to worship anyone other than YHWH.

Part of what we will explore in this chapter is when the idea that Jesus is *kyrios* originated. It is important to know how early it came about, because if it happened evolutionarily over a long period of time then chances increase that it shouldn't be traced back to the original disciples. Where the idea originated is also important. If it originated outside of Jerusalem, then again the chances increase that it isn't connected to Jesus' first disciples who resided in and around Jerusalem. We need to know if these innovative ideas came from Jesus' initial disciples or if they came from people who were not personal eyewitnesses to the crucifixion and resurrection.

What we are going to see is this: the idea of Jesus as *kyrios* emerged extremely early and can be traced back to the original disciples in and around Jerusalem. As to when, it happened suddenly, in a way we'd expect if the disciples had been shocked about seeing the risen Jesus. New Testament scholar Larry Hurtado describes it as an historical "big bang" that is so early it is completely taken for granted by the time our earliest Christian texts are written (Paul's letters).[1] As we will see, worship and devotion to Jesus are presupposed as *already normal* within the Christian congregations by the time Paul's first letters are penned, which means that it has to be traced back to the first years of the Christian movement.

Evidence from Paul

As usual, our earliest material comes from St. Paul. In what follows, we will look briefly at three texts demonstrating that Jesus was viewed as fully divine and worshipped within the earliest Christian community.

Romans 10

What is important to notice about our first example is that Paul applies a ruthlessly monotheistic Old Testament text about Israel's God, YHWH, directly and unequivocally to Jesus. So that you can see how, here are the two texts:

> Then My people will never be put to shame. Thus you will know that I am in the midst of Israel, And that I am the LORD [YHWH]

---

[1] Hurtado, *Lord Jesus Christ*, 135–36.

> your God. And there is no other. And my people will never be put to shame. . . . And it will come about that whoever calls on the name of the LORD [YHWH] will be delivered. (Joel 2:26–27, 32)

> That if you confess with your mouth Jesus is Lord, and believe in your heart that God raised Him from the dead, you will be saved. . . . For the Scripture says, "WHOEVER BELIEVES IN HIM WILL NOT BE DISAPPOINTED." For there is no distinction between Jew and Greek for the same Lord is Lord of all, abounding in riches for all who call on Him; for "WHOEVER WILL CALL ON THE NAME OF THE LORD WILL BE SAVED." (Romans 10:9, 11–13)

As you can see, the Old Testament text in Joel is YHWH centered and deeply monotheistic: "And there is no other." Since YHWH is sole creator and sole ruler, only those who call on the name of the Lord (YHWH) will be saved. Any first-century Jew would be familiar with the text, as it was as much part of their diet as social media is to us. Now look at the text in Paul's letter to the Romans. Remember that when the Old Testament was translated into Greek (which was called the Septuagint), the Greek word used to translate the sacred name of YHWH was *kyrios*, which Paul applies to Jesus in the Romans passage.

From the context, Paul includes Jesus in the very identity of YHWH himself by claiming that confession of Jesus as Lord equals being saved. The same monotheistic language used in Joel about believers not being put to shame is in both texts. Paul also identifies the Lord in both final verses as referring to Jesus. This is huge. Bauckham puts it this way: "Paul's God and the God of Israel are the same God only if YHWH is so identified with Jesus and Jesus with YHWH that the first two commandments are not violated."[2] In other words, to be aligned with the basic Old Testament principle that there is only one God, Paul includes Jesus within YHWH's very identity—who he is—as sole creator and ruler. He is saying that by

---

[2] Richard Bauckham, *Jesus and the God of Israel: God Crucified and Other Studies on the New Testament's Christology of Divine Identity* (Minneapolis, MN: 2008), 196.

seeing the historic Jesus, you see YHWH. It doesn't get any clearer than that, and you can only imagine the effect it had on his Jewish contemporaries. They would have thought it blasphemous.

Philippians 2

One of the defining characteristics of Jewish monotheism is that only the one God, YHWH, is to be worshipped. To worship another would have been a violation of everything Jews were taught. What is interesting about the next example is that Paul paints the picture of Jesus being worshipped by the whole creation, which is associated with his exaltation to the position of divine sovereignty over the whole creation. Remember that in Jewish monotheism, sovereignty over the whole creation defines who YHWH is and can therefore be ascribed only to him. Let's look at the passage:

> Who, although He existed in the form of God, did not regard equality with God a thing to be grasped, but emptied Himself, taking the form of a bond-servant, and being made in the likeness of men. Being found in appearance as a man, He humbled Himself by becoming obedient to the point of death, even death on a cross. For this reason also, God highly exalted Him, and bestowed on Him the name which is above every name, so that at the name of Jesus EVERY KNEE WILL BOW, of those who are in heaven and on earth and under the earth, and that every tongue will confess that Jesus Christ is Lord, to the glory of God the Father. (Phil. 2:6-11)

Take a look at the beginning verses, specifically the ideas of emptying and not regarding equality with God a thing to be grasped. Paul's main point is to show Jesus in antithesis to the fall of Adam in Genesis 3. Adam, in his sin, wanted to be like God and completely independent of him and grasped at making God's divinity his own like a predator hunting down its prey; whereas Jesus did not have to grasp at being like God because he actually is God. Instead, he humbled himself (as Adam did not) even to the point of death on the cross in obedience to God.

For Paul and the early Christians, our deliverance from sin depended on whether Jesus subordinated himself to the rule of God with the same unconditionality he required of others, but which Adam and Eve (and the rest of us) failed to give.[3] If he'd saved his life by recanting before Pontius Pilate, he would have made himself independent of God in the same way Adam had. Only as he let his earthly existence be consumed in service to the Father could Jesus show he was one with God. Although his unconditional obedience to God led him into extreme separation from the Father and into death on a cross, it became for us deliverance from sin and alienation from God.

Paul continues by saying that because of Jesus' unconditional obedience, God exalted him and gave him "the name which is above every name." What is critical here is that Paul appeals again to a monotheistic Old Testament text, and there can be no doubt that "the name which is above every name" is YHWH, as it would have been inconceivable for any Jewish writer to use the name for any other than God's own unique name.[4] Confessing that "Jesus Christ is Lord" is a surrogate for calling him by his name YHWH. We find this same idea echoed in Hebrews 1:3-4, which says: "He is the radiance of His glory and the exact representation of His nature, and upholds all things by the word of His power. When He had made purification of sins, He sat down at the right hand of the Majesty on high, having become as much better than the angels, as He has inherited a more excellent name than they." Only the divine name itself can be superior to the names of the angels.

As the background of the Philippians text, Paul assumes the furiously monotheistic text of Isaiah (45:21-23). There we read:

> There is no other god besides me, a righteous God and a Savior; there is none besides me, Turn to me and be saved, all the ends of the earth! For I am God and there is no other. By myself I have sworn; from my mouth has gone out in righteousness a word that shall not return: "To me every knee shall bow, and every tongue shall swear allegiance."

---

[3] Wolfhart Pannenberg, *Systematic Theology*, vol. 2, trans. by Geoffrey W. Bromiley (Grand Rapids, MI: 1994), 373-76.

[4] Bauckham, *Jesus and the God of Israel*, 197-206.

That every knee shall bow refers directly to YHWH—with the Greek Bible using *kyrios*—yet Paul applies it to Jesus by using the same word *kyrios*, thereby including Jesus in the divine identity and proclaiming that he has the sovereignty over all creation only YHWH can claim. It is in the exaltation of Jesus, in his identification of YHWH, that the unique deity of Israel's God comes to be acknowledged by all creation. Thus the expectation of Isaiah is fulfilled through Jesus' inclusion in the identity of YHWH. In other words, it is fulfilled only in a christological monotheism.

What is important is that, from the beginning, the early Christians had a very developed sense of who Jesus was and what he revealed about the one God, YHWH. Not only did Paul clearly identify Jesus as YHWH, but he insists that Jesus' suffering, death, and exaltation are the way in which the sovereignty of the one true God is acknowledged by all. The radicalness of the idea can hardly be overstated. No one before this point had so much as hinted at such a view, and we can find no parallels within Judaism during this period.

1 Corinthians 8

As you can imagine, life in the first century was quite different than it is today. One of the questions Paul had been asked, and to which he here responds, was how Christians should think about food offered to idols. At the time, pagan rituals were common in which sacrifices were made to the gods in the form of meat offered on an altar. Part of the animal was burned on the altar while the rest was prepared for a feast that followed. Any meat that wasn't eaten would be taken home and consumed afterward, but this is where it became a pressing question for Christians who denied the existence of these gods. Oftentimes, because they had pagan friends and family, they were offered the meat when invited to dine at the person's home. Adding to the problem was that some of the leftover meat found its way into the butcher shops and was sold like ordinary meat. So the Christians at Corinth were concerned they might be committing idolatry by unwittingly eating meat offered to idols.

Understanding the backdrop, you'll understand why Paul is talking about loyalty to the one true God over against the pagan worship of many gods. More interesting than the background is how he approaches the issue. Every Jew of this period knew by heart and recited daily what is called the Shema: this was the central Jewish daily prayer that confessed their strictly monotheistic faith in the form, "YHWH our God, YHWH is one." That Paul uses it isn't surprising; it is how he uses it that is. He gives the two words in the Shema "YHWH (*kyrios* in the Greek)" and "God (*theos* in the Greek)" different referents than the standard Jewish ones, so that *theos* now refers to "the father, from whom are all things and we to him" and *kyrios* refers directly to "Jesus the Messiah, through whom are all things and we through him."[5] With unparalleled innovation, Paul maintains Jewish monotheism but one in which loyalty to the only true God means also loyalty to the Lord Jesus Christ.[6] Here is the passage:

> Therefore concerning the eating of things sacrificed to idols, we know that there is no such thing as an idol in the world, and that there is no God but one. For even if there are so-called gods, whether in heaven or on earth, as indeed there are many gods and many lords, yet for us there is but one God, the Father, from whom are all things and we exist for Him; and one Lord, Jesus Christ, by whom are all things, and we exist through Him. (1 Corinthians 8:4–6)

First off, notice the passage "we know that there is no such thing as an idol in the world, and that there is no God but one." This is a typically monotheistic statement, in that the idea of other gods as "idols" can only be Jewish. For instance, Deuteronomy 4:35, 39 says that "YHWH is God; there is no other besides him . . . YHWH is God in heaven above and on the earth beneath; there is no other." Paul sets the context for a strictly Jewish monotheism within which his following words have to be understood. What is remarkable is that he incorporates Jesus into the identity of YHWH and formulates his most explicit statement of christological monotheism—a fact now widely accepted by New Testament scholars.

---

[5] Wright, *The Resurrection*, 571.
[6] Bauckham, *Jesus and the God of Israel*, 210–18.

Because of the polytheistic context within which Paul's letter is written, he acknowledges pagan beliefs but specifically makes a contrast between their allegiance to the many they call gods and lords and the exclusive, monotheistic loyalty of the early Christians (he does so by the phrase "but for us"). Over against the many gods and lords of pagan worship, Paul reminds believers in Corinth to worship God alone whom the Old Testament affirms as one, and whom he identifies directly with Jesus.

He makes this clear in his reference to creation. Of the Jewish ways to characterize YHWH's uniqueness, the most unequivocal was to affirm that he alone created all things. It would have been unthinkable that any other being than God did so or even assisted him in his creating activity. Yet Paul includes Jesus within the creative activity of God by including him in the traditional monotheistic formula: the Father, from whom are all things and we exist for Him; and one Lord, Jesus Christ, by whom are all things, and we exist through Him (v. 6). "No more unequivocal way of including Jesus in the unique divine identity is conceivable within the framework of Second Temple Jewish monotheism."[7]

Worship and Liturgy

The worship of the early church in its liturgy speaks volumes about how quickly (and how far) the belief that Jesus is *kyrios* spread in the early years. Liturgy refers to the rituals and words the early congregations repeated in the worship service and includes things like the chanting of psalms or the words leading up to celebration of the Lord's Supper. Because such evidence comes from the liturgy, we know it was understood as worship, which is important since it tells us that Jesus was indeed worshipped. Being steeped in Judaism, the disciples understood anything related to the liturgy as connected to the worship of God. Remember that what we are asking is how quickly the early Christians came to believe that Jesus is YHWH. If you think about the church's liturgy, it had to have developed later than the actual beliefs about Jesus (since putting ideas in rituals takes

---

[7] Bauckham, *Jesus and the God of Israel*, 213.

time), so placing dates on the liturgy tells us that at very least, the beliefs had to exist some years *prior* to their appearance in worship.

Let's look at a few examples, starting with Romans 1:8, in which Paul thanks God "through Jesus Christ." For a monotheistic Jew, the phrase signified the important place Jesus occupied in the prayers of the early churches. What is interesting is that Paul makes no attempt to explain why he includes Jesus in the prayer; he simply assumes the Christians in Rome are already familiar with the liturgy he is citing, meaning, of course, that it had been used in worship for quite some time before he wrote the letter. Reinforcing this are the numerous prayer passages reflecting the liturgical prayers of the early churches, in which God and Jesus were addressed and invoked together.[8]

In 1 Thessalonians 3:11–13, for instance, Paul recites the following prayer:

> Now may our God and Father Himself and Jesus our Lord direct our way to you; and may the Lord cause you to increase and abound in love for one another, and for all people, just as we also do for you; so that He may establish your hearts without blame in holiness before our God and Father at the coming of our Lord Jesus with all His saints.

Notice the inseparable connection between Jesus and God. Jesus is to bring believers successfully to God's final appearance with his holy ones. Paul's characteristic "grace and peace" greetings perform the same function of linking God and Jesus. For instance: "The God of peace will soon crush Satan under your feet. The grace of our Lord Jesus be with you." Scholars widely accept these as Christian liturgical formulae already in use within the earliest congregations. At the very latest they show that already in the 50s it was common and uncontroversial to link Jesus with God as the source of the blessings invoked in worship.

There are also explicit references of direct prayers to Jesus in Paul (2 Cor. 12:8–9) as well as Stephen's dying words as he is stoned to death (Acts 7:58–60, and ironically at the full approval of the

---

[8] Hurtado, *Lord Jesus Christ*, 139–42.

pre-Christian Paul). And while we already mentioned Romans 10:9–13 (confessing with the mouth that Jesus is Lord), we should point out that it was also part of the early church's liturgy. In his impressive six hundred–plus-page study, Larry Hurtado repeatedly reports that we know of no analogy in Roman-era Jewish groups for what was the instant and common practice of linking Jesus with God in the liturgy and prayer life of the early church. Lest its significance be missed, these practices show that because they were so uncontroversial—incredible given they were the confession of monotheistic Jews—that we have every reason to believe they were there from the earliest moments of the Christian movement. Again, this is huge, because we see no evolutionary development of what was actually a revolutionary idea.

One last observation before moving on. First Corinthians 16:22 preserves an important practice of the earliest Christians still in use in the liturgy of the Lord's Supper. It comes in the form of the *marana tha*, which roughly means, "Our Lord, come!" An appeal for Jesus to be present in the liturgical worship of the church, it simultaneously beseeches him to wrap up human history and make his final appearance. Since only YHWH can consummate history, it demonstrates that all power has been given to the crucified one. All of this shows that invocation of Jesus was widely known and accepted by the earliest believers, so much so that by the 50s when Paul's letter was written, it was already commonplace even among the Gentile churches (which were geographically farther dispersed than the first congregations). That demonstrates an incredibly rapid and widespread unity of confession for both Jewish-Christian and Gentile-Christian believers. This is an unbelievable pace from any historical standpoint, which points to their origin in the very earliest Christian communities, beginning with the Aramaic-speaking disciples in Jerusalem.

Hymns

Hymns are commonly recognized as a basic part of early Christian worship (as they are today). What is interesting is that scholars think that many passages in the New Testament were originally hymns used within the early congregations before they were quoted in the written text (e.g., Phil. 2:6–11, Col. 1:15–20, John 1:1–18, Eph. 5:14, 1 Tim. 3:16).[9] These hymns, which were adapted from the Old Testament psalms and made into psalms of Christ, have identifying marks that betray their hymnic qualities. As a whole, they're formulated in the third person and talk about the identity of Jesus and the events surrounding his death and resurrection. Thus they were particular in their content: they spoke of Jesus' preexistence, his mediation of creation, his incarnation and death on the cross, and his resurrection and exaltation.[10] Important for our purpose is their focus on the divine identity of Jesus and the significance of his death and resurrection.

Let's take the Philippians passage as an example (which we also talked about above). It speaks specifically of Jesus' divine nature, being "in the form of God" along with his surrender even to the point of crucifixion, and then proclaims that God exalted Jesus to an equal status, which entitles him to universal reverence. The passage (and others like it) shows that singing/chanting in the worship of Jesus was a characteristic feature of Christian worship from the earliest years. Again, the dates must be early because they show up in our earliest records, but already by the time of Paul's writing they were imbedded in the worship service. We might recall the report of the Roman administrator Pliny about Christian worship, referring to the antiphonal singing "to Christ as to a god" as a chief feature of Christian worship. He was right. Exclusive worship of Jesus signified the sort of reverence otherwise reserved for God the Father alone.

Pliny's complaint was that Christians worshipped Jesus but refused to reverence any other "gods" and the emperor. He derived his information from interrogating apostate Christians as well as torturing two Christian deaconesses. Anyone accused of being a Christian was released if he or she reverenced the Roman gods, made supplication to the emperor's image, and then "cursed Christ." Knowing Christians could not deny their Lord, he had a sure way of weeding out false cases. Reports like this extend beyond Pliny,

---

[9] Hurtado, *Lord Jesus Christ*, 606–08.

[10] Hengel, *Studies in Early Christology*, 286.

though. All descriptions we have from critical outsiders in the first two centuries, pagan or Jew, characterized Christian worship as directed toward Jesus. Though we mentioned the critic Celsus earlier, he correctly saw what was central to the early Christian movement in its "adoration of one unique God, rejecting as impiety all polytheism, and uniting in the same worship the Son of God with his Father."

With that said, let's take a closer look at our early evidence. Starting again with St. Paul, he writes the following in Colossians 3:16-17: "Let the word of Christ richly dwell within you, with all wisdom teaching and admonishing one another with psalms and hymns and spiritual songs, singing with thankfulness in your hearts to God. Whatever you do in word or deed, do all in the name of the Lord Jesus, giving thanks through Him to God the Father." Here is why the passage matters. All in the context of worship, which can be directed to God alone, Paul insists that the "word of Christ" is to govern everything when the community meets for worship. It is to be present and found in abundance within the Christian congregation.[11] While he uses three terms, "psalms and hymns and spiritual songs," he is not referring to three different types of music but uses the most important terms the Greek Old Testament used for religious singing. They all refer to the same type of song, which was the psalm singing typical of the Jewish tradition.

The "word of Christ" that produces the song in the heart through the Spirit is aimed at the praise of God. By making the word of Christ dwell in its midst through the singing of psalms to Christ—which again is through the hymnic narration of the saving action of Jesus—the early church gave glory to God the Father, thus intimately linking YHWH to Christ in the act of worship. In the same vein Paul ends another hymn with, "to the glory of God the Father" (Phil. 2:11). Striking is that at the end of Ephesians 5:19, Paul replaces "to God" with "to the Lord," which certainly refers to Christ. We actually have more evidence of hymns to Christ than to God in the New Testament. Moreover, it wasn't intended just as

---

[11] Martin Hengel, *Between Jesus and Paul: Studies in the Earliest History of Christianity* (Eugene, OR: 2003), 79–81.

a liturgical separation from the Jewish synagogue but expressed the fact that God has disclosed his final salvation only through his Son. That is why liturgical hymns were an essential part of the earliest Christian worship.

Clearer still is the hymn found in Paul's letter to the Colossians:[12] "He is the image of the invisible God, the firstborn of all creation. For by Him all things were created, both in the heavens and on earth, visible and invisible, whether thrones or dominions or rulers or authorities—all things have been created through Him and for Him. He is before all things, and in Him all things hold together" (1:15–17). Emphasizing Jesus' preexistence, the hymn declares him to be the agent of creation who then also reconciled all things to himself through his death on the cross. Stop and think about that for a moment. The hymn has to be extremely old by this point because Paul makes no attempt to justify the extraordinary notion that not only is Jesus the preexistent Son of God, but that by his brutal death on a Roman cross he reconciles all things to himself. Once again the pace of christological development is lightning fast and betrays no evidence of a long evolutionary path that we expect when facts get swallowed up in myth.

Perhaps our most detailed description of an early Christian worship service comes from St. John in Revelation 4–5. While depicting heavenly worship before the throne of God, it is likely that John is echoing the liturgical practices of his own community. Chapter 5 begins the scene's climax with the appearance of Christ, the "Lamb who has been slain." He alone is worthy to receive the book of judgment from God. Signifying Jesus' authority over all things, the four creatures and the twenty-four elders fall down and worship Christ by singing a new song: "Worthy are You to take the book and to break its seals; for You were slain, and purchased for God with Your blood men from every tribe and tongue and people and nation. You have made them to be a kingdom and priests to our God; and the will reign upon the earth" (v. 9–10).

Following this dramatic scene, the choir of all the heavenly beings sing the hymnic narrative of the saving action of Christ, giving

---

[12] Hengel, *Studies in Early Christology*, 113.

the "Lamb once slain" the absolute worship that is given only to God himself. The climax of the heavenly liturgy—which is at the root of all earthly liturgy[13]—occurs in the final doxology (a word coming from the Greek word *doxa*, meaning glory), and now all creatures "in heaven and on earth and under the earth and in the sea and all that is in them" praise God and Christ as one choir: "'To Him who sits on the throne, and to the Lamb, be blessing and honor and glory and dominion forever and ever.' And the four living creatures kept saying, 'Amen.' And the elders fell down and worshipped" (v. 13–14). Unambiguously, the liturgy makes clear that from the earliest times Christians understood Christ to be YHWH himself and worthy of absolute allegiance and worship.

In a similar way and drawing on several hymns (including from the Old Testament), Hebrews 1:3ff. explicitly demonstrates Jesus' unique status as divine over against all heavenly and earthly creatures: "And He is the radiance of His glory and the exact representation of His nature, and upholds all things by the word of His power. When He had made purification of sins, He sat down at the right hand of the Majesty on high, having become as much better than the angels, as He has inherited a more excellent name than they." Given the fact that it draws on other, and therefore older, hymns, we know that they were already in use within Christian liturgy and, like the others, extremely early. Though we won't go into any more detail here, there are other hymns and hymn fragments, which include 1 Peter 3:18–22, Ephesians 1:20–22, and Romans 8:34.

We will end by summarizing one of the foremost experts on the subject, Martin Hengel.[14] He points out that the hymns to Christ grew out of the early worship services and liturgy of the very earliest Christian community after the Easter event and are therefore as old as the community itself. That is a significant point. It means that there was no evolutionary development in which one idea mutates and changes into another. The hymns were an immediate reaction to the resurrection, which took the disciples by surprise, and a spontaneous formulation of the new reality with which they were

---

[13] Hengel, *Studies in Early Christology*, 236.

[14] Hengel, *Between Jesus and Paul*, 93.

confronted. While in their form they took the character of Jewish psalmody, hymns were part of the community's praise of God, and in their content, they presented the work, nature, and destiny of the crucified and exalted Lord—and therefore they all took on a narrative character about the crucial events. Accurate history mattered, because it served as the vehicle by which God delivered his people from their sins, and the hymns in turn served as the conduit for delivering that critical message. Beyond that the hymns tell us in no uncertain terms that, for the earliest Christians, Jesus was fully divine and worthy of all honor, worship, and praise.

Where and When?

Let's now pinpoint as much as possible where and when a fully divine Jesus developed. Both are important because if the idea of Jesus as *kyrios* originated with any group other than the disciples in Jerusalem, who'd been the primary eyewitnesses, then we might suspect the historicity of the claim.

Again, our earliest evidence is from Paul, whose first letter was written probably about AD 50 and the last around AD 56–57.[15] What is significant is that we can't detect any development in his christological views in his letters, and he presupposes that the titles for Jesus, the formulae and conceptions he uses, are already known by the communities he is writing to. That means we have to assume all of the features of Paul's view of Christ were already fully developed toward the end of the 40s. Do the math and there are less than twenty years available for the development of primitive christology up to the time of its earliest witness in St. Paul.

But we need to consider one more fact. Paul's conversion to the Christian movement occurred between AD 32–34, which we know from Galatians 1:18 and 2:1. We have reasons to believe that Jesus' death should be dated to Friday, April 7 (14 Nisan), AD 30. It is reasonable to assume that Paul would have received some of the early Christian formulae and liturgical hymns soon after his conversion. In fact, in Galatians he reports that three years after his conversion he

---

[15] Hengel, *Between Jesus and Paul*, 31.

went to Jerusalem and spent fifteen days with Cephas (Peter), where he would have verified what he knew (he also saw James, the brother of Jesus). Again, do the math and now there are only between two and four years separating us from the death/resurrection and our earliest material. At very least, the time between Jesus' death and resurrection and Paul's letters is only about eighteen years, which is an incredibly short timeframe for this huge jump in linking Jesus with YHWH. Hengel remarks that "more happened in christology within these few years than in the whole subsequent seven hundred years of church history. Philippians 2:6ff., 1 Cor. 8:6; Gal. 4:4; Rom. 8:3 and 1 Cor. 2:7 already bear witness to the preexistence and divine nature of Jesus and his mediation in creation."[16]

Where did the development occur? During these brief years it took place in the Greek-speaking Jewish-Christian communities of Jerusalem, Caesarea, Damascus, Antioch, Syria, and Palestine. We know at that time these areas were limited both socially and geographically, meaning corrupting outside influences are improbable. Jerusalem, home of the disciples, would have definitely played a controlling role over fact and fiction. We find evidence of this in Paul's letters, where he recognizes the principle that it is from Jerusalem that the word of God proceeds. It matters because that is where Peter, James, John, and the rest of the eyewitnesses resided. He even goes so far as to point out that Jerusalem was the point of departure for his own missionary activity (Rom. 15:18ff.).[17]

Further, Paul treats the Gentile Christian congregations as imitators of the Jerusalem churches and the rest of Judea. He makes clear that the Gentile churches receive the word of God from Jerusalem (the seat of the apostles) and they're to imitate their practices. Because of this, he adds in Romans 15:25–27 the following responsibility: "but now, I am going to Jerusalem serving the saints. For Macedonia Achaia have been pleased to make a contribution for the poor among the saints in Jerusalem. Yes, they were pleased to do so,

---

[16] Hengel, *Between Jesus and Paul*, 39–40.

[17] Birger Gerhardsson, *Memory and Manuscript: Oral Tradition and Written Transmission in Rabbinic Judaism and Early Christianity with Tradition and Transmission in Early Christianity* (Grand Rapids, MI: 1998), 274–75.

and they are indebted to them. For if the Gentiles have shared in their spiritual things, they are indebted to minister to them also in material things." In other words, because the Gentiles received the Jesus tradition from the Jerusalem church, they're indebted to support it with material things. It is an application of the rule Paul expresses in Galatians 6:6: "The one who is taught the word is to share all good things with the one who teaches him." Here the Jerusalem church is the teacher of the other churches. Paul's insistence on taking collections for the Jerusalem church is powerful evidence that the church must be unified in its traditions and that the Jerusalem congregations take precedence over the others.

Birger Gerhardsson points out that in 1 Corinthians 14:36 Paul makes a comment that would have been immediately understood by his audience. The Corinthians were developing a tendency to play foot-loose and fancy-free with public worship and teaching. Paul goads them by asking, "Was it from you that the word of God first went forth? Or has it come to you only?" Why were his words recognizable? Because from a long tradition of Scripture and the Rabbis they knew two principles well. First, that the chosen people of God have one common "law" (in other words, the word of God found in the Old Testament, Lev. 24:22), and that the law proceeds from Jerusalem (Deut. 17:8ff., Isa. 2:3). It was there the sacred text had its home, and it was there the prophets appeared and had their sayings transmitted and interpreted. With this it is not surprising that Jerusalem played the role it did for Jesus and the early church.[18] There is a close parallel in rabbinic sources that reads as follows: "Does the Torah proceed from Babel, and the word of God from Nehar-Paqod?" For the early Christians, the center around which all historical and doctrinal questions about Jesus were vetted was Jerusalem with the eyewitnesses.

Before wrapping up, we should mention an important detail from Paul. It comes from his Galatians letter (2:1ff.) and reads as follows:

---

[18] Gerhardsson, *Memory and Manuscript*, 214–15, 275–77, 279.

> Then after an interval of fourteen years I went up again to Jerusalem . . . and I submitted to them the gospel which I preach among the Gentiles, but I did so in private to those who were of reputation, for fear that I might be running, or had run, in vain . . . But those who were of high reputation . . . contributed nothing to me. But on the contrary, seeing that I had been entrusted with the gospel to the uncircumcised, just as Peter had been to the circumcised . . . and recognizing the grace that had been given to me, James and Cephas and John, who were reputed to be pillars, gave to me and Barnabas the right hand of fellowship, so that we might go to the Gentiles and they to the circumcised.

Again, Paul clearly recognized the apostles in Jerusalem as the church's highest doctrinal authority.[19] In a relationship he would have understood as a former Pharisaic Jew, Paul understood that his own authority was based on that of the eyewitnesses along the lines of the rabbi and his students. The collection of eyewitnesses in Jerusalem has authority over against a single person or church. His phrase, "contributed nothing to me," implies he was in no need of correction. He'd been taught accurately, which he now confirmed with them in person.

Conclusion

Everything we have seen shows there was a fully developed view of Jesus as *kyrios* by the time Paul started writing his letters in the 50s. Working backward, we know the beliefs were in stone well before his writings appear, and it is highly likely that a fully developed belief in Jesus as *kyrios* originated in Jerusalem simultaneously with the appearances of Jesus to the disciples. In what would have been common, the beliefs were codified immediately in the form of formulae (a set form of words allowing little room for originality and used for teaching and worship), teaching, written material, and the earliest church's liturgy and hymns, all in the fashion of their Jewish background.

---

[19] James D. G. Dunn, *Jesus Remembered* (Grand Rapids, MI: 2003), 190–91.

In light of all of this, we can conclude that the confession of Jesus as *kyrios* erupted with a suddenness best explained by Jesus' physical appearances shortly after his crucifixion. We find no evidence of evolutionary development in their early beliefs, indicating that they were forced to realign old conceptions around the Easter event. So, once again, the resurrection accounts for the relevant data and provides the keystone idea that makes the different pieces fall into place like a key does a lock. We will end with the conclusion of New Testament scholar Larry Hurtado after his painstaking six hundred–page work on the subject: "Moreover, devotion to Jesus as divine erupted suddenly and quickly, not gradually and late, among first-century circles of followers. More specifically, the origins lie in Jewish Christian circles of the earliest years."[20]

---

[20] Hurtado, *Lord Jesus Christ*, 650.

CHAPTER 8

Transmission of Jesus' Words and Deeds

We are now at the point of asking if we have reason to think that the disciples took care to preserve what they witnessed, and if so, how that information was passed on to others. It is a legitimate question because the earliest Christian writings started to be published in the 50s, with Jesus being executed around twenty years earlier. What we want to know is how carefully those early accounts were preserved from the time of the actual events to when they were fixed in writing. Also, in what was preserved, how far back can the key facts of the crucifixion, empty tomb, and resurrection appearances be traced? Answering these questions will help us determine if our accounts accurately reflect the original events.

To do so, we are going to jump into how ancient culture captured and conveyed important information. While the New Testament was put into written form quite early, a lot of the information in the written text originated and was transmitted first in "oral tradition." As the phrase implies, information about important events was captured in memory and then orally preserved by passing it down through word of mouth and fixing it in the memories of successive generations.[1] Much of what we know about history stems from oral tradition. (A quick note before proceeding. Because scholars refer to the traditions of early Christianity as "Jesus tradition," I'll do so as well throughout this chapter.)

---

[1] Jan Vansina, *Oral Tradition as History* (New York: 1997), xi–xii.

Why Oral, and How Faithful Was It?

If you think about writing, it is actually a form of what today we call information technology (IT). Of course, it isn't as high tech as businesses now require, but it is no less a form of capturing and conveying information with current technology. No matter what period of history, ancient or modern, IT has always been costly and required trade-offs. Anyone who's dealt with modern IT issues understands this. The first century was no exception. Writing, their form of IT, was costly due to the time and expense of documenting information on scrolls. In addition to many people being illiterate, it is one reason why telling and retelling important facts was the most effective way of keeping records; it communicated all sorts of things, ranging from historical, moral, cultural, to religious. It also kept information in the public domain because of its inherently social nature. Traditions would be told and retold from mouth to mouth, making it a communal—not just private—body of knowledge. Keeping history this way meant that it lived in communal memory, and because its meaning could be explained in real-time it was considered to be living as opposed to the dead history found in written texts. "Ancient things are today" would have been a commonly accepted idea, implying that as people repeated tradition, the past became a living, breathing thing in the present life of the community.[2] So you can see why oral tradition was a communication linchpin for most cultures throughout history.

It is not that books were never used. They were, especially for mission-critical information like the Torah, which contained the words of God. But even when they were used, they served mainly as an aid to memory, in that though they were written they were meant to be spoken aloud. Knowledge through the written text was considered a dead thing if not imprinted on the memory, which happens best by hearing the spoken word and allowing it to pierce the heart. This may sound foreign because we can just open a web browser and instantly search anything we want. But we need to recognize it is only in our day that memory has been unloaded into books and web browsers, and in which education consists in finding material

---

[2] Bauckham, *Jesus and the Eyewitnesses*, 254.

without the need to memorize it. "Not until our day has the pedagogical revolution taken place which has been called 'the dethronement of memory.'"[3]

The modern shift hasn't all been good as memory and attention spans decline. TED talks are kept between fifteen to twenty minutes because research shows that we can't focus longer. Yet as recently as the nineteenth century (not long ago, really) people gathered in huge crowds to hear political candidates for hours. In lock-step, modern attention span and memory have declined together. Not so for the ancient world, where memory was critical to the life and values of the community, which remained unaltered from the centuries before Christ to the end of antiquity. Having an exceptional memory was a matter of honor and shame. Children competed for memorization prizes at school, and as we will see, rabbis were known for their extreme attention to memory. This was true of both Judaism and the classical world.[4]

Remembering the Teacher's Words

We know it was critical for the sayings of important teachers to be conveyed in their own words. Authentic statements contained the authority of the one who originally uttered them.[5] Because of this, ancient schools did not provide summaries of the older masters; rather, their words were quoted together with the name of the person who said them. One of the rules for students of the rabbis was, "It is a man's duty to state (a tradition) in his teacher's words." The rule was cited in reference to what the great Jewish teacher Hillel (who died in AD 10 and whose famous grandson, Gamaliel, was the teacher of St. Paul) said about purification. What is important is that Hillel passed on a unit of measurement no longer used in his time, showing that repeating the actual words of former masters was expected.

In fact, rabbis were unwilling to correct the wording of either the written or oral Torah, instead giving old sayings a new interpretation

---

[3] Gerhardsson, *Memory and Manuscript*, 123–24, 332.

[4] Byrskog, "A New Perspective on the Jesus Tradition," 66.

[5] Gerhardsson, *Memory and Manuscript*, 129–31.

that sometimes differed from the original. Deliberately manipulating the words of great teachers—of whom Jesus would be numbered—was unthinkable. What they said was preserved and passed on with a faithfulness that is difficult for modern people to comprehend. In the case of the Torah, it was understood that students should first learn it and meditate on it later, reading and repeating it aloud, even though they may not yet understand it. Such was the importance of getting the exact wording correct even though comprehension may have to follow.

Given the Jewish culture in which Christianity arose, it is completely unrealistic to think that forgetfulness and wild imagination had too much of a hand in transforming authentic memories beyond all recognition in the course of just a few years or decades.[6] We shouldn't forget that Jesus was regarded as a great teacher, and his closest followers were called disciples, meaning those who are taught and learners. There can be little doubt they understood themselves to be committed to remembering their master's words.[7]

We see plenty of evidence of this. John 14:26 and 15:27 indicate that the disciples were expected to remember all Jesus said because they were witnesses with him from the beginning. Second Peter says that remembering the teaching first given was a central concern of the earliest Christians (1:15; 3:2). Paul stresses the importance of remembering the traditions he was taught as he passes them on to the Corinthians (1 Cor. 11:2; 2 Thess. 2:5). That this would have been a normal expectation is well established. It is also instructive to point out that Papias (an early Christian who lived from AD 60–163) repeatedly emphasized the importance of remembering the transmission of the earliest traditions from Jesus' disciples. All of this tells us that, from the beginning, those who established new churches would have taken care to pass on accurate Jesus traditions. It also provided new Christians, particularly Gentiles, a solid basis of tradition they were expected to remember and live out.

---

[6] Gerhardsson, *Memory and Manuscript*, 329–30.

[7] Dunn, *Jesus Remembered*, 177–80.

Accuracy and Control of Tradition

Was there any control over Jesus tradition by authoritative eyewitnesses who could vouch for its accuracy? We know that Jesus' earliest disciples had a particularly authoritative position in the young church. Luke has ample evidence in Acts, but Paul independently confirms it. Jerusalem, where the critical events took place, served as the center of early Christianity for some time, and evidence shows that Jesus' disciples lived there until the late 50s; thus they were there between fifteen to twenty years after the crucifixion and resurrection. As we will see, eyewitness testimony was embedded in their earliest traditions and considered essential to its accuracy. Against a hostile environment, both Jewish and pagan, the disciples were compelled to offer eyewitness accounts of "what we have heard, what we have seen with our own eyes, what we have looked at and touched with our hands" (1 John 1:1). As we talk about the communal side of tradition, we shouldn't forget that, for the early Christians, tradition gained authority only through its specific eyewitness character.

Because of this, accurately passing on testimony was a central concern. It is certainly one reason why teachers played such a prominent role within the earliest Christian communities. They were even the first regularly paid ministry.[8] Their positions were critical because they would have served as the repository of early Jesus tradition and the liturgy of the church. In this oral society, few had access to textbooks and written material, so they had to rely on individuals whose role was to function as a walking library.

Easily Remembered

In the first century, not only would people deliberately remember what they heard, but masters would formulate their teachings to make them easily remembered.[9] Jesus' teachings had many of these features. His sayings are typically short and incisive, and the parables have a clear and simple plot. They're also recognized as having a

---

[8] Dunn, *Jesus Remembered*, 176–77.

[9] Bauckham, *Jesus and the Eyewitnesses*, 281–82, 284–85.

poetic structure in their original spoken language (Aramaic). We can see this even in their Greek translations (the form in which we have them). It is apparent that Jesus carefully drafted and designed them as concise formulations of his teaching his hearers could remember, ponder, and live by.

It would have been self-evident that Jesus expected his sayings to be deliberately learned by his hearers, especially his disciples. As was customary, his sayings would be memorized word for word. But narratives such as his act of stilling the storm (Matt. 8:23–27; Mark 4:35–41; Luke 8:22–25) were probably memorized as a narrative structure, meaning that key phrases along with the overall flow would be memorized.[10] This is exactly what we see in the different traditions in Matthew, Mark, and Luke. We find consistency in the flow of the story and near word-for-word similarities, but there are variations. The basic features of the event are fixed, guaranteeing the story does not turn into another, but we find variation around nonessential details. We should also note that Jesus would have said the same things on many different occasions as he broadcast the message of the kingdom to the villages he entered.[11] So some of the variability we see is probably due to Jesus' own delivery of the same teaching on different occasions.

New Testament scholar Craig Blomberg notes that what is remarkable is the extent to which the main contours of oral tradition remained solidly intact. It is impressive, and it shows how aligned they are with other ancient historical accounts in displaying a substantial commonality in plot, setting, people, and order.[12] Separating them distinctively from tales, the allowed variability with historical accounts is much less pronounced. The concern for

---

[10] Dunn, *Jesus Remembered*, 217.

[11] Craig L. Blomberg, "Orality and the Parables: With Special Reference to James D. G. Dunn's *Jesus Remembered*," in *Memories of Jesus: A Critical Appraisal of James D. G. Dunn's Jesus Remembered*, eds. Robert B. Stewart and Gary R. Habermas (Nashville, TN: 2010), 98–99; Bauckham, *Jesus and the Eyewitnesses*, 256.

[12] Vansina, *Oral Tradition*, 53.

accuracy is clear from the key elements that give the oral tradition its stability.[13]

How Soon?

When did the remembering of Jesus tradition begin? Did it start years or decades after Jesus' death and resurrection appearances? Gauging this is vital to know if what we have accurately reflects history. We can answer by stating what we know generally of the period and specifically what we know about early Christian practice. Regarding the period in general, we know that, as events occurred, an oral history was typically developed by gathering eyewitness testimony from people involved in the incidents.[14] It was common to amass testimony and cross-check the main elements against other relevant testimonies. Eventually this newly composed oral history would become oral tradition of past events. As you might imagine, not all oral tradition is equal. Some lose their historical roots more than others, and we have to be careful about how far removed the tradition is from the original event and if there is other corroborating evidence. But you can see why memory was so critical for ancient people: their histories and identities were passed on through these traditions.

Specifically regarding Jesus tradition, we have every reason to believe that the process of fixing Jesus' words and deeds in memory would have begun at the *very same time* Jesus spoke or acted. His hearers would not have waited years or decades to fix tradition. Jesus would have made an enormous impact, such that the impact would *include with it* the formation of tradition. Thus from the first moment it would have been common to begin deliberately committing what was witnessed to memory. As we noted, the exact words were memorized and orally recited with others, or the key elements of the events were fixed for easy recall. New Testament scholar James Dunn remarks:

---

[13] Dunn, *Jesus Remembered*, 206–07, 223–24, 239–41.

[14] Vansina, *Oral Tradition*, 12–13.

Subsequently we may imagine a group of disciples meeting and requesting, for example, to hear again about the centurion of Capernaum, or about the widow and the treasury, or what it was that Jesus said about the tunic and the cloak, or about who is greater, or about the brother who sins. In response to which a senior disciple would tell again the appropriate story or teaching in whatever variant words and detail he or she judged appropriate for the occasion, with sufficient corporate memory ready to protest if one of the key elements was missed out or varied too much.[15]

The disciples had a shared experience they would have discussed and formulated into fixed tradition right away. In addition to aiding the memorization process (a little like college students discussing the day's lectures), it served as the bond holding them together as a community of disciples. We see it already before Easter, evidence of which is in the formal transmission (a word-for-word memorization) of Jesus' teachings during his ministry. In the Gospels of Matthew (9:36–10:15), Mark (6:7–13), and Luke (9:1–6; 10:1–16), Jesus sends the disciples to spread his message while he is still alive. Making it obvious that he equates their message with his own, he says, "He who receives you receives me." It is only reasonable to assume that the disciples would have used the exact message Jesus used in his own teaching, which at any rate would have already been memorized by that point.

Formal Transmission

We have evidence in Paul's letters that early Christians practiced a "formal" transmission of tradition.[16] By formal we mean that there were specific methods to ensure tradition was faithfully handed on from a qualified authority. The evidence is found in Paul's use of the technical terms for handing on (*paradiddomi*, 1 Cor. 11:2, 23, corresponding to the Hebrew *masar*) and receiving tradition (*paralambano*, 1 Cor. 15:1, 3; Gal. 1:9; Col. 2:6; 1 Thess. 2:13; 4:1; 2 Thess. 3:6, corresponding

---

[15] Dunn, *Jesus Remembered*, 119.
[16] Bauckham, *Jesus and the Eyewitnesses*, 264ff.

to the Hebrew *qibbel*). Pregnant with technical meaning, these terms were used for the formal transmission of tradition and would have been familiar to Paul's readers. We know this is what Paul intended because he was educated in the Pharisaic school of Judaism, and it is obvious he took the technical terminology from his training.

Here is why it matters. To "hand on" tradition isn't just to tell it or speak it, and to "receive" a tradition isn't just to hear it. Rather, handing on tradition "means that one hands over something to somebody so that the latter possesses it," while receiving tradition "means that one receives something so that one possesses it." While this sometimes meant verbatim memorization, it always entailed some process of teaching and learning so that what was communicated was accurately retained. Also, it is clear that tradition required an authorized person to hand it down, so the *who* is a necessary precondition of its accuracy. We already mentioned the prominence of teachers within the early church who would have been authorized agents of Jesus tradition. In 1 Corinthians 15:3, Paul says he received the tradition from competent authorities and thereby places himself in a chain of transmission. In doing so, he provides us with the earliest evidence of how traditions were transmitted, and it shows that a considerable degree of precise memorization was involved.

We have many examples of formal transmission, but an interesting one involves independent material both Paul and Luke report, and its early date makes it worthwhile to highlight. It concerns the ancient tradition of the Lord's Supper. In 1 Corinthians 11:23-25, Paul "hands on" the words of institution he no doubt received directly from Peter during his two-week visit to Jerusalem shortly after his conversion. Beyond the fact that it is extremely early, here is what is interesting. Luke and Paul each report the tradition, and although they're completely independent of one another, the verbal similarity between the two accounts is striking (1 Corinthians 11:23-25, Luke 22:19-20). Clearly an instance of formal transmission (here almost word-for-word similarity), the two accounts can't be explained any other way because they could not have been aware of the other's text. Luke's Gospel—which was written later than Paul's letter—could not have been available to Paul. And Luke shows no familiarity with Paul's letters. Only strictly memorized oral tradition explains the high degree of verbal resemblance.

The Last Supper, which forms the basis of the Lord's Supper in Paul's letter, is on similar ground. It appears in multiple texts (Matt. 26:26–29; Mark 14:22–25; Luke 22:17–20), yet we know it was an earlier formalized oral tradition. Evidence shows that the communion language in these accounts was already embedded in the church's liturgy long before the Gospels or Paul's letters were written, meaning we know they were disseminated through the formal handing on of tradition early and quickly. The Lord's Prayer is in the same position. As Dunn remarks, "it was a matter of fundamental tradition, the sort of tradition which Paul took care to pass on to his newly formed churches (1 Cor. 11:23), the sort of tradition which gave these churches their identity . . . It was tradition remembered as begun by Jesus himself, and remembered thus from as early as we can tell."[17]

One other quick point before moving on. Much of what Paul says in his letters implies that his hearers already know what he is talking about. He assumes they know the traditions of Jesus' death and resurrection, as well as liturgical practices and how Christians should live their lives.[18] Given that he wrote his letters in the 50s, they had to have received the traditions much earlier, especially because many of them were already part of the liturgy. Thus we can surmise that the passing on of tradition was part of the founding of churches from the very beginning. And Paul was careful to refer his churches back to those foundational traditions, which included things pertaining to Jesus' identity and resurrection from the dead (2 Tim. 8; Rom. 1:3–4), community tradition (1 Cor. 11:2, 23), and how new converts should live (Phil. 4:9; 1 Thess. 4:1; 2 Thess. 3:6).

First Corinthians 15:3–7

One of the more significant sections from Paul involves his *handing on* of the resurrection appearances in 1 Corinthians 15:3–7. So you have the context of the passage, here is what it says:

---

[17] Dunn, *Jesus Remembered*, 226–31.

[18] Dunn, *Jesus Remembered*, 176–79.

> For I delivered to you as of first importance what I also received, that Christ died for our sins according to the Scriptures, and that He was buried, and that He was raised on the third day according to the Scriptures, and that He appeared to Cephas, then to the twelve. After that He appeared to more than five hundred brethren at one time, most of whom remain until now, but some have fallen asleep; then He appeared to James, then to all the apostles.

What is interesting is that it is a textbook case of a preexisting formula Paul hands on to his Corinthian audience. Scholars agree that the tradition probably reaches back into the first five years after Jesus' crucifixion. Here are the reasons.[19] First, the words Paul uses to introduce verses 3–7 correspond to the technical rabbinical terms used to transmit tradition (1 Cor. 11:23) referenced earlier. Second, the verses contain many non-Pauline traits, meaning that the style and syntax aren't consistent with the rest of Paul's writings. In other words, it is obvious he did not write them. Third, what is cited as evidence for Jesus' resurrection way exceeds what was necessary in the context of the letter. Paul simply hands on a set tradition he probably received when he first became a Christian one to three years after the crucifixion.

The tradition's origin is also significant. First Corinthians 15:11 states that the apostles preached the same tradition, which points to Jerusalem as the place of origin for the resurrection formula. Since the church began in Jerusalem, the Twelve, which included Peter, would have acted as guarantors of the tradition. We know Paul probably received the formula in Damascus immediately after his conversion. We also know from Galatians 2 that Paul personally met with Peter and James in Jerusalem three years after his conversion. He spent two weeks with Peter in particular. Since Paul had been educated a Pharisee, his natural inclination would have been to seek out doctrinal authorities who were able to transmit authentic tradition, which is exactly what Jewish teachers and students did. Thus, we can have no doubt why Paul went to Jerusalem: to gather

---

[19] William Lane Craig, *Assessing the New Testament Evidence for the Historicity of the Resurrection of Jesus* (New York: 1989), 15–20.

and validate the tradition he'd already received. Even the word Paul uses to describe the visit speaks to his intent. It is used only here in the New Testament and implies that it was a fact-finding mission. Elsewhere, the word indicates a fact-finding mission to well-known cities and other points of interest with a view to acquiring firsthand information. His purpose was to get information about the resurrection from firsthand eyewitnesses.

But here is what is so important about the timing of his visit: it was only six years after Jesus' crucifixion, and given the incredibly short period, it would be infeasible to regard the formula with its list of named eyewitnesses—who were still alive and could be questioned—as legendary. And because the formula is a unity, we know that the original apostolic preaching included the naming of eyewitnesses. So given its early date and Jerusalem origin, it is most probable it goes back to the apostles themselves.[20]

Thus, we can conclude that with the formula, Paul was passing on firsthand eyewitness testimony of Jesus' resurrection from the dead. Greek historians like Herodotus regularly employed the method of naming witnesses to demonstrate historical trustworthiness. As Dodd comments, "There can hardly be any purpose in mentioning the fact that most of the 500 are still alive, unless Paul is saying, in effect, 'the witnesses are there to be questioned.'"[21] Note that Paul does not appeal to any subjective experience but to historical fact that can be verified by his readers. Last, we should note that the majority of the appearances and the sequence of events—death, burial, resurrection, appearances—are multiply attested in other Gospel sources.

Early Written Material

Up to this point we have talked primarily about oral tradition and how it was transmitted. One thing we have not covered yet is the evidence we have for many of those traditions being fixed in written

---

[20] Gerhardsson, *Memory and Manuscript*, 297–98.

[21] Craig, *Assessing the New Testament Evidence*, 15-20.

form.[22] Samuel Byrskog says it is highly likely there were written accounts with eyewitness reports integrated into small narratives well before any New Testament writings appeared.[23] It is also evident that the early Christian teachers and authors were well educated, and their oral practices intersected with scribal practices.[24] One of the clearest examples is the passion narrative found in the Gospel of Mark, which scholars refer to as a "pre-Markan" account of Jesus' crucifixion that Mark used to compile his Gospel. It is incredibly early and probably dates right back to the time of the crucifixion itself.

We know this because there are details of places and names that situate the narrative in Jerusalem. It probably originated with the Galilean members of the early church in Jerusalem soon after Jesus' death, no later than AD 37. Jesus' disciples were identified as Galileans in Jerusalem. Because of its incredibly early date, it is highly unlikely it would have been corrupted so early on. We have to remember that the accounts were circulated not just among Jesus' followers but among critics as well, who would have been all too eager to correct misleading or false information since everything occurred in the public space. Another fascinating detail about the narrative is that, oddly, it does not name the high priest, which the parallel accounts in the other Gospels do. Such a strange omission seems explicable only if the account was circulating between AD 18-37, the time in which everyone would know Caiaphas currently held the office.

It is likely that Peter's testimony stands behind the narrative, which is where its Galilean imprint comes to the foreground. While we will look at this more later, it is sufficient here to point out that Peter stands out prominently in Mark generally but specifically here in the pre-Markan passion account. It seems most plausible that the Galilean disciples, and particularly Peter, produced a narrative about Jesus' death and resurrection. The combination of its early date, its

---

[22] Brown, *The Death of the Messiah*, 51.

[23] Samuel Byrskog, *Story As History—History As Story: The Gospel Tradition in the Context of Ancient Oral History* (Boston: 2002), 269–72.

[24] Byrskog, "A New Perspective," 75.

location in Jerusalem, and the testimony of the eyewitnesses behind it is nothing short of astonishing. In it we have an unadorned account of Jesus' crucifixion with high historical value that few question. On top of these examples there were probably other private written notes of the disciples and other witnesses that may have been worked up into written sources.[25]

Conclusion

Based on the evidence, we can conclude with high probability that the disciples would have begun memorizing Jesus' words and deeds *as* he spoke or acted. It would have been expected for the disciples to learn their master's sayings word-for-word, and then to fix the main elements of plot, setting, people, and order of the critical events. We have plenty of evidence of both. Those traditions would have in turn been carefully passed on from an authorized person to the early churches, and we have seen how important the office of teacher probably was toward that end. Accurately handing on Jesus tradition was enormously important because they were rooted in eyewitness testimony, a fact that served to guarantee their historical trustworthiness.

In the earliest written records, we saw how careful Paul was to use the technical rabbinic terms for handing on and receiving tradition. He'd received the resurrection formula soon after his conversion and spent two weeks with Peter and James to verify the accuracy of the tradition. He makes the point in Galatians that the Jerusalem apostles had nothing to add to what he'd already received, meaning it was accurate and in no need of revision. Given the culture in which he lived, this shouldn't come as a surprise. It was the expectation that tradition should be safeguarded against corruption, which we saw abundantly demonstrated by the rabbis of the period.

Finally, concerning how far back we can trace Jesus tradition, Jan Vansina points out that recent oral traditions of one or two generations beyond the eldest living members in a community suffer only small damage, if any. Obviously timing of a tradition matters,

---

[25] Blomberg, "Orality and the Parables," 126.

because the longer the interval between its original telling and where it is presently increases the chance that successive communities have inserted their interpretations.[26] Predictably, if it is a short interval between the event and the tradition, it still resembles its original form. As they get older, they tend to accrue interpretive elements from the then-present community. This does not mean they lose all historical value, because whatever is carried forward from previous retellings still reflects the original event.

Generally, we can say that memorized wording fares better than loosely remembered accounts. Whether it was one or the other depended on how important it was to the individual and community as a whole. The strict memorization we see throughout the Gospels and Paul's letters speaks to the significance the disciples attached to Jesus tradition. The fixed formula in 1 Corinthians 15 is universally recognized as being, at the latest, composed just a few years after the crucifixion. Evidence also shows that the pre-Markan passion narrative was composed probably on top of the events themselves. Poetry and song also remain rich sources when they contain historical data, which we also saw in the narrative hymns in Paul's letters. Previously we had the opportunity to point out how ancient many of the hymns and liturgical formulae were and indicated that a good portion of the material should be dated from within just a few years of Jesus' death. From an historical perspective, that is impressive and greatly increases the probabilities that we have tradition rooted in eyewitness testimony. Because of their early dates, we are well within the first generation of eyewitnesses and when they were still alive. Thus, given the remarkably short period and the independent traditions, any serious doubts about the accuracy of the core Jesus tradition would be historically unsound.

Before ending we should add that this is all on top of the fact that the earliest Christian records started to be published in the 50s, only twenty or so years after the crucifixion. Relative to other historical records, this happened at lightning speed. Thus, we see Jesus tradition was frozen in time extremely quickly and during the lifetime of the eyewitnesses.

---

[26] Vansina, *Oral Tradition*, 191–93.

CHAPTER 9

How We Are Wired

Memories, Biology, and Social Influence

How accurate is human memory? How sure can we be of our own memories, and how long, if at all, do they reflect what actually happened days, months, or years ago? Certainly not all memories are equal. Think about what you had for breakfast this morning, and maybe even how the kitchen looked. Compare that with memories of a childhood family vacation and see how dim the latter is in contrast. And what about the possibility of memory bias—do the groups we identify with influence what we remember? These are important questions as we talk about the disciples' eyewitness testimony and whether their memories were sufficiently accurate to establish the central elements of the appearances. To get a handle on the issues, we are going to look in this chapter at what memory research suggests. Specifically, based on the data we will try to answer two questions: Do the memories transmitted in the Jesus tradition have the characteristics that produce accurate and stable memories, and what would we expect to see if the disciples reported something that did not happen?

Answering these allows us to make predictions about what we should have expected if Jesus had been raised from the dead, as well as what was probable if he did not. To get there, we will need to look at the data around if and how memory is reliable over time. If it is, what characteristics do we normally see? Based on those, we will see if the resurrection events fit the parameters. To answer what we'd expect if the resurrection did not occur, we will look at research on our biological and social influences and how memory and attitudes are shaped by them. Doing this will allow us to say with some probability what we should expect if Jesus hadn't risen from the dead.

Recollective Memory

New Testament scholar Richard Bauckham points out that the type of memory we see throughout the Gospels is what experts refer to as recollective memory.[1] It is a form of autobiographical memory involving a recollection of a particular episode from a person's past. It usually seems to be a "reliving" of the original event and can have a strong visual imagery component.[2] While recollective memory does not have a direct representation of time, it typically contains information about place, actions, persons, objects, thoughts, and emotion. Information is normally expressed as a mental image and may have irrelevant details, but it can also have nonimage components. It is also accompanied by a belief that the event was personally experienced by the person in that person's past. Generally, recent memories are fairly accurate unless they've been influenced by what experts call schema-based beliefs (which we will discuss below). Last, recollective memories cause high confidence in their accuracy, and that confidence frequently predicts memory accuracy.

Overall, research has shown that recollective memory is accurate about the central details of an event, while somewhat less so in its periphery details. In an experiment that bore this out, research participants were asked to carry an alarm clock device for several weeks. When the alarm went off, they were instructed to write down events that were occurring (actions and thoughts) and other descriptive information (location and time). During the next few months, they were tested to see how accurately they recalled the details. Aside from periodically recalling the wrong event, only 1.5 percent of the time did they make true errors in which they recalled something

---

[1] Bauckham, *Jesus and the Eyewitnesses*, 324.

[2] William F. Brewer, "What is Autobiographical Memory?" in *Autobiographical Memory*, ed. David C. Rubin (New York: 1986), 30, 34–35.

that wasn't part of what they originally recorded.[3] That is fairly impressive.

Flashbulb memories—memories about where you were when you heard unusual news—appear to tell a different story, however. At least that is the impression given in popular literature. It is based on a 1992 study on memories of the space shuttle Challenger explosion. In the study, researchers gathered information within one day of the event and carried out recalls two to three years later. They found that 25 percent of people were in error while only 7 percent were completely correct,[4] a finding often used to show memory's fallibility. And of course, memory can be fallible. A closer examination, however, of the space shuttle data reveals a more nuanced picture. Turns out that some participants recalled a vivid event that occurred the same day, but it wasn't related directly to the initial reception event the researchers were scoring against. So while a large number of people were technically in error, they were probably accurately recalling different scenes from the same day. While we will talk about emotion below, other studies on flashbulb memories highlight that when events are emotionally charged, recall is rather accurate.[5]

Some of the memory errors people make involve what experts refer to as schema-based beliefs. A schema is a pattern-seeking device in our mind that allows us to quickly distill the information of everyday experience. It filters what we experience and determines how we interpret things, and it makes a new experience meaningful by normalizing it according to our preexisting mental schema. Built through past experiences and intertwined with our social setting, schemas lead us to expect certain things based on history. "When we perceive and store experiences we are already shaping them with structures of meaning that belong to us because they belong to our

---

[3] William F. Brewer, "What is Recollective Memory?" in *Remembering Our Past: Studies in Autobiographical Memory*, ed. David C. Rubin (New York: 1995), 41.

[4] Brewer, "What is Recollective Memory?" 42, 48.

[5] Sven-Ake Christianson and Martin A. Safer, "Emotional Events and Emotions in Autobiographical Memories," in *Remembering Our Past: Studies in Autobiographical Memory*, ed. David C. Rubin (New York: 1995), 222.

social context."[6] On the one hand, schemas are beneficial because they instantly organize new experiences into meaningful patterns; on the other hand, because they're based on our own limited knowledge and relatively small social setting, they can bias memory formation and our ability to absorb new knowledge. In other words, although schemas have their upsides, they can also create resistance to change.

A simple example of schema-based errors involved an experiment on rooms people had visited previously. In this case it was the graduate student office. When asked to recall the room and what was in it, participants frequently reported books that weren't actually there. Preexisting schemas created the *expectation* of seeing books, so participants included them in later recollections. In other words, they retroactively included in their memory the plausible presence of books. In the Challenger study, it is possible that some people reconstructed details around the plausible idea that they had initially heard about the explosion on TV.[7] Because television is where most of us got news at the time, it makes sense why someone would reconstruct details around television media. Over time and with strong schema-based processes, an original experience can be reconstructed to produce a new memory that retains most of the characteristics of other memories (strong visual imagery and strong belief value).[8]

However, we shouldn't overlook an obvious point: researchers uniformly assume the accuracy of the flashbulb memory itself. In other words, *that* the space shuttle exploded is accurately remembered. Otherwise, how would they be able to ask about the circumstances around the event? Notwithstanding the more irrelevant details, participants accurately remembered the main event. Thus, William Brewer notes that "for private flashbulb events (i.e., those personally experienced) the event itself should produce a classic recollective memory, and one would think that they would show an extremely low level of forgetting."

---

[6] Bauckham, *Jesus and the Eyewitnesses*, 335, 337.

[7] Brewer, "What is Recollective Memory?" 44–45, 50.

[8] Brewer, "What is Autobiographical Memory?" 44–45.

Before moving on we should also mention a schema-based error that retroactively makes a person look better than he should. A famous example involves the reminiscence of Rossini about his only meeting with Beethoven. When he first related it a few years after Beethoven's death, Rossini said he'd gone to Beethoven's house, had a hard time being admitted, and did not end up speaking to the master, whose command of Italian (Rossini's language) wasn't sufficient. However, toward the end of Rossini's life, the story had become quite a tale. Now the master, tortured and in the throes of creation, received Rossini and advised him to continue his great work and then praised *Il Barbiere di Siviglia* as the greatest comic work ever written.[9] This shows that reminiscences can project a consistent picture of the narrator and, in some cases like Rossini's, an ego-boosting justification for his or her life.

Emotion-Arousing Events

Not all aspects of experience are remembered equally well. Memories can be selective and emotional arousal can improve accuracy in some cases, but it can also affect how we remember unimportant details. If you're robbed at gunpoint, for instance, you'll remember the robbery better than other things that happened the same day. While the central elements of the event will probably be remembered well, periphery details may be less so. Your memory's accuracy will be higher on what your focus was during the episode, which could have been the gun or the perpetrator's face. Periphery details like hair or eye color might be less accurate. Emotional arousal seems to put an indelible imprint in our memories of the broad features of such events. "Explicit memories are very closely related to what gets attended to during the experience."[10]

Generally, research shows that people are more likely to remember emotion-arousing events than neutral, everyday events. One study examined witness memory and emotional reactions from

---

[9] Vansina, *Oral Tradition*, 8–10.

[10] LeDoux, *The Emotional Brain*, 209.

twenty-two post office robberies.[11] Those who'd observed a robbery, as either a victim or a bystander, filled out a questionnaire about their emotional reactions during the robbery and their memory for specific information. The consistency of their account was measured against police reports and the recollections given four to fifteen months after the robberies. Results showed that witness recollections of detailed information about the robbery (action, weapon, clothing) were consistent with police reports. Recollections of specific circumstances (date, time, other people) were less consistent. Interestingly, the accuracy rates of the victims were significantly higher than bystanders. What the study indicates is that highly emotional events are well retained over time with respect to the central event but less so in peripheral details.

Although similar results have been demonstrated in other studies, one in particular is worth mentioning. It involved Nazi concentration camp survivors in which testimonies of seventy-eight former prisoners were collected from 1943–1947 and 1984–1987. Comparison of the testimonies from these two periods revealed that almost all victims remembered the concentration camp experiences in great detail even after forty years. Although errors occurred, researchers found recall of the conditions in the camp and smaller details to be "remarkably consistent and accurate."[12] Thus we can conclude that the critical details of emotionally arousing events and some circumstantial information are less susceptible to forgetting than their neutral counterparts.

Summary of the Data

To understand the big picture, let's summarize the research so far. First, accurate recollections of past events show stronger visual imagery than inaccurate recollections. Second, memories with high confidence ratings show strong imagery reports.[13] The data provide clear evidence that confidence judgments are valid indicators

---

[11] Christianson and Safer, "Emotional Events and Emotions," 219–22.

[12] Christianson and Safer, "Emotional Events and Emotions," 222, 226.

[13] Brewer, "What is Recollective Memory?" 35–36, 43, 47, 49.

of memory accuracy. Thus, there is a link between confidence and accuracy, as well as between image vividness and accuracy. In fact, in the Challenger study, researchers found that imagery vividness reliably related to memory accuracy. Third, an event's uniqueness is an indicator of better remembered events. Fourth, if an event is rare, it is better remembered over time, demonstrating that low-frequency events consistently show better recall than high-frequency events. Fifth, if an event is important for a person's life then it tends to be better remembered. Sixth, emotionally charged events make them better remembered over a longer period. Seventh, frequent rehearsal consistently factors into more accurately retained memories.[14] This may involve the memory being constructed in a story form that is remembered as a piece of information rather than a recollection that is "relived." Interestingly, memory vividness correlates strongly with emotion, importance, and the amount of rehearsal. It has been shown that the best predictors of vividness for younger people is emotionality and importance, but for elderly people the amount of rehearsal is the most powerful factor. Here remote memories are vividly preserved because they're thought and talked about often.[15]

With that summary, we need to deal with two additional subjects before drawing any conclusions about the disciples. The first involves how the brain is wired. It turns out that the human brain has built-in automation affecting both memory and our attitude to new concepts. The second is the impact of group influence. Humans are inherently social creatures and the extent to which groups influence what we think and the memories we attend to is enormous. Recent research on both areas is fascinating and adds texture to the data we have surveyed on memory. Let's talk first about the brain.

The Brain's Automation

Researchers tell us we have built-in machinery, especially suited to minimize the energy and effort it takes to form and retain memories, find identity and meaning in social groups, and think. Consider

---

[14] Bauckham, *Jesus and the Eyewitnesses*, 334–35.
[15] Brewer, "What is Autobiographical Memory?" 44.

how you process decisions. Do you take your choices apart, look at the details, and perform a cost/benefit analysis of every option before coming to a conclusion? Sounds like the best way, but ponder the reality. You'd have to evaluate the consequences of each option at different points in the future and weigh the losses and gains, from which you'd infer logically which is a good and bad outcome. Considering all the possibilities, though, both in our available choices and the potential losses and gains, such a process is unrealistic.

Luckily this isn't how most of us make decisions, but it is what happens with patients who have prefrontal brain damage. Neuroscientist Antonio Damasio gives an account of one such patient who was presented with two simple options for a follow-up appointment. After consulting his calendar, he proceeded for almost thirty minutes to list reasons for and against each date, considering even possible weather conditions. He was walking through a tiresome cost/benefit analysis involving an endless comparison of his options and their consequences. He was unable to make a decision, and someone had to finally suggest which date to pick.[16]

Something different happens with normal brain function. The key components unfold in the mind instantly, and before applying a cost/benefit analysis, we experience an unpleasant gut feeling as a bad outcome comes to mind. Damasio calls it a somatic marker because feelings are directly tied to our body (*soma* being the Greek word for body) and because it marks an image in our minds. A somatic marker forces attention on a negative outcome and then sounds the alarm. That leads to *immediate* rejection. A cost/benefit analysis only happens *after* this automated step dramatically reduces the number of options. Damasio argues that somatic markers increase the accuracy and efficiency of the decision process while their absence reduces them.[17]

There is a downside, however, in that because they operate even when we are unaware, they can bias decision-making without our realization. By creating a bias against objective facts, they can interfere

---

[16] Damasio, *Descartes' Error*, 172–73, 193–94.

[17] Damasio, *Descartes' Error*, 173–74, 179, 185.

with rational decision-making and working memory.[18] Damasio thinks that they're probably driven by our biological drive of obedience, conformity, and self-esteem, which are ultimately manifest as emotions. On the one hand, we can be thankful to be wired with efficiency-producing machinery. It is hard to imagine how humans would have fared without it. Our ability to make actionable decisions is critical, and the idea of progress depends on it. And as we saw, the alternative isn't comforting. But its downsides of foreclosing and favoring certain options are notable.

There may be a more precise reason why the brain tends to do this, and it could have to do with energy consumption. We know the brain regulates many functions necessary for survival, such as our five senses, the continuous monitoring of our surroundings, learning and new memory, breathing, and heartbeat. Although it comprises only 2 percent of the body's mass, the brain consumes about 20 percent of its energy. Each unit of brain tissue requires almost twenty-five times the amount of energy as a similar unit of muscle tissue. "Consequently, for the brain to perform all functions necessary to survival, it must manage its limited energy resources very efficiently."[19] Because of this, it has built-in expense-minimizing capabilities, affecting the reception of both new information and memory.

Initially memories are unstable and subject to change but later become stabilized and resistant to disruption. The older the memories, the more resistant they are. We can see this as we compare children to older adults, with children being much less resistant to new ideas than adults. Technically, it is believed that memory formation changes the transmission effectiveness at the synapse level (a synapse is a structure that allows a neuron to pass a signal to another neuron); and of the brain's many components, synapses consume the most energy.[20] The point is that memory formation requires a

---

[18] Damasio, *Descartes' Error*, 177, 192.

[19] Onojighofia Tobore Tobore, "On Energy Efficiency and the Brain's Resistance to Change: The Neurological Evolution of Dogmatism and Close-Mindedness," (2018), 2. https://journals.sagepub.com/doi/abs/10.1177/0033294118792670?journalCode=prxa, 2.

[20] Tobore, "On Energy Efficiency," 3–4.

lot of energy, and the increased resistance we see as our memories get consolidated (particularly past early childhood) can be seen as the brain's way of efficiently using its limited resources. Absent that, the brain is likely to use more than 20 percent of the body's energy, which would be energy expensive and compromise its ability to manage other essentials.

But here are the practical consequences. Since ingrained memories are resistant to disruption or replacement, contrary information tends to be rejected. In contrast, information consistent with existing knowledge tends to be absorbed quickly, which would explain why dogmatism and close-mindedness are universal.[21] We seem to be wired to reject or be suspicious of new things.[22] When in familiar situations, the cells in our brain's core (the hippocampus) fire hundreds of times faster than they do in new situations. Because the hippocampus is connected to the area of the brain driving emotions (the amygdalae), it explains why sameness literally feels better. In other words, we have a biological default setting against what is new, against innovation.

The simple fact is we don't like creativity, even though we'd never say it out loud or admit it to ourselves. The new scares us because new things create uncertainty, and uncertainty is an aversive state we avoid. And because our social setting is part of normality for us, we prefer not only what we already know but also the groups that share our values. With assistance from the brain's automated processes, our social setting and the groups we identify with help form the schemas we talked about before.

Social Influences

Over the years many theories about why people make schema-based errors have been floated, particularly why they think in groups. Some argued that resistance to change stems from people valuing the groups they belong to, and changing one's attitude is the same as abandoning the comfort group-think provides. Others add that

---

[21] Tobore, "On Energy Efficiency," 4–5.
[22] Kevin Ashton, *How To Fly A Horse* (New York: 2015), 86.

people avoid tension and seek out information in line with their pre-existing views and are therefore likely to be persuaded by sources similar to themselves. A discomfort with uncertainty plays a large part in change resistance because it reduces predictability and creates feelings of chaos.

For social psychology, the power of group influence is one of the most durable lessons of human behavior. Evidence shows that we interpret things in light of the emotional expressions of others as early as twelve months old. Because social groups are a primary source of personal values, people safely assume that members of their group have values similar to their own. What is interesting is that although people deny it individually, they vastly underestimate the influence a group has over their thinking.

The extent to which this is true was demonstrated in well-known experiments in which participants, both politically conservative and liberal, were asked about welfare policy.[23] They were randomly assigned to one of two versions of the policy report. Naturally appealing to liberals was the "generous policy" with its lavish welfare spending, while the "stringent policy" appealed to conservatives with its strict spending limits. No existing program was more generous than the generous one in the study, and no existing program was more stringent than the stringent one. Participants were asked to comment on the randomly assigned policy.

Naively we'd expect their reactions to be based solely on content, as in fact they were when party opinions weren't mentioned. Here is what happened, though, when party preferences *were* mentioned. For both liberal and conservative participants, information from political parties completely overrode policy content. If they were told their party endorsed the plan, then liberals supported even a harsh welfare policy and conservatives supported even a lavish one. Once a policy was defined as liberal or conservative, its objective content was reduced to nothing. In other words, participants assumed the position of their group as their own and gave no weight

---

[23] Geoffrey L. Cohen, "Party Over Policy: The Dominating Impact of Group Influence on Political Beliefs," *Journal of Personality and Social Psychology* 85/5 (2003), 808–10.

to policy content. Further, they denied being influenced by the stated party positions and instead claimed that their opinions were based on policy content (as well as by personal government philosophy).[24] Even more interesting is that participants understood the power of group influence in a general sense: they could accurately estimate its impact on the attitude of others. However, they believed that they themselves were exempt from its effect.[25] Self-deception, it turns out, arises from the failure to apply a valid social theory to oneself.

Bottom line is that schema-based beliefs, partly driven by biological and social factors, are powerful enough that even when we know better, we can't escape their influence. In the business world, group-think is a constant threat and relentlessly talked about in the literature. Even so, it is continually credited with taking the lives of many once-great companies. Think Kodak and Blockbuster. Few if any organizations are risk free.

But what about the scientific community? Shouldn't this of all groups be free from schema-based errors? While science has built-in mechanisms for challenging group-think, it is not completely free either. It may be more immune than other less-structured disciplines, but it is still at risk. And the reason is due to the inherent bias humans have against change, which threatens preexisting schemas. To illustrate the extent of its effects, let's look at two fascinating medical cases highlighted by Kevin Ashton in which experts in their field wrongly interpreted otherwise clear evidence.

Vienna General and Royal Perth Hospitals

The first occurred in 1846 when a large number of women and infants were dying during childbirth in Vienna.[26] The cause was puerperal fever. What did not make sense was that the hospital had two maternity clinics and only one of them was experiencing the high death rate. In fact, more women and infants survived giving birth in the street than in this clinic, the deaths of which all came at the hands of

---

[24] Cohen, "Party Over Policy," 811–12.

[25] Cohen, "Party Over Policy," 820.

[26] Ashton, *How To Fly A Horse*, 72–75, 91–95.

doctors. Midwives delivered babies in the unaffected clinic, but the stark contrast between the two made no sense.

Vienna General happened to be a teaching hospital where doctors learned by cutting up cadavers. It was common then for doctors to go straight from dissenting corpses to delivering babies, proudly wearing their blood-stained gowns and without washing their hands. A doctor by the name of Ignaz Semmelweis started to wonder if the disease was being carried from the corpses to the maternity ward. He hypothesized that some kind of organic matter was being transferred from the morgue to the mothers but had no idea what it was. In spite of his colleagues' resistance, Semmelweis persuaded them to wash their hands before delivering babies, and the results were immediate. The death rate plummeted from 18 to 2 percent, the same as the other clinic.

His colleagues nevertheless remained skeptical and outraged, with one of them telling his students that a doctor's hands could not possibly carry disease because doctors are gentlemen, and a gentlemen's hands are clean. Because Semmelweis could not specify why it was saving lives, only that it apparently did, colleagues questioned the new procedure. As the medical community began to reject it, Semmelweis took a tragic downhill turn and eventually ended up in a lunatic asylum. With him out of the picture, doctors stopped washing their hands, and the death rate rose by a staggering 600 percent. Why did they throw up such resistance in the first place? Because it went against two thousand years of medical dogma. And it was that dogma that stunted progress until Louis Pasteur finally answered the why with his now-famous germ theory. What is important here is that prevailing ideas were and are fortified and vigorously defended by incumbency and familiarity.

Just as fascinating is our second and more recent case involving Robin Warren, a pathologist at the Royal Perth Hospital in Australia in 1979. For years scientists had known that bacteria can't grow in the stomach. Because stomachs are acidic, experts thought, they had to be sterile. It was practically dogma in the field of medicine. The problem began when Warren spotted what looked like bacteria in a patient's stomach. When he showed his colleagues the sample through a high-powered electron microscope, they eventually saw what he was talking about but did not get the point. Whatever it was, they reasoned, it could not be bacteria. But Warren started seeing it more and more, in fact in one out of every three stomachs. For two years he collected samples until he found someone who believed him. That man was Barry Marshall, a newly hired gastroenterologist.

Collaborating over the next year, the two collected evidence showing that 90 percent of patients who had the bacteria had ulcers. Further, they found that every patient with a duodenal ulcer had the bacteria. Despite widespread skepticism, they finally got the proof they needed. Armed with the data, they tried to publish their findings in a leading medical journal. Not surprisingly, the editor could not find any reviewers who agreed. Every expert in the field knew that bacteria can't grow in the stomach. Fortunately, however, the editor was a bit of a renegade and published the piece anyway. Warren and Marshall went on to show that the bacteria *H. pylori* causes ulcers, and through the research of others, it was learned it can be killed with antibiotics. In 2004, the duo won the Nobel Prize for their discovery.

But here is the backstory that illustrates just how powerful pre-existing schemas can be. Warren was able to gather stomach tissue because of the emergence of the flexible endoscope—a tube with a light, camera, and cutting tool that doctors fed down the patient's throat—which became available in the 1970s. The same endoscope was being used all over the world, and thousands of pathologists were looking at similar stomach biopsies. Yet they weren't seeing what Warren was. "*H. pylori* was staring them all in the face," notes Ashton, "But they saw dogma, not bacteria." Moreover, at the same time Warren first saw *H. pylori*, a group of American scientists were conducting a study on an epidemic of stomach disease. Looking for a virus—again because everyone knew bacteria can't grow in the stomach—they tested the blood and stomach fluid of the research participants. Certainly not beginners, they were led by a decorated professor of medicine. After Warren and Marshall's work was published, the research team revisited their biopsies, and lo and behold, *H. pylori* was clearly visible. They literally could not "see" it before because long-established dogma veiled their eyes. What is more, in 1940 a Harvard researcher found *H. pylori* in more than a third of ulcer patients, but his supervisor told him he was wrong and stopped him from further investigation. We now know that the bacteria had been found in medical literature dating back to 1875. For over one hundred years, it had been seen but not believed.

Cases like this abound, and the implications are clear. Human beings are highly susceptible to their social context, be that familial, religious, or the larger social structure in which they live. With neural wiring preset to favor existing and ingrained memories and knowledge, stepping outside of group norms is the exception. This isn't to suggest that individuals can't and don't do precisely that at times but to point out that the probabilities are stacked in favor of the status quo. Try making swift changes to an organization and you'll likely see how the status quo reigns supreme. As we noted earlier, it is what Peter Drucker, the famous management consultant, meant when he said that "culture eats strategy for breakfast." He was right.

Implications for Jesus' Disciples

Here are some of the questions we need to answer now that we have looked at the issues. First, could the memories of the disciples have been distorted in the same way as Rossini's later recollection? Second, did the memories of the disciples betray influences of schema-based errors? And third, what is the probability their memories were accurate in the central details? That is, did the events the disciples describe have the elements we'd expect to produce accurate long-term memories? Remember that we are only attempting to establish the core facts and that incidental details won't concern us. The core issues are around the *fact of* Jesus' resurrection appearances, nothing else.

First then to our opening question: could the reminiscences of Jesus have followed the same tale-making pattern as Rossini's? Could those resurrection stories have come as a result of the justification of their own life trajectory, becoming ever more fanciful and non-historical as time went by? The evidence does not support such a notion on multiple levels. What we find in Rossini's late account is a self-aggrandizing tendency, the opposite of what we see in the reports of the disciples. The Gospels paint an unflattering picture of them as fearful, faithless, and frankly a bit clueless. This was definitely not even close to egocentric reconstructions. It is because of this difference that scholars regard the Gospel accounts as historically credible; the church would not have created embarrassing portraits of their first leaders. Unhistorical tales go the opposite direction. The bottom line is that we find no evidence in the record of the Rossini effect.

A more serious possibility lies in schema-based errors. As we have seen, these arise from the strong biological and social tendencies to cling to the groups and information with which we feel at home. I believe we see precisely these influences in their attitudes and behavior in the days following the crucifixion, but then witness a violent shift as the appearances begin. Let me explain.

Evidence from this period shows that Jews expected a Messiah to deliver Israel from the political and social bonds of foreign rule. He was supposed to come, sword in hand, to complete a military victory and achieve independence from pagan culture and restore Temple worship. There is no evidence anyone expected the Messiah to fail, and there was definitely no expectation he would die. Beyond that, crucifixion was the most humiliating death imaginable and reserved for society's outcasts, slaves, and criminals. Not only could people of this period not imagine a dying Messiah, but no one ever suggested a resurrected Messiah, especially one that had been rightfully executed as a Messianic pretender by the state. Anyone who suggests that the disciples could have connected the ideas of crucifixion and Messiah, Messiah and one man's resurrection from the dead, and resurrected Messiah and his identification with Israel's God, YHWH, is ignoring these well-established facts.

As a reminder, we see plenty of evidence of this in the Gospel accounts. For instance, before the crucifixion Jesus asks the disciples, "But who do you say that I am?" to which Peter responds, "You are the Christ." Jesus then plainly tells them he'll soon suffer and be killed, and then rise again (Mark 8:29–33). Peter immediately rebukes him and protests, after which Jesus in turn rebukes Peter, "Get behind Me, Satan." Painfully obvious is that Peter could not process what Jesus said precisely because of what the disciples could not then fathom: the brutal crucifixion and resurrection of Israel's God—an understanding that would not emerge until the shocking confrontation with the risen Jesus. Time and again the disciples as a group fail to understand Jesus' prediction about his impending death

(Mark 9:32; 10:32–41). And all of them end up deserting Jesus as he is taken into custody, soon after which Peter completely denies him (Mark 14:37–50, 66–72).

After Jesus is crucified, the disciples are justifiably terrified. Jesus was executed as a criminal and Messianic pretender, and they knew full well the same punishment could come their way. Everything they had hoped for, based around their preexisting Jewish expectations, had been crushed. So they fled. Later on the road to Emmaus, Cleopas and one other disciple lament, "But we were hoping that it was He who was going to redeem Israel," betraying their continuing fixation on traditional Jewish Messianic teachings that formed the heart of their early education (Luke 24:13–42). Soon after this Jesus appears in the midst of the disciples, and the Gospels describe them as "startled and frightened," resulting in Jesus' acknowledgment of their fear and doubt. Even after he shows them his hands and feet as proof of his crucified body, they still can't believe it "because of their joy and amazement." Separately John reports the disciples being shut in a room with closed doors "for fear of the Jews" (John 20:19). Thomas, after being told by the others that Jesus had risen from the dead, refuses to believe: "Unless I see in His hands the imprint of the nails, and put my finger into the place of the nails, and put my hands into His side, I will not believe" (John 20:24–25).

That they maintained schema-based Jewish beliefs is an understatement, and historically this is exactly what we'd predict. All along they had interpreted the words and deeds of Jesus *within the construct* of a first-century Palestinian worldview. Warren and Marshall's colleagues knew from a lifetime of reinforcement that bacteria can't grow in the stomach. Jesus' disciples knew from a lifetime of education and social reinforcement that no one rises from the dead before the general resurrection at the close of human history. They knew the Messiah would deliver Israel from foreign rule, and they most certainly knew that the Messiah would not be shamefully crucified. And just as we'd predict, they behaved in accordance with those ingrained beliefs until violently shaken from their preconceptions. If the appearances never took place, we have every reason to think that their schemas would have taken over. Like others in this period, Jesus would have been regarded as another in a long line of murdered prophets who was translated to heaven, and no doubt his disciples would have made regular visits to his tomb for the veneration so prevalent during the first century.

Schema-based beliefs derive their plausibility from individual and social expectations, which is what we see immediately after the crucifixion. Based on history and what we know about biological and social influences, there is nothing to support the notion that the disciples expected a resurrected Jesus shortly after his execution. And there is nothing to support the contention that they would have connected the three ideas of crucifixion and Messiah, Messiah and one man's resurrection from the dead before the end times, and resurrected Messiah and his identification with Israel's God, YHWH.

If the disciples had fabricated the appearances, either unwittingly or willfully, as some maintain, we have every reason to think that the stories would have morphed to fit their long-standing pre-existing first-century Jewish schemas. Lest Rossini be put forth as an example to the contrary, we should note that he too fell back on a well-documented schema-based tendency: an ego-boosting self-schema. Absent a life-altering event, it was highly likely the disciples would return to their socially ingrained schemas. They never did. And further, many of them suffered horrible fates maintaining Jesus' physical resurrection from the dead.

Finally, what is the probability that the memories of the disciples were accurate in the central details? Did the described events have the elements that produce accurate and long-term memories? I believe so. We saw that well-recalled memories have strong visual imagery (or vividness), high confidence, uniqueness, rareness, importance, the provoking of emotions, and frequent rehearsal.

We find the majority of these elements in the eyewitness testimony. Let's take them one at a time, starting first with what we don't find in most of them. Because the narratives had to be concise collections of Jesus tradition, most lack visual imagery. The reason is probably due to the size limit and expense of the papyrus scrolls used during this period.[27] It was important to keep scrolls to a manageable length so it wasn't prohibitively expensive to copy and use them. As you can well imagine, visual imagery is costly because of its

---

[27] Bauckham, *Jesus and the Eyewitnesses*, 342.

wordiness. Making the necessary trade-offs, the evangelists slimmed the descriptions down to fit the large amount of material they needed to include. But we also know that high confidence is the other side of vividness, and I don't think the evidence could be stronger in the case of the disciples. We saw last chapter how durable the Jesus traditions were, and it is because of that confidence. We know that many of the disciples were executed for not backing down on their recollections. So confidence would have to be ranked as extremely high. Based on this, and on the fact that the traditions have most of the characteristics facilitating accurate memory retention, we can infer that the eyewitnesses had strong visual imagery associated with their personal memories.

Moreover, that Jesus' words and deeds were unique is an understatement. The sick were healed, the dead were raised, Jesus walks on water and appears to them alive after he was executed. Nothing about it is ordinary or trivial, and much of it would have been considered rare indeed. In addition, the events would have been enormously consequential and thus highly significant both at a personal and group level.[28] Based on the durability of the disciples' testimonies and their eventual deaths, it is easy to see that their experiences with Jesus were the most significant events of their lives.

Last, frequent rehearsal is demonstrated by the well-preserved Jesus traditions. We can be sure that eyewitnesses would have deliberately remembered and told their stories about what happened soon after the events. We see this in several places, and it would have been natural for people to spread the news about miracles they had witnessed or about being healed themselves. In Matthew 9:27–31, for instance, Jesus heals two blind men, and despite his wish to the contrary they "went out and spread the news about Him throughout all that land." This was so common that we even hear reports from contemporary pagan sources about Jesus being known as a miracle worker. So too would the disciples have told stories to other disciples, rehearsing and committing the events to memory, thereby fixing them into tradition. We saw previously that Jesus' words would likely have been memorized verbatim, while narrative

---

[28] Bauckham, *Jesus and the Eyewitnesses*, 342.

events would be memorized as a structure. "As a general rule, frequent rehearsal would have the effect of preserving an eyewitness's story very much as he or she first remembered and reported it."[29]

Because these would have been the most significant events of the disciples' lives, there can be no doubt of indelible emotional tags fixing them in memory. Not only would the healings and exorcisms during Jesus' ministry fit this condition, but the radical unexpectedness and rarity of Jesus appearing alive days after his execution would have guaranteed accurate reflection. Evidence shows that the crucial events were quickly fixed in traditional formulae and carefully passed onto the early churches. We have seen specific examples requiring dates from within a few years of the crucifixion, but we can be sure they were fixed as the events occurred. And finally, in line with the research, the central details reported in the Gospels—death by crucifixion, burial, empty tomb, multiple appearances of the risen Jesus in multiple settings—remain consistent, which is exactly what we'd expect with stable recollective memory. New Testament scholar Richard Bauckham concludes that "the memories of eyewitnesses of their history of Jesus score highly by the criteria for likely reliability that have been established by the psychological study of recollective memory."[30]

---

[29] Bauckham, *Jesus and the Eyewitnesses*, 345–46.
[30] Bauckham, *Jesus and the Eyewitnesses*, 346.

CHAPTER 10

What Are the Gospels, and Who Stands behind Them?

Think about any past event and consider how we know it. Napoleon's defeat at the battle of Waterloo or Julius Caesar's crossing of the Rubicon are things we are fairly certain of, but what are our reasons? No one living today can personally vouch for either event, yet historians are confident they occurred. There might be several ways we know things like this. Archeologists could unearth clues from distant history with the potential of changing the way we think about a particular culture. Such evidence could come from an inscription on stone that sheds light on a society's language or ancient earthenware that reveals how a people otherwise shrouded in mystery lived from day to day. Another important piece of evidence is oral tradition, which has proved invaluable for our understanding of ancient culture generally. And then there are written texts. Obviously the degree to which each can help is limited to what they are. A sole piece of earthenware, while perhaps valuable, is probably not as impactful as someone's eyewitness testimony of an important event transmitted either orally or in writing. We have always put a premium on hearing people with firsthand knowledge of an event.

One thing we *can* say is that our understanding of the past would not be as rich if we lacked testimony from people who lived through it. Consider the first Roman rulers as an example. Without a minimal amount of eyewitness testimony, how would Suetonius have written his important history, *Lives of the Caesars*, with its famous account of Nero's death? Though not reliable in every respect, it still provides valuable information on the personal habits, lives, careers, and even the physical appearance of the Roman emperors. Minus any accounts from people who witnessed many of those events, we'd lack some valuable knowledge. Of course eyewitness testimony is no silver bullet. Alongside its historical value, Suetonius's work includes information based on gossip and hearsay, and at times we can detect evidence of subjective bias. So historians face many problems sifting through eyewitness testimony. People who witnessed the *Titanic* sink disagreed over whether the ship sank in one piece or broke in two as it plunged into the sea. In fact, it wasn't until 1985 when the ship was found that researchers concluded it must have split apart just before sinking.

When a fire ravaged the city of Rome in AD 64, it burned 70 percent of the city over a six-day period, leaving half its population homeless. Rome's emperor was the unpopular Nero, and many speculated that he himself started the fire, a rumor fueled by the fact that he used some of the land cleared by the fire to build his Golden Palace and surrounding gardens. In contrast, Nero blamed Christians for the fire and had many of them arrested and executed. Of course the charge was far-fetched, but again we see conflicting testimonies. Whether or not we will ever know the fire's cause is hard to predict, but one thing we can say about both the *Titanic* and the fire of Rome is that, despite disagreement over the details, we can establish the *fact that* Rome burned and that the *Titanic* sank.

Thus, despite the problems around the periphery details, eyewitness testimony plays an essential role in our knowledge of past events. This is as true today as it was thousands of years ago. Read any current historian and you'll find considerable dependence on eyewitness testimony of some sort. For instance, Doris Goodwin's recent book *Leadership* documents the lives of Abraham Lincoln, Theodore Roosevelt, Franklin Roosevelt, and Lyndon Johnson. In the opening pages, she talks about her sources, and here is what she says:

> By immersing myself in manuscript collections, personal diaries, letters, oral histories, memoirs, newspaper archives, and periodicals, I

searched for illuminating details that, taken together, would provide an intimate understanding of these men, their families, their friends, their colleagues, and the worlds in which they lived.[1]

Think about her history without eyewitness testimony. Much of what she cites depends on it in some way. Without it we'd lack the rich details that pull us into the lives of four American presidents and we would not have a firm foundation for understanding many of the events that shaped the country. Eyewitness testimony is clearly the linchpin of much of our historical knowledge.

Our understanding of Jesus is no exception, and because of that we need to ask some basic questions. First and foremost, because what we know comes from ancient documents, what type of literature are the Gospels? Just like today, the ancients had different types: they had poetry, history, philosophy, biography, moral, tragedy, comedy, and so forth. Though there was often an overlap in genres (for instance between biography and history), one usually dominated. Which one the Gospels fall into determines how we should understand what the authors intended to convey. In other words, answering the genre question will help us to predict if the authors included history as part of their work. Obviously if they intended the Gospels as myth or drama then asking about eyewitness testimony is a nonstarter. Second, do we have evidence that eyewitness reports stand behind any of the New Testament? And third, is there any corroborating external testimony about the sources used by the Gospel authors? As you can see, the question of eyewitness testimony stands at the center of what follows.

The Gospels: What Are They?

Let's talk about the idea of literary genre. If you read a best-selling novel, you won't expect historical truth to be front and center. That is because you know at the outset the author created the world you inhabit while immersed in the story. If done well, the book takes

---

[1] Doris Kearns Goodwin, *Leadership In Turbulent Times* (New York: 2018), xii.

you on a journey of the ups and downs of the main character and hurls you toward a climactic ending. On the other hand, read a biography of George Washington and you'll intuitively expect something different: there you'll expect to be engaged with research and reliable historical truths. While poetry is enjoyable, you would not expect it to necessarily convey history. There might be a blending of the different genres, but it is usually clear which dominates and what to expect. Though we may not explicitly think through a book's genre, we do so implicitly and without giving it much thought, such that if its content does not match our expectations, we are surprised. So what about the Gospels? What was their intended genre, and what should we expect in terms of history?

It was fashionable throughout the twentieth century for scholars to place the Gospels in their own literary genre for which there was no precedent. As late as the 1970s, the Gospels were considered a category of their own that could not be compared with other ancient literature.[2] The thinking went that they're not ancient biographies since, scholars alleged, the Gospels don't distinguish between the past—or the real history of Jesus—and the present of the first-century Christian community. In other words, they alleged that we can't get much history out of the Gospels because Jesus' actual past had been reformulated to meet the present needs of the Christian churches. Thus the past had been swallowed by the present, leaving little trace of the Jesus of history.

Then, in 1992 New Testament scholar Richard Burridge published a seminal book demonstrating that the Gospels should be seen as ancient biography and not as a unique genre. Turns out that allegations of the Gospels being a unique genre reflected more the biases of certain scholars than the Gospels themselves. This shouldn't surprise us at this point, as we have seen that preexisting biases can powerfully influence both individuals and groups. Despite the then-widespread bias on Gospel genre, Burridge demonstrated that the status quo was wrong. Here is why he drew his conclusions.

---

[2] Richard A. Burridge, *What Are the Gospels? A Comparison with Graeco-Roman Biography* (Grand Rapids, MI: 2004), 15–16, 211, 246–47.

After a detailed study of ancient biographies, he was able to isolate and document certain generic features they all shared. First, they all concentrated on one individual (much like they do today) and were flexible in how they handled the person's life, with some giving even-handed coverage of the person's life and others stressing just one period. Second, some biographies concentrated on the person's deeds and life chronology, while others focused on certain topics, teachings, or virtues in a nonchronological way.[3] Third, they all tended to be of a similar appearance, length, and structure. Taken together, these features communicated its biographical nature to readers. Burridge then demonstrated that the Gospels fit squarely within the genre of Graeco-Roman biography. At the generic level, he pointed out that the framework of the Gospels have a chronological sequence with topical material inserted, have a geographical and social settings focused on Jesus, and convey a serious and respectful atmosphere—all of which were typical of ancient biography.[4]

Digging deeper, he showed additional characteristics linking the Gospels to biography. First, Luke begins with a formal preface stating his intention to give an accurate account of Jesus, while Mark and Matthew start with their subject's name (Jesus), both of which were common for biography. Second, Jesus is clearly the subject of the Gospels, with each devoting a large amount a space to his passion and death. Again, this uneven allocation of space to a particular period was common among biographies. Third, the Gospels have similar size, structure, and scale that we find in other ancient biographies. They use a similar range of literary units, and they select from oral and written sources to characterize Jesus in his words and deeds. Fourth, the settings, topics, atmosphere, quality of characterization, and range of purpose are similar to other ancient biographies. The bottom line is that Burridge settled the issue by demonstrating that the Gospels belong to the genre of Graeco-Roman biography. In fact, they exhibit more of the features of biography than that of Isocrates, Xenophon, and Philostratus. His study has now been widely accepted by New Testament scholars.

---

[3] Burridge, *What Are the Gospels?*, 184.

[4] Burridge, *What Are the Gospels?*, 210–12.

But here is why this is important. Ancient readers would have expected biographical works to accurately represent the past, *as past*, and to not be overly confused with the present needs of the community. In other words, they would have expected the narratives to recount Jesus' real past and not to confuse it with the present. If the early church hadn't been interested in the historical person of Jesus, then it would not have produced biography.[5] Thus by creating biography, the authors clearly signaled its historical basis.

Autopsy in the Earliest Texts

Ancient Greek and Roman historians adhered to Heraclitus' maxim that "eyes were surer witnesses than ears," and in doing so they related to the past visually. Being an eyewitness or interrogating someone who had been was the most reliable way to understand past events. The term for this was *autopsy*, which can be thought of as a visual way of gathering information through the direct testimony of people who witnessed an event.[6] In seeking out eyewitnesses, ancient historians acted like oral historians, in that they aimed to hear the living voices of those who were present. But this primacy of sight wasn't restricted to just historians; it was part of both ancient Greek culture and the cultural setting of the New Testament. Sight was essential for reaching back to the past. Thus autopsy was necessary for anyone interested in finding out and recording what happened at an earlier time.

What is important is that autopsy runs throughout the New Testament to the point that it is elevated as a central apostolic credential.[7] The eyewitness testimony of those who could speak from firsthand experience was therefore critical to the formation of the earliest Christian churches.[8]

---

[5] Burridge, *What Are the Gospels?*, 249.

[6] Byrskog, *Story As History*, 48, 64–65.

[7] Byrskog, *Story As History*, 232.

[8] Bauckham, *Jesus and the Eyewitnesses*, 122.

The Testimony of Peter

In addition to Peter's letters, we have reason to believe that he stands behind much of Mark's Gospel. He is given special prominence, and Mark mentions him twenty-six times (Simon occurs seven times, and references to Simon Peter and Peter just occur nineteen times), which is considerably higher than the other Gospels. An example occurs in chapter 16 as the women go to Jesus' tomb to anoint his body. Once they are there, an angel appears and tells them Jesus has been raised, and then says, "But go, tell His disciples and Peter, 'He is going ahead of you to Galilee . . .'" Since Peter was just one member of the group of disciples, this singling him out from the rest is surprising. Richard Bauckham notes two things about this. First, it surely points ahead to the resurrection appearance of Jesus to Peter individually, which both Paul and Luke mention (1 Cor. 15:5, Luke 24:34).[9] Second, because Mark brackets the entirety of his Gospel by highlighting Peter at the beginning (1:16) and here at the end (16:7), it is likely that Peter is the witness whose testimony runs throughout. Bauckham says it is a striking confirmation of Papias' later testimony (see below) that Peter was the source of Mark's Gospel.

On top of this, scholars have documented the so-called plural-to-singular narrative device in Mark that gives readers the effect of approaching a place with Jesus from *within* the group of disciples. In other words, it gives readers a vantage point of being there with the disciples as Jesus approaches and a personal view of what happens next. This was first shown by Cuthbert Turner in 1925 but has now gained widespread attention because Mark seems to adopt the "point of view" of the group of disciples, most likely that of Peter.[10] In addition to what we saw above, Mark has an undue focus on Peter in several places, including 8:27–33 and 14:27–31, where Jesus addresses Peter individually, 9:5–6, where Peter's inner motivation is explicitly disclosed, and in 14:54, 66–72, where Peter denies Jesus and the reader goes with Peter into a situation physically removed from the other disciples. In addition, we previously pointed out that Peter probably stands behind much of the pre-Markan passion narrative

---

[9] Bauckham, *Jesus and the Eyewitnesses*, 125.
[10] Bauckham, *Jesus and the Eyewitnesses*, 161, 168.

in Mark's Gospel, which was an early written account dated no later than AD 37.

Last, Peter's perspective in Mark may be visible in what is referred to as a "Servant christology," which emphasized Jesus as God's faithful servant who suffered on the cross in our stead.[11] Here is why scholars think Peter stands behind it. There are several places in the New Testament where he is either directly or indirectly associated with the idea of Jesus as God's suffering servant (Acts 3:13, 26; 4:27, 30). Isaiah's suffering servant (53:2ff.) also clearly stands behind his comments in 1 Peter 2:21–25. This would be all the more understandable if Peter's emphasis came from the painful memory of rebuking Jesus for predicting his suffering and death by crucifixion. After his restoration by Jesus after Easter, he very likely verbalized in a special way that such suffering was in accordance with God's purposes.

Luke's Perspective

F. F. Bruce informs us that Luke was the only Gentile among the New Testament writers and a physician by profession. He inherited the high traditions of Greek historical writing and had a rich trove of excellent sources for the information in the Gospel of Luke and its companion, the book of Acts. Many scholars have pointed out his careful attention to historical details, including his familiarity with the proper titles of notable people. As Bruce notes, anyone relating to the wider context of world history as Luke does is courting trouble if he is not careful because it affords critics opportunities for pointing out falsehoods.[12]

It is clear that Luke has done his homework with no less rigor than Greek historians like Thucydides. He makes this point in the first verses (the prologue) of his Gospel:

> Since many have undertaken to set down an orderly account of the events that have been fulfilled among us, just as they were handed

---

[11] Byrskog, *Story As History*, 270–271.

[12] Bruce, *The New Testament Documents*, 46, 88ff.

on to us by those who from the beginning were eyewitnesses and servants of the word, I too decided, after investigating everything carefully from the very first, to write an orderly account for you, most excellent Theophilus, so that you may know the truth concerning the things about which you have been instructed. (1:1–4 NSRV)

Luke has done his research and did not rely on hearsay, with most scholars agreeing that he took the time to interview eyewitnesses. We know this for several reasons. First, the prologue is written so his readers understand he is writing a form of historiography, meaning that he has investigated the facts from people who were with Jesus from the beginning of his ministry. The Greek word he uses for "eyewitnesses" (*autoptai*) refers to those who were firsthand observers of the events, while the phrase "from the beginning" (*ap arches*) refers to eyewitnesses who'd been present throughout the events being related.[13]

Thus he is qualified to tell the story from the beginning because he is familiar with the traditions from eyewitnesses who were physically present at the events.[14] As Baukham points out, "the principle of eyewitness testimony 'from the beginning' was remarkably important for the way that the traditions about Jesus were transmitted and understood in early Christianity."[15] Notice that Luke acknowledges he was one of many attempting to compile an account and gathering tradition from eyewitnesses. Given the cultural emphasis on sight, this is exactly what we'd expect.

Interesting too is that Luke follows Mark in making Peter the first and last disciple to be individually named (4:38; 24:34), thus incorporating Peter's witness in his own Gospel. But he does something just as interesting in contrast to Mark by highlighting the testimony of the women, which for Luke is second only to Peter (8:2–3; 24:6). "The implication is surely that Luke owed some of his special traditions to one (most likely Joanna) or more than one of them."[16]

---

[13] Bauckham, *Jesus and the Eyewitnesses*, 117, 124.

[14] Byrskog, *Story As History*, 228–32.

[15] Bauckham, *Jesus and the Eyewitness*, 124.

[16] Bauckham, *Jesus and the Eyewitnesses*, 131.

So his sources expanded beyond the disciples to include others who were present as well.

As we move to the book of Acts we find the same emphasis on autopsy. Early on (1:21–22), Luke includes an account of the apostles having to replace Judas, who had betrayed Jesus. What is interesting is the criterion they used to select Matthias, which he records as follows:

> Therefore it is necessary that of the men who have accompanied us all the time that Jesus went in and out among us—beginning with the baptism of John until the day he was taken up from us—one of these must become a witness with us of His resurrection.

For inclusion in the group of apostles, it was necessary to have accompanied Jesus during his whole ministry, which is how the twelve are presented in the Gospels. An apostle had to be an eyewitness to the history of the earthly Jesus as well as his resurrection from the dead. "Autopsy is raised to a level of essential importance. It is a central apostolic credential."[17] Thus when Peter and John are called to defend their preaching of Jesus' resurrection, they can't refrain from speaking about what they've seen and heard (Acts 4:20). Peter repeats his report of autopsy in Acts 10:39–41:

> We are witnesses of all the things he did both in the land of the Jews and Jerusalem. They also put Him to death by hanging Him on a cross. God raised Him up on the third day and granted that He become visible, not to all the people, but to witnesses who were chosen beforehand by God, that is, to us who ate and drank with Him after He arose from the dead.

Last, you might remember that teachers were the first paid ministry of the early church. We can now see the reason. Acts makes clear that the apostles are eyewitnesses and ministers of the word, or eyewitnesses *become* ministers of the word. This service consisted primarily in teaching, reflecting the importance of the office as it was

---

[17] Byrskog, *Story As History*, 233–34.

commissioned with transmitting Jesus tradition that was founded in autopsy. The word was the concrete manifestation of what they themselves observed. Consequently, it makes sense why the teaching office rose to a central position in the earliest congregations.

The Testimony of John

Although John often speaks of seeing with the eyes of faith, the physical observance of the historical Jesus was always the *basis of faith*, especially for those who followed but did not themselves witness the events. In his prologue, he emphasizes autopsy when he says that "the word became flesh and dwelt among us." This idea also underlies the doubting Thomas incident in John 20:29, in which Thomas insists that unless he sees physical proof that Jesus rose he won't believe. It is noteworthy that *as* Jesus quells Thomas' doubt, he adds, "Because you have seen Me, have you believed? Blessed are they who did not see, and yet believed" (John 20:29). With the episode John does not downplay the importance of autopsy but makes the point that Thomas, like those of us who follow, should believe based on the eyewitness testimony of the disciples who'd already seen the risen Christ.

But John's main emphasis on autopsy is primarily found toward the end of his Gospel. Seeing becomes his authorial qualification for everything he has said to that point, making clear that "he who has seen has testified, and his testimony is true; and he knows that he is telling the truth, so that you may also believe" (19:35). While the context refers to the piercing of Jesus' side, in 21:24 he includes everything in his Gospel. There he enlarges his authority by specifically naming himself as the witness, claiming, "This is the disciple who is testifying to these things and wrote these things, and we know that his testimony is true" (21:24).[18] John's eyewitness testimony is corroborated by his presence at three critical events: the last supper where he is next to Jesus (13:23, 25), in the courtyard with Peter (18:15–16), and at the cross (19:26–27). In addition, at the empty tomb John is the only one to perceive what had happened (20:8)

---

[18] Byrskog, *Story As History*, 236–38.

and the first to recognize the risen Jesus at the appearance in Galilee (21:7).

Even more forceful is John's reference to autopsy in his first letter (1 John 1:1-4):

> What was from the beginning, what we have heard, what we have seen with our eyes, what we have looked at and touched with our hands, concerning the Word of Life—and the life was manifested, and we have seen and testify and proclaim to you the eternal life, which was with the Father and was manifested to us—what we have seen and heard we proclaim to you also, so that you too may have fellowship with us; and indeed our fellowship is with the Father, and with His Son Jesus Christ. These things we write, so that our joy may be made complete.

There are four verbs for seeing in this brief section, with the first two being followed by statements that stress even further the reality of sensual perception. Autopsy is of primary importance.[19] As Samuel Byrskog notes, it indicates that the reference to seeing for oneself, with its stress on sensual perception by touch, clarifies that the glory "we looked at" (John 1:14) was of one who was so real we could feel it with our own hands. Jesus could be heard, seen, and touched. Autopsy is meant to defend the Jesus event as an event in history, and John claims to have been an eyewitness himself as well as the other disciples implied by the "we." While John claims to have been an individual eyewitness, he maintains a collective self-understanding and thus regards himself as carrying on the oral history of the community.

So you can see that for the early Christians, having eyewitness authority behind the traditions was essential. They insisted on having reports from witnesses that were attached to individuals who could vouch for their authenticity. Thus, when the disciples of the original Apostles preached or taught, they fell back on the witness of the Apostles and constantly referred to them in their preaching and teaching.[20]

---

[19] Byrskog, *Story As History*, 239-42.

[20] Gerhardsson, *Memory and Manuscript*, 282-83.

Personal Names

In addition to the apostolic eyewitnesses, Richard Bauckham points out that the personal names in the Gospels were likely attached to the stories they were included in.[21] It is reasonable to assume that the names were of well-known people in the early communities and that many of them were themselves the eyewitnesses behind the accounts. Cleopas is a good example. The story he appears in (Luke 24:13ff.) does not require him to be named; in fact, his companion in the story isn't. There does not seem to be any plausible reason for naming him other than he was the eyewitness source behind the tradition. Bauckham notes that he is probably the same person as Clopas whose wife, Mary, appears with the other women at the cross (John 19:25). "The story Luke tells would have been essentially the story Cleopas himself told about his encounter with the risen Jesus. Probably it was one of many traditions of the Jerusalem church which Luke has incorporated in his work."[22]

Also fascinating is the role of the women as eyewitnesses in the Gospel accounts. They see Jesus die, they see his body being laid in the tomb, and they find the tomb empty. Because some of the women were present at all three events, they could testify that Jesus was dead when laid in the tomb—and that it was the tomb he was buried in that they later found empty. All the accounts use the verbs of seeing when referring to the women.[23] They saw the events as Jesus died (Matt. 27:55; Mark 15:40; Luke 23:49), they saw the tomb he was laid in (Mark 15:47; Luke 23:55), they went on the first day of the week to see the tomb (Matt. 28:1), they saw the stone rolled away (Mark 16:4), they saw the young man sitting on the right side (Mark 16:5), and the angel invited them to see the empty place where Jesus' body was lain (Matt. 28:6; Mark 16:6). It is reasonable to suppose that the women were well known and remained accessible and authoritative sources of these traditions as long as they lived.

---

[21] Bauckham, *Jesus and the Eyewitnesses*, 46–47.

[22] Bauckham, *Jesus and the Eyewitnesses*, 47.

[23] Bauckham, *Jesus and the Eyewitnesses*, 48, 51.

There are also the recipients of Jesus' healing who continued to be the eyewitness sources behind the Gospel accounts. It is interesting that only in a few accounts of healings are the recipients named. Those are Jairus, Bartimaeus, and Lazarus. There are also three women named in Luke 8:2–3 who were cured of evil spirits and infirmities, and then Simon the leper. It is likely that Jairus and Bartimaeus were both well known in the early Christian community, but by the time the other Gospels were written their names were omitted because they weren't as well known (although Jairus is mentioned by Luke). Mark could expect his readers to know Bartimaeus as a living miracle who made Jesus' healing still visible to the churches of Jerusalem and Judea. After his death and the fall of Jerusalem, however, Bartimaeus was no longer widely known, and so Matthew and Luke omitted his name.

That named individuals continued to serve as the authoritative sources behind the healings is corroborated by a reference from the early historian Eusebius, who cites the early second-century remarks of Quadratus. Probably around the same generation as Papias (whose life would have spanned the late first and early second century), Quadratus remarked that those who were healed by Jesus were always present and survived "even to our own times."[24] Thus around the same time (end of the first century) that Papias was collecting information from still-living disciples, Quadratus claims that those healed performed a similar function of eyewitness testimony. What is important about his comment is that, however long these people lived, they served as sources for their own experiences with Jesus.

Finally, it is probable that the twelve disciples are listed by name because they were the official eyewitnesses who formulated and authorized the core traditions in the Gospels. The group was evidently so important for the transmission of Jesus tradition that their specific names are carefully listed in the Gospels. Luke identifies them by name as those who are "eyewitnesses and ministers of the word" (1:2) while Matthew and Mark imply the same in their accounts.

---

[24] Bauckham, *Jesus and the Eyewitnesses*, 52–54, 97.

External Testimony: Papias and Polycarp

Because autopsy was so important in ancient culture, drawing a direct line from those with firsthand experience of Jesus' ministry, death, and resurrection was critical. Having traditions that can be traced back to eyewitnesses became more important as time went on, especially as the first generation began to die off. First and foremost, the object was to produce eyewitnesses, but second was to find witnesses to what the eyewitnesses had said. While this would have been a normal expectation, it was particularly the way transmission functioned among the rabbis. That is why we see an organic line from the apostolic claim that the risen Lord was seen by Peter and the other disciples to the post-apostolic concern to prove that one's information came from "Mark, who was the interpreter of Peter," from "Polycarp, who was a disciple of John," or from "the elders, the disciples of the Apostles."

That concern for a connection leading back to original eyewitnesses is what we find in the years after the apostles die. And because there is a legitimate link between the apostles and the next generation, we have some important evidence in later writings. That is what concerns us here, and we will highlight five examples.

First, Eusebius preserves an account of the origin of Mark's Gospel by Papias—bishop of Hierapolis—who in turn heard it from the "Elder," who was most likely John the Elder, who had been a personal disciple of Jesus and the author of the Gospel of John. In terms of the connection we mentioned, when Papias heard John's remarks, it could not have been later than AD 100 and must have been from someone who was in a good position to know how Mark's Gospel related to Peter's teaching.[25] Here is what Papias says:

> The Elder used to say this also: Mark, having been the interpreter of Peter, wrote down accurately all that he [Peter] mentioned, whether sayings or doings of Christ; not, however, in order. For he was neither a hearer nor a companion of the Lord; but afterwards, as I said, he accompanied Peter, who adapted his teachings as necessity required, not as though he were making a compilation of the sayings of the

---

[25] Bauckham, *Jesus and the Eyewitnesses*, 204.

Lord. So then Mark made no mistake, writing down in this way some things as he [Peter] mentioned them; for he paid attention to this one thing, not to omit anything that he had heard, nor to include any false statement among them.[26]

We don't have any compelling reasons to reject Papias' remarks about the author and eyewitness source behind Mark's Gospel. In fact, there is a lot to support it.[27] First, it is supported by 1 Peter 5:13 in which Peter calls Mark "my son," indicating a close relationship between the two. Second, Peter's prominence and the number of times he is mentioned in Mark's Gospel is striking when compared to the others. Mark mentions him twenty-six times, mostly at vital points, with nine of those at the beginning of the passion narrative. Third, we have independent confirmation of Papias' remark toward the middle of the second century in a comment made by Justin Martyr. Also, between AD 160–180 there is a fragmentary introduction to Mark's Gospel that says, "He [Mark] has been the interpreter of Peter. After the death of Peter himself, he wrote down this gospel in the regions of Italy."

Our second example comes from what Papias says about Mark's method of composition. That Mark made it his concern "not to omit anything that he had heard, nor to include any false statement among them" was a common statement for someone doing historiography. It described the character of reliable eyewitness testimony, which is precisely what Papias claims of Peter's role. Mark puts readers into direct touch with Peter's oral teaching and does not falsify anything by adding to it.

Third, Papias commented on his own method for collecting information, which should now make sense against his ancient background. It reads as follows:

I shall not hesitate also to put into properly ordered form for you (sing.) everything I learned carefully in the past from the elders and noted down well, for the truth of which I vouch. For unlike most

---

[26] Bruce, *The New Testament Documents*, 32.

[27] Byrskog, *Story As History*, 276–77, 282–83.

people I did not enjoy those who have a great deal to say, but those who teach the truth. Nor did I enjoy those who recall someone else's commandments, but those who remember the commandments given by the Lord to the faith and proceeding from the truth itself. And if by chance anyone who had been in attendance on the elders should come my way, I inquired about the words of the elders—[that is,] what [according to the elders] Andrew or Peter said, or Philip, or Thomas or James, or John or Matthew or any other of the Lord's disciples, and whatever Aristion and the elder John, the Lord's disciples, were saying. For I did not think that information from books would profit me as much as information from a living and surviving voice.[28]

In keeping with good historiographic practice, Papias is interested only in traditions formulated and transmitted by named eyewitnesses, preferably from their own mouths. We know that Philip the evangelist and his daughters settled in Hierapolis, and Papias would have personally known Philip. Once Philip arrived, Papias would have received a whole body of tradition from people who knew many of the eyewitnesses. For Papias, the closer to an eyewitness the better. While he received the words of the apostles from their followers, Irenaeus says he actually heard Aristion and John, "often being able to quote them by name and give their traditions in his writings."[29] Obvious for Papias is that oral traditions directly from living witnesses were preferable, and that the written compositions were the outcome of the oral history of those who were present.

Fourth, Papias comments on the way Mark, Matthew, and John handle the chronological sequence of events in their Gospels. Mark, he notes, lacks a detailed sequence of events but should be praised for limiting himself to recording Peter's testimony. By recording an eyewitness source, he accomplished the first stage of the historian's task. Matthew's Gospel is valuable because it was written by an eyewitness. However, it too lacked the strict chronological sequence Papias appreciated in John's Gospel. In that Papias heard John around AD 90 and about the time when his Gospel was published, it might

---

[28] Bauckham, *Jesus and the Eyewitnesses*, 218–30.
[29] Byrskog, *Story As History*, 244–45.

have been what prompted John to talk about the different styles of each Gospel.

Our final example comes from Irenaeus, bishop of Lyons. His following remarks are significant because they corroborate Gospel authorship and their autopsy foundation:

> So Matthew published a written Gospel among the Hebrews in their own language, while Peter and Paul were preaching at Rome and founding the church. After their departure [i.e., their death, which occurred during the Neronian persecution in 64], Mark, the disciple and interpreter of Peter, did also hand down to us in writing what had been preached by Peter. Luke also, the companion of Paul, recorded in a book the Gospel preached by him [Paul]. Then John, the disciple of the Lord, the one who leaned back on the Lord's breast [a reference to John 13:25 and 21:20], himself published a Gospel while he resided in Ephesus.[30]

Irenaeus' remarks are valuable because he was a student of Polycarp, bishop of Smyrna (martyred in 156), and Polycarp in turn had been a disciple of the apostle John himself. Irenaeus had often heard Polycarp relate eyewitness accounts of Jesus from John and others who were personally acquainted with Jesus. Concerning his memories about this, he adds:

> For I distinctly recall the events of that time better than those of recent years (for what we learn in childhood keeps pace with the growing mind and becomes part of it), so that I can tell the very place where the blessed Polycarp used to sit as he discoursed, his goings out and his comings in, the character of his life, his bodily appearance, the discourses he would address to the multitude, how he would tell of his conversations with John and with the others who had seen the Lord, how he would relate their words from memory; and what the things were which he had heard from them concerning the Lord, his mighty works and his teaching. Polycarp, as having received them from the eyewitnesses (*autopton*) of the life of the Logos, would declare altogether in accordance with the scriptures. To these things

---

[30] Bauckham, *Jesus and the Eyewitnesses*, 456.

I used to listen diligently even then, by the mercy of God which was upon me, noting them down not on papyrus but in my heart.[31]

What is important is that Polycarp as a young man heard a disciple of Jesus named John, who was likely the author of the Gospel of John, as well as others who'd seen Jesus (including Aristion). Irenaeus would hardly have been mistaken about this important detail, and he valued his memories of Polycarp because they put him in touch with Jesus by only two intermediaries, Polycarp and John. This was possible because both lived long lives. John survived into the reign of Trajan (beginning in AD 98), and Polycarp was eighty-six when he was martyred in Smyrna somewhere between AD 156 to 167. Irenaeus also had a written source in the works of Papias, whom he calls "a hearer of John and companion of Polycarp." He would have had further corroboration about John being the author of the Gospel of John through the independent confirmation of Polycrates of Ephesus, who wrote about the same time as Irenaeus.

Thus we find ample evidence from second-generation sources about both the authorship of the Gospels as well as their direct connection to eyewitnesses. Not only this, but these external sources confirm that many of the Gospel accounts can be traced directly back to specific individuals who could vouch for their authenticity.

Conclusion

We have now seen that because the Gospels were composed in the genre of ancient biography, readers would have expected the past to be represented accurately. If the early church hadn't been interested in the past *as past* they would not have written biography. In keeping with this, we have found many examples of autopsy reports in both the Gospels and the early letters of the apostles highlighting their experience of seeing the risen Jesus. With their deliberate use of the language of autopsy, there can be no doubt that they were testifying to what occurred in human history. No spiritualizing tendencies can be detected in the reports. "What we have heard, what we have seen

---

[31] Bauckham, *Jesus and the Eyewitnesses*, 456–58.

with our eyes, what we have looked at and touched with our hands" was their constant refrain.

Further, we have ample evidence from disciples of the disciples corroborating the eyewitness authority behind the Gospels. In light of the cumulative weight of the evidence, there is no reason to doubt these second-generation reports. All in all, we can conclude with a high degree of historical probability that the early reports came directly from those who personally witnessed the Jesus events and continued to stand behind them throughout their lives.

CHAPTER 11

The Conversion of Paul the Persecutor

In her lively book on the pre-Civil War Congress of 1830–1860, historian Joanna Freeman reveals surprisingly violent incidents between congressmen in both the United States House and Senate. She shows that by the time the Civil War broke out in 1861, congressional violence had become something of a spectator sport among the public and provided much fodder for newspapers countrywide. Thanks to a well-regarded House clerk named Benjamin Brown French, who was personally present for much of what Freeman documents, we get a front row seat on events that would profoundly shape the country's history.

Though the violence is interesting in its own right, my interest relates to French's evolving views on slavery. We are fortunate because French was unusual in the amount of detail and discipline he brought to his diary entries. He was unusual in the sense that he wasn't content with merely relating what he did that day, or how he felt. While we get this too, he also included detailed information about what went on in Congress behind the scenes, as well as his evolving political views. We learn a great deal about how Congress and the nation changed over time, and we also witness his own evolution—most dramatically in his conversion from a loyal Democrat eager to appease Southern pro-slavery allies to a devoted Republican with a deep-seated hatred of the Southern "slave-ocracy."[1]

---

[1] Joanne B. Freeman, *The Field of Blood: Violence in Congress and The Road to Civil War* (New York: 2018), 5, 9–11.

Notably, by 1860 he'd switched to the other side of the slavery question, ready to stand up to the brutality and bullying of Southern congressmen. It was a long evolutionary road given that he'd been a Washington insider since 1833. Early on, his diary shows him kowtowing to Southerners to save the Union and serve himself. At that time there was a domineering block of slaveholders at the heart of the national government who regularly deployed violence to get what they wanted, and a large number of Northerners were bullied into silence in French's earlier years. But the diary also reveals his evolution, which was a gradual and difficult one. Pro-slavery Southerners, we learn, were all too willing to threaten personal violence against congressional colleagues who attacked their way of life.

Central to the emerging congressional violence was party membership, and early on the Democratic party had a powerful hold on French. It embraced his entire worldview. It was during this period that the first structured national parties rose to power; party membership wasn't just a label but a fraternal pledge. It bound men together in loyalty to a worldview and in reputation and purpose. Manhood and honor were at the heart of this band-of-brothers form of politics. To abuse one party member meant that all members had been abused. In a sense, the first battles of the Civil War were fought in the halls of Congress but were also merely representative of the battles raging across the country.

Freeman points out that in the 1830s most fighting centered around party differences, but by the '40s and '50s, it was slavery-centric. Because Southerners regularly threatened and bullied their congressional Northern colleagues to stifle debate about slavery, French began to change his views. Having one's rights challenged within the Union, and even more within the very walls of Congress whose responsibilities include free and open debate, was a form of degradation that required resistance. French's evolving fears and growing sense of betrayal from his Southern colleagues precipitated a dramatic change in beliefs. "By 1860," Freeman notes, "this most genial of men was armed and ready to shoot Southerners, a change of mind and heart experienced through the North."[2]

---

[2] Freeman, *The Field of Blood*, 9-11.

While today's issues are different, we can all empathize with French's long (even painful) thought evolution. We can empathize because it is the norm for personal evolution to take lots of thought, pain, and time. Think about your own views. No doubt they've matured over time, oftentimes rather dramatically. Age and experience tend to do that.

In contrast, take Preston Smith Brooks, a member of the House of Representatives from 1853–1856. A Southern Democrat from South Carolina, Brooks was a zealous advocate of slavery. Actually, zealous is an understatement. His speeches and conduct on the House floor would seem atrocious to us now, but in his mind he was defending the Southern way of life and fought (often literally) accordingly. Willing to do whatever it took to uphold the Southern code of honor, he earned widespread popularity and approval from the South when he attacked his fellow House member, Republican Charles Sumner, in 1856. Sumner, an abolitionist, had previously delivered an intentionally inflammatory antislavery speech that prompted the attack.

In his mind Brooks had no choice but to defend his Southern constituents, and he also felt that one of his relatives had been unfairly impugned in Sumner's speech. For days Brooks tried to assault Sumner on the streets (which at the time was common) but was unable, so he made the decision to confront Sumner within the House chamber. Waiting impatiently until the women left the gallery, he approached Sumner's desk, made a quick statement, and started brutally beating him with his cane. Pinned down by his desk, which was bolted to the ground, Sumner wasn't able to free himself quickly enough and was hit over the head multiple times. Blinded by his own blood, he ended up unconscious before the assault ended. Incredibly, Brooks was cheered in the South for defending its way of life. He was even reelected in 1856, but he died in 1857 before the new term began.

Brooks' road to that moment of attack was marked by a dogged adherence to particular beliefs about who was human, what his and the South's rights were, and a larger sense of purpose (wrong though it was). He believed from a lifetime of training that what he did to Sumner that day was justified and moral. An attack on Sumner was an attack on the North, and a clear statement that no one would threaten the Southern way of life without retribution. It proved to be an ominous foreshadow of the bloodbath created by the Civil War when it claimed over 625,000 people. The tendency to react with violence characterized Brooks' life. He was a hothead, as we might put it today. So the road that took him to Sumner's desk in 1856 was almost predictable. Brooks had a history of defending slavery and the right to expand it to other territories. He lacked no uncertainty.

In his conviction and zealotry, the pre-Christian Paul (known then as Saul of Tarsus) was more like Brooks than French. Paul was raised to believe certain things about man, God, and how Israel would finally be delivered from pagan rule. He was as certain and zealous for his traditions as was Brooks, and while their beliefs were different, we can't imagine either switching to the other side—let alone in an instant—as they travel their respective roads to exact violence on the opposition. Given their history and no evidence of any evolution in their thinking, such a cataclysmic change would have been inconceivable.

Yet this is where it gets interesting and where the comparison stops. Dramatically unlike Brooks, Paul *was* changed, in an instant—on a road leading to Damascus where he was as bent on punishing Christians as Brooks had been Sumner. On their roads, they were both sufficiently zealous and willing to do whatever it took. But only in St. Paul's case do we have something requiring an explanation. That Brooks beat Sumner makes sense. His whole life led to that moment. That Paul *did not* persecute and imprison Christians in Damascus is the shocker. Like Brooks, his whole life led to the Christian persecutions. Had he been like French and followed an evolutionary path to the early Christian movement, we would not be talking about him. No doubt his theological insight might still prove historically interesting, but the mystery surrounding his sudden about-face would be absent. And that is what we are trying to grapple with here.

What we will see in this chapter is that the young Paul was much more like Brooks than French in his radicalness and perhaps even demeanor. His dramatic change on the Damascus road—which he claimed was forced by the sudden appearance of the crucified Jesus—is therefore as shocking as it would have been if Brooks, already approaching Sumner's desk that fateful day and within just a few seconds, suddenly converted to a fiercely anti-slavery position and immediately began preaching an abolitionist message. That no doubt would have caused a national stir and cried out for explanation, no less by Democratic colleagues who would have been dumbfounded by his sudden defection. As did Paul, he would have found quickly that his former friends are now sworn enemies plotting his downfall. It is not surprising that Brooks did not defect, but it *is* that Paul did.

His sudden conversion to Christianity, the movement he devoted his life to destroying, demands an explanation. Scholars agree that his about-face was sudden, even shocking. But we have to ask the obvious: what would have convinced the young Paul not only to convert to a movement he wanted to destroy but to simultaneously abandon his previously cherished beliefs? Let's not underestimate this. He was educated by the best of his time and equipped to give the rationale for persecuting the early Christians. And like everyone else in this period, he would have found the idea of a crucified Messiah absurd and deeply offensive, which no doubt fueled his stream of violence. It is therefore reasonable that the evidence convincing him otherwise was significant, so strong, in fact, that it precluded all other considerations. I'll argue that the best explanation for his turn-around, and the one best fitting the surrounding facts, is that the crucified Jesus actually appeared to him on that road to Damascus.

To make sure that we are examining the relevant data, though, we need to take a closer look at Paul's background. Only against that can we begin to answer our questions with any degree of probability. And as a reminder, I'm not concerned with what is possible; anything is possible. Possibilities get us nowhere other than a quick trip to fantasy-land. What is probable is what we are after, because whatever that is will be best positioned to explain all the relevant data.

A quick word about our sources before proceeding. Our information comes from the testimony of both Paul himself and separately from Luke. On the whole scholars don't question Paul's testimony. He was more often than not brutally transparent about his past, even going so far in 1 Corinthians 15:9 to say, "For I am the least of the apostles, and not fit to be called an apostle, because I persecuted the church of God." If only our politicians were that transparent. Luke's independent testimony is also considered trustworthy with regard to Paul's checkered past. New Testament scholar Martin Hengel points out that Luke knew his facts. His incidental details show he was familiar with the Pharisaic-scribal environment of which he speaks. Generally, Luke "gives the most accurate and positive accounts of Jewish situations of any non-Jew in the ancient world." Thus, in addition to what we know about this period generally, we have a strong historical basis for what follows.

Paul's Background

To understand the pre-Christian Paul a little better, let's begin with his education. In addition to his childhood schooling, Paul received advanced education—which would have begun around age fifteen—under the tutelage of the best-known Pharisee of his day, Gamaliel I (Acts 22:3). Just as today, when a student who wants the best education studies under a well-known scholar, so in first-century Palestine the young Paul went to Jerusalem to sit at the feet of the famous Gamaliel.

That Jerusalem was where Paul's studies occurred under Gamaliel is well attested; it was the only proper place for a strict Jew of this period, and Paul came from a strict Jewish family. As an advanced student in Jewish teaching, which Paul describes in Galatians 1:13–14, he surpassed his contemporaries and was extremely zealous for the traditions of the fathers.[3] He describes it as follows: "I used to persecute the church of God beyond measure and tried to destroy it; and I advancing in Judaism beyond many of my contemporaries among my countrymen, being more extremely zealous for my ancestral traditions." Elsewhere he says, "As to the law, a Pharisee; as to zeal, a persecutor of the church; as to righteousness which is in the law, found blameless" (Phil. 3:5–6).

It is very possible that the young Paul witnessed Jesus' death in Jerusalem. As a Pharisaic teacher, he would have found both the

---

[3] Martin Hengel, *The Pre-Christian Paul* (London: 1991), 27–28, 40–42.

message of Jesus and his humiliating death on the cross repulsive.[4] Fueled by his self-described "zeal" for his traditions and his hatred of the Christian message, he got approval to persecute the early Christians in Jerusalem and surrounding territories. As an upstanding Pharisee, he had the firm conviction he was acting according to God's strict law and will. And in obedience to the law, Paul was prepared to use force if necessary, even to the point of killing the lawbreaker.

But what about Paul's environment? What more can it tell us? As in the case of Brooks in the years leading to the Civil War, which included his upbringing in Southern racist ideology, it is important to understand Paul's wider context—how he was raised and what he was taught. While how we are raised and educated is universally important, it was doubly so for Jews in the first century. It was everything, forming the basis of their identity, how they related to the outside world, and where their sense of purpose came from. Fortunately, we know a good deal about what the young Paul would have been taught. From his earliest days he would have heard how Israel had departed time and again from YHWH, wanting to be more like the pagan nations around them, instead of being set apart and distinct as God had called them to be.

That is what the food laws were all about. Other nations might eat all kinds of things (including blood), but Jews eat only clean foods, with careful attention to how animals are killed and cooked.[5] Other nations have no rhythm to their lives, but Jews keep the Sabbath and look forward to God's promised future when he'll once again come to rest in the Temple and cleanse Jerusalem of foreign corruption. Paul knew from Israel's history that, anytime it forgot, bad things happened. He would have seen his own time in just this way. Jews had again forgotten and committed idolatry, which is why some Jews (including Paul) were especially zealous for ancient tradition and the Torah.

Because they ate and drank such ideas, Jews living in the first century considered idolatry a pressing issue. Ever since Roman

---

[4] Hengel, *The Pre-Christian Paul*, 63–67, 71–72.

[5] N. T. Wright, *Paul: A Biography* (New York: 2018), 28–29.

soldiers marched through the sacred lands, Jews felt again that they were in exile, cut off from the dream of worshipping YHWH without pagan corruption.[6] And in fact they were in a sort of exile. Perhaps not like the Babylonian captivity, but as long as pagans ruled over the Jews (which the Romans did) they weren't truly free. As long as they were paying taxes to Caesar, they were in exile. As long as Roman soldiers could make obscene gestures while they worshipped in the Temple, they were in exile. And every Jew knew, as did Paul, that it was because of Israel's idolatry.

Yet they were still full of hope that God would rescue Israel and forgive their sins. Though not all Jews were as zealous or had the intellectual gifts of Paul, they all shared this same hope. Through scripture and the liturgy they were aware of the tension between their present reality and YHWH's promise to deliver his people. "One way or another, it was a culture suffused with hope. It may have been long deferred, but it was hope nonetheless."[7] At hope's center was the Jerusalem Temple, which held together heavenly and earthly realities. It was a small working model of the entire cosmos. It is where Israel's one God of creation, YHWH, would dwell in the midst of his people.

Gamaliel, one of the greatest rabbis of the period, would have made sure Paul was steeped in these ancestral traditions. His sources would have included the Old Testament and the unwritten Torah, which was a living discussion of the finer points that accumulated as oral tradition (later codified in what is called the Mishnah). N. T. Wright reminds us that during this time, there was a divide between two schools of thought about the Torah that was getting wider. Paul would have been shaped by these debates. Gamaliel appears to have advocated the policy of "live and let live," a picture we get in Acts 5:34–40. If people wanted to follow Jesus, then let them, and if the new movement is from God, it will prosper. If not, it will fail all on its own. Gamaliel's advice about the early Christian movement was thus fairly mild. Overall, this had been the teaching of the previous generation's famous teacher, Hillel.

---

[6] Wright, *Paul*, 46–47.

[7] Wright, *Paul*, 47–48.

Paul's Radical Turn

Our records indicate that Paul disapproved of his teacher's advice. We first hear about him in Acts 7 playing a subordinate role in the stoning of Stephen, who'd been accused of severe transgressions of the law, and Paul's zeal seethed against such violations. The Christian poison about a crucified and resurrected God had to be stopped, which was seen by Paul as an attack on the Temple and, therefore, on YHWH himself.[8] From a lifetime of hearing the Old Testament stories and traditions, Paul knew that the Temple was where heaven and earth were joined, where God promised to be present. And it was there that a year or two earlier a false Messiah named Jesus had caused trouble with his symbolic demonstration.

Now Jesus' followers, Stephen being one of them, preached that heaven and earth were joined in this condemned criminal who had been executed by crucifixion. For these early Christians, God had done something new. To make things worse, Stephen—on trial for his life—uttered the unimaginable: "Behold, I see the heavens opened up and the Son of Man standing at the right hand of God" (Acts 7:56). Blasphemy could be the only word that came to Paul's mind, and Stephen was rushed out of the city and stoned. An interesting note about this is that, in doing so, Paul's group acted illegally, because Roman law decreed that executions belonged under the jurisdiction of the regional governor. Zealous lynchings like Stephen's weren't condoned by the authorities, and it is very possible that there were additional instances.

From then on, Paul played a leading role as Christians were arrested in their homes and carried off to prison or flogged in the synagogues (Acts 8:3; 22:19), thus becoming the driving force behind their condemnation. As a judge authorized by the high priests, he voted for the death penalty while "breathing threats and murder against the disciples" (Acts 26:10; 9:1). Now in contrast to his famous teacher, Paul's zeal aligned him with the school of Hillel's rival, Shammai, who said that if God was going to establish his reign on earth then his followers needed to get ready for action by saying

---

[8] Wright, *Paul*, 37–39.

their prayers and sharpening their swords. Action against both pagans and renegade Jews might be necessary.[9]

As you might imagine, after Stephen's execution, many believers fled Jerusalem, and as they went they continued to establish groups and spread the Christian message. To pursue them, Paul proactively asked for authorization from the high priest and traveled to Damascus. Unbeknownst to him, the trip would change his life in the blink of an eye. Approaching Damascus, he encountered the crucified Jesus, the one he'd been persecuting with such fervor. To get the context, here is Luke's report (Acts 9:1–6):

> Now Saul, still breathing threats and murder against the disciples of the Lord, went to the high priest, and asked for letters from him to the synagogues at Damascus, so that if he found any belonging to the Way, both men and women, he might bring them bound to Jerusalem. As he was traveling, it happened that he was approaching Damascus, and suddenly a light from heaven flashed around him; and he fell to the ground and heard a voice saying to him, "Saul, Saul, why are you persecuting Me?" And he said, "Who are you, Lord?" And He said, "I am Jesus whom you are persecuting, but get up and enter the city, and it will be told you what you must do."

In light of the dual testimony of Luke and Paul himself, and given the historicity of his radical about-face, we know that something cataclysmic happened that day. Paul could never be the same again. In an instant his life had been rocked to the core. The false Messiah he thought was justly crucified was now calling him to account.

The Historian's Dilemma

Here is where we leave the story and ask the historian's question: what could possibly account for Paul's sudden turnaround? Historically we know two things for certain. First, before the Damascus road appearance, Paul ruthlessly persecuted the early Christians. We have

---

[9] Wright, *Paul*, 36–37.

every reason to suppose that he had his mind set on further persecution and violence as he traveled to Damascus. All the evidence points to his firm belief he was doing God's will in bringing Christians to justice. He was defending Israel's God. Second, we know that after the Damascus road appearance, Paul's world was flipped upside down in a moment. The movement he'd persecuted was now what he preached with confidence and with great personal sacrifice, and he did so without pause until his death.

Just to be clear, the dilemma isn't that he changed his position. People change. During the Civil War many people changed from being wishy-washy about slavery to being fully antislavery. President Lincoln himself evolved on the issue and how to deal with slaves once freed, much to the frustration and impatience of Fredrick Douglas. But normally when people change, it happens over a period of time. Rarely, if ever, do we see someone make a dramatic about-face in a mere moment. Yet still, it is not only Paul's sudden shift that is so strange—though it is that too—but it is also that it happened in the context of the appearances of Jesus to people completely unconnected with Paul one to three years earlier. Thus, it is not simply Paul's Damascus encounter that increases the probability of Jesus' resurrection, it is that it happens with other unconnected but similar appearances and in such a dramatic fashion—and in both cases, against the background of contrarily held beliefs.

Certainly alternative theories about Paul's conversion abound. Wright points out that since the rise of psychology, everyone seems to be amateur psychologists. Thus psychological theories have come and gone: Saul's vision was actually just the moment when his "twice-born" personality kicked in; no, it was when residual guilt came back for Stephen's stoning; no, it was the inevitable explosion of the tension between his inner lusts and the outer demands of holiness; no, it was dehydration in the midday sun. I think you get the point. It is what is referred to as armchair psychoanalysis, and it is generally frowned upon by professionals, for good reason.

Here is why. Even for trained psychologists who personally see patients weekly and over a long period of time, it can be very difficult to get at root causes. And that is all assuming the patient shares the same cultural beliefs and values. "How much more impossible is it with someone who lived two thousand years ago in a culture very different from our own."[10] Fortunately, this type of study isn't necessary for the historian, because there is a ton we can know from the implicit narratives that run through a culture or through the mind of the person of interest. We know plenty about Paul's culture and his mindset against this backdrop. There is absolutely no need to weigh into misguided speculation that could never yield probable conclusions when we already have what we need. This is the case for any historical figure, from Aristotle, to Shakespeare, to Washington. New Testament scholar Martin Hengel concurs and points out that we have no evidence of any psychological conflict to explain Paul's sudden conversion.[11]

But besides the flaws of armchair psychoanalysis, even more important is that these theories completely ignore the surrounding evidence about Paul's background and his zealous attitude as a Pharisee, not to mention the critical details around Jesus' crucifixion, the empty tomb, and appearances to the disciples. We need to keep our feet firmly on the ground and anchor theory in the facts we are sure of. Paul was zealous for the law and the tradition of his fathers and more than willing to do what was necessary to maintain their strict adherence. His young life as a first-class persecutor of the new movement is proof. But this moment on the Damascus road shattered his dreams, and yet as Wright says, ironically fulfilled them at the same time. This was the fulfillment of Israel's ancient hope, yet the complete denial of the way he'd understood it to that point. "*God the Creator had raised Jesus from the dead, declaring not only that he really was Israel's Messiah, but that he had done what the One God had promised to do himself, in person.*"[12] While the young Paul was right in his devotion to the one God, he'd been wrong in his understanding of who that one God was and how his purposes would be fulfilled.

From this moment on, everything was focused on the person from whom streamed blinding light, the figure he recognized as the crucified Christ. Rather than the Jerusalem Temple, he now

---

[10] Wright, *Paul*, 41–43.

[11] Hengel, *The Pre-Christian Paul*, 79–80.

[12] Wright, *Paul*, 52–53.

saw heaven and earth come together in Jesus of Nazareth, who was commanding him to acknowledge that fact and completely reorient his life accordingly. The Temple, he now understood, had merely pointed to what Jesus himself was in reality. Death had been defeated personally in his person and had launched a new creation—a creation that would spring forth in the faith of believers.

Given that Paul's early activity as a persecutor occurred in Jerusalem, we can understand why he waited years to return there, and even when he did, he stayed for only fourteen days, getting to know only Peter and James (Gal. 1:17).[13] Keenly aware of the danger he was in, he would have recognized that his former friends considered him an apostate for embracing the very thing he'd condemned. Rightly bitter at his about-face, they now sought his life as he'd once sought out those of Jesus' disciples.

Considering the facts, I believe the best explanation of Paul's about-face is the actual appearance of the crucified and risen Jesus, which struck him like lightning and turned his previous life upside down. His radical conversion was a fundamental reversal of all the previous values that determined his life. We need to remember that the young Paul persecuted the Jewish Christians because he saw them as threats to what was most holy in Israel. It was deeply personal. The very idea of someone like Paul, or like Brooks, radically changing belief systems in the twinkling of an eye due to some psychological conflict is on its face absurd. It completely ignores all the social constructs that were part of his thinking, including his most cherished beliefs, his closest friends, and the religious ceremonies and symbols reinforcing those beliefs. More could be added to be sure. But the idea of such a radical change without some cataclysmic, all-encompassing event or enough evolutionary time and space flies in the face of the evidence. The proposal that inner conflict produced the radical change severely misstates and underestimates the very idea of change.

---

[13] Hengel, *The Pre-Christian Paul*, 77.

The Nature of Change

To keep our feet on the ground, let's quickly review what the research suggests about change. For one thing, it unequivocally demonstrates that change is hard, and it is because of the way we are built from the bottom up. We are wired to reject or be suspicious of new things.[14] We noted previously that when we are in familiar situations, the cells in our brain's core (the hippocampus) fire hundreds of times faster than they do in new situations. Because the hippocampus is connected to the area of the brain that drives emotions (the amygdalae), it explains why sameness feels better. We have a biological default setting against what is new, against innovation, and it explains why organizations struggle to maintain creative cultures. Bottom line is that we don't like creativity. New things create uncertainty, and uncertainty is an aversive state we avoid.

We saw earlier how powerfully schema-based beliefs impact our attitudes and how they can sabotage change. Rooted in our biological and social makeup, they continually bias our judgments in favor of the status quo, even when we think they are not. They operate under the covers and covertly align our attitudes toward the groups with which we identify. Experts have argued that change resistance stems from valuing those groups, such that changing our attitude is the same as abandoning the self-reinforcing comfort they provide.

That is why change takes long periods of time and why it is naive to suggest that someone can make radical and life-altering change in mere moments. St. Paul lived in one of the more historically cohesive social structures that provided meaning and ordered existence down to the smallest detail. Changing his core beliefs would have entailed something far more dramatic than some mysterious psychological conflict, which of course itself would had to have evolved over time. We find no evidence of anything like it.

The disciples spent years with Jesus and still interpreted him *within the constraints* of their first-century Jewish schemas. Like the medical researchers in our prior chapter, they could not "see" through their preconceived dogma. After all that face-to-face time, they fled in horror at the spectacle of the cross and

---

[14] Ashton, *How To Fly A Horse*, 86.

commiserated on the Emmaus road that they had hoped he would have redeemed Israel. But he did not, at least not to their liking, and they were crushed. Their faith had been destroyed. If they missed it after three years then it is pure fiction to suggest that Paul was driven to upend his entire life because of some mysterious internal conflict. But the armchair theory also implicitly suggests that, in his conflict, Paul was different from the rest of us. After all, it takes the rest of us a lot of pain and deliberation to change. He wasn't different, though. We all have conflicts, one emotion and desire battling another, which is precisely what makes change so hard. That is why real and lasting change takes time. Read any current expert on the topic—Kotter, Duhigg, Heath and Heath, for instance—and you'll find agreement that *because* we all live with conflicting desires and beliefs, we have to effect change slowly and incrementally if we want to see any improvement at all. Paul wasn't any different from us, and his sudden about-face can't be explained by such conflict proposals.

Even when people want change, it takes a long time to transfer the desire—itself an evolutionary outcome—to action. Take small changes, the kind people make for their New Year resolutions, and consider the massive failure rates. Around 80 percent of New Year's resolutions fail by February. Go to any gym before and after the first of January and you'll see a sharp spike in attendance, but already by mid to late January, it is emptied out and back to normal. Change is extremely difficult. It involves moving both head and heart, and that is no small thing. Its difficulty accounts for the myriad of books written on the topic and for all the interesting research that has been published recently.

One thing researchers agree on is that change takes time and effort. That is why French's change on slavery makes perfect sense. He had the time to evolve little by little. Such incremental development is required because each of us lives within particular social constructs with our own habits, friends, stories, and beliefs. The many obstacles for any change, even small ones, are well documented and beyond dispute. And that is just for minor changes, not the entire replacement of one's belief system. So I'm not particularly moved by psychological arguments about Paul's conversion. It seems to me the "possibility" thinking that could only come from the ivory tower of academics. Get into the real world, however, the world of Paul and the rest of us, and things are not so simple. They get messy, as life is messy. Without some truly cataclysmic event, head and heart have to be moved in very small increments, and this applies to Paul as well.

In the corporate environment where decisions can affect the lives of employees, possibility thinking is deadly. Ray Dalio, founder of the financial firm Bridgewater, could not have been more right when he insisted: "Don't mistake possibilities for probabilities. Anything is possible. It is the probabilities that matter. Everything must be weighed in terms of its likelihood and prioritized. People who can accurately sort probabilities from possibilities are generally strong at 'practical thinking'; they're the opposite of the 'philosopher' types who tend to get lost in the clouds of possibilities."[15] Ask what is probable, not merely possible, if you want a firm grasp on reality and make your decisions on that.

Conclusion

Based on the evidence we have examined, it would have taken a catastrophic event on the Damascus road to change Paul's entire belief system. To keep our imaginations from taking flights of fancy, let's recall what Paul himself said twenty years after the appearance of Jesus when he stressed that the crucified Christ is a stumbling block to the Jews (1 Cor. 1:23). He is not just describing his present experience with unbelievers but to the personal offense he'd taken as a Pharisaic Jew to the idea of a crucified Messiah. Hengel says it best: "At that time he really did see the crucified Jesus of Nazareth, the blasphemer who had led the people astray, as the one who had been rightly 'accursed' by God."[16] To the young Paul, the Christian agitators were accursed lawbreakers and followers of an accursed deceiver who'd led people astray. That was his conviction and mindset as he rode into Damascus on that fateful day.

But think about how radical Paul's transformation was. After his Damascus encounter with the risen Christ, his new thinking was based on a wholesale reversal of his former beliefs, which he'd

---

[15] Dalio, *Principles*, 254.
[16] Hengel, *The Pre-Christian Paul*, 83–86.

held and cherished with extreme fervor. This Jewish Pharisee now becomes the Christian missionary to the Gentiles. His zeal for the righteousness of the law is replaced by the justification of the godless by faith apart from the law, and without the works of the law; faith is now by grace alone through the creative power of the word. And hatred of the accursed and crucified false Messiah is replaced by a theology of the cross that delivers salvation to Jew and Gentile alike. Radical does not even begin to describe his transformation.

Thus based on all the evidence, Paul's history, environment, and convictions, along with the empty tomb and resurrection appearances to a completely unconnected group of people, the probabilities are heavily tilted toward an actual encounter with the crucified Jesus of Nazareth. No other explanation does justice to all the relevant data. Once again, facts prove to be stubborn things.

CHAPTER 12

Alternative Theories and a Response

Having established the case for the historicity of Jesus' resurrection from a minimal set of bedrock facts, we are now in a position to look at some of the more popular objections. What we will see is that many, if not all, of them seem to stem from an assumption that dead men can't rise. While the assumption gives the surface appearance of a modern scientific view of the world, you'll soon see that it is actually a metaphysical position that seems to underlie the majority of modern critical thinking. However, in and of itself it is no argument against Jesus' resurrection. Philosophical yes, but having its basis in science no.

Because of its constant background presence, we will start by examining naturalism. Once we have given a broad overview, we will be in a position to look at the more trendy counter-theories to Jesus' physical resurrection from the dead. Some will seem silly while others will have more plausibility. However, as you'll see, none of them stand against critical scrutiny. In the end, we will show that the resurrection is the simplest and best explanation of the bedrock facts surrounding Jesus' death and resurrection appearances.

Naturalism as a Worldview

Some bar the very possibility of Jesus' resurrection due to a philosophy called naturalism, which denies the existence of any entities or events lying outside the scope of science. As an axiom, it excludes any notion of the supernatural, making miracles an impossibility. Whatever Jesus' resurrection was, according to the eyewitnesses, it was definitely some sort of miracle since men don't ordinarily rise from the dead. What is important to note is that despite its scientific sound, naturalism is every bit as much a metaphysical belief as supernaturalism. Both make philosophical claims about the foundation of knowledge and the constituent elements of the known world.

Naturalism holds that what is real is only what can be known through the natural sciences, but how do we know that the world that is known by the five senses is the whole of reality? How do we know that nothing outside our limited sense perception exists? And based even on what we do know, how can we be certain that no miracles have ever occurred? Because of our limited understanding of the known universe, which includes the human brain that thinks such metaphysical theories, we are simply not in a position to foreclose what can and can't happen, or what can and can't exist. Science has a history of making sport of our generalizations. Naturalism's strong metaphysical claims go beyond what can be reasonably claimed as a scientific outlook. Pointing this out, Alister McGrath notes, "Naturalism smuggles an essentially materialist philosophy into its allegedly 'scientific' account of reality. It places an embargo on the transcendent, without offering any scientific justification for doing so."[1] In other words, naturalism precludes in advance of any evidence what can and can't occur in the known universe—which is something that can *only* be assessed on the basis of empirical evidence. It is circular reasoning to assume at the outset that miracles are impossible and then conclude on that basis that we can't justify any particular miracle.

These sweeping assumptions about the nature of the universe can be called *a priori* beliefs, which claim to be knowledge of how the world works independent of any evidence for or against. It is one thing to say that 2+2=4 is known *a priori*, or independently of verifying it through experience (because given the definition of the term 2 and 4, the answer is *necessarily* 4), but an entirely different thing to claim that all miracle claims should be rejected outright

---

[1] Alister E. McGrath, *A Scientific Theology*, vol. 1 (Grand Rapids, MI: 2001), 128–30.

because we already know that the universe does not allow miracles. How could you know no miracle has ever occurred unless you examine the evidence for or against a particular claim? Science's success and its remarkable progress can't be explained by sweeping assumptions. On the contrary, as McGrath rightly says, the success of science rests on its refusal to make *a priori* prejudgments about what can be known, and the manner by which that knowledge is established. Precisely by refusing to be limited by grandiose assumptions, the natural sciences have been able to grow without the encumbrance of preconceived theories. Thus, despite its appearance, there is nothing scientific about naturalism.

Historically, the natural sciences accumulated an understanding of reality primarily in an *a posteriori* manner—meaning as a result of our actual experience of the world—and as a consequence of empirical testing and assessment of evidence. "The fundamental point to be made here is that the natural sciences have not allowed themselves to be inhibited by a preconceived epistemology [theory of how we know things], which lays down what can and what cannot be known in advance of an engagement with the natural world."[2] Accordingly, the only way we can know if a miracle has occurred in history is to evaluate the evidence for and against it. Merely stating that Jesus' resurrection is impossible as a matter of course is an unjustified opinion, not an argument.[3] It simply highlights one's presuppositions about what can and can't happen in the world.

Bottom line is that the universe has always had a tendency to invalidate our assumptions about it and will continue to do so for a long time to come. What we will see in the following objections seems often to be the result of an unjustified naturalism, which causes the critic to proliferate ad hoc ideas to support counter-theories to Jesus' resurrection. Let's look at a few fringe theories and then examine the popular hallucination proposals.

---

[2] McGrath, *A Scientific Theology*, vol. 2, 270–72.

[3] Licona, *The Resurrection of Jesus*, 506–07.

A Variety of Alternatives

Over the years there have been many alternatives to the empty tomb and resurrection of Jesus, not all of which are equally plausible. Some of the more far-fetched theories suggest things like the disciples stealing the body and then claiming he'd risen; or the swoon theory suggesting that Jesus did not actually die on the cross, and after being revived in the cool of the tomb, he "appeared" to the disciples; or the women going to the wrong tomb; or some third party stealing Jesus' body. None of them have gained widespread support for different reasons. Let's take them one at a time.

First, the idea that the disciples came and stole Jesus' body isn't anything new. In fact, Matthew reports it his Gospel. After Jesus was crucified, the chief priests and Pharisees went to Pilate and asked for the tomb to be secured with a guard, the reason for which was that Jesus had predicted his resurrection and they did not want the disciples stealing the body and then claiming he'd risen. Pilate grants their wish and tells them to make it as secure as possible. Matthew then reports that when the women come to the tomb, they find it empty and soon after encounter the risen Jesus. When the guard reports what had happened to the chief priests, they pay the soldier off and tell him to say that the disciples came and took Jesus' body while he was asleep. Interestingly, Matthew reports the incident in a rather tangential way and does not make much of it, adding "and this story was widely spread among the Jews, and is to this day" (28:11–15).

Before addressing the theft theory, we should point out some things we can surmise from Matthew's report. For one, the Jewish polemic presupposes the empty tomb. From this information unintentionally furnished by Matthew, we know that Jewish opponents did not deny Jesus' tomb was empty, implied by the fact that they concoct the theft story to explain it. "The fact that the Jewish polemic never denied that Jesus' tomb was empty, but only tried to explain it away is persuasive evidence that the tomb was in fact empty."[4] The Jews did not respond to the preaching of the resurrection by pointing to the tomb or displaying Jesus' body but rather got bogged down in a hopeless series of absurdities trying to explain

---

[4] Craig, *Assessing the New Testament Evidence*, 371ff.

away the empty tomb. This shows that not only was the tomb known but also that it was empty. Corroborating this is the fact that Jesus' tomb was never venerated, which would have been inconceivable given Jesus' stature as a great prophet.

What about the charge that the disciples slipped in unnoticed by a Roman guard and stole the body? The question itself gives a clue to its implausibility. Not only was the tomb guarded by one of the most highly trained soldiers of the day, but we also know from the record that the disciples fled after Jesus' arrest. Only Peter remained, and only until he denied Jesus during the trial. It was the women who tarried and followed Joseph of Arimathea to the tomb, and it is to them Jesus first appeared. That the disciples fled in terror is granted by the vast majority of scholars, so from a locational standpoint, they could not have stolen the body. Further, the record shows that they were in no psychological state to confront a Roman guard, concoct a story they knew to be a lie, and then preach the resurrection fearlessly to the point of their own martyrdom. The theory is untenable in the extreme and contradicts well-attested facts.

There is only one theft theory with any plausibility, namely that some third party stole the body. Its possibility comes from the fact that tombs were sometimes robbed for valuables during this period. But while that is seemingly plausible, William Lane Craig notes that the theory does not stand up to scrutiny for several reasons.[5] First, we know of no third party who would have had any motive for stealing the body, and robbers would not have any reason to break into the tomb since there wasn't anything of value interred with the body. Not to mention the obvious fact that they would not cart away a dead man's body. There is no group that would have gained anything by taking the corpse and hiding it. Second, it is unlikely that anyone but Joseph and the women knew where the body was. Third, since the women found the tomb empty on Sunday morning, the thieves would have had to hatch their conspiracy, steal the body with a guard at the tomb, and get rid of it sometime between Friday night and Sunday morning. All of this would had to have taken place during the tumultuous confusion at Jesus' trial and execution,

---

[5] Craig, *Assessing the New Testament Evidence*, 377–78.

and during Passover, nonetheless. Highly unlikely. Fourth, the fact that the graveclothes remained in the tomb seems to preclude any theft of the body (Luke 24:12). Fifth, conspiracies like these almost always get exposed. It is hard to believe that when the disciples began preaching Jesus' bodily resurrection that the thieves would have kept their secret. Jewish authorities would have been more than happy to receive such information, but there is not even a hint of it in any of the traditions. Sixth, the theory only explains half the evidence (namely the empty tomb) but does not explain the appearances.

The swoon theory has reappeared recently but not among specialists. It claims that Jesus lost consciousness on the cross, causing onlookers to conclude he was dead. When taken down, he revived in the cool of the tomb and was treated. Aside from the absurdity that Jesus survived the long process of Roman torture and crucifixion—a fact granted by virtually all scholars—it seems equally nonsensical that, after brutal torture and crucifixion, Jesus' disciples believed after seeing him that he was resurrected. Not only have professionals from the medical community balked at the possibility of surviving crucifixion, but overall the theory is too far-fetched to give much consideration. For these reasons, it has never gained traction. On the basis of his painstaking cataloging of scholarly opinion, Habermas notes that "Certainly the majority of scholars think that Jesus' body was placed in a tomb."[6] In other words, his death on the cross is a given.

The idea that the women went to the wrong tomb is equally implausible. Are we to believe that some of Jesus' most devout followers were so careless that, after having gone to the lengths of being present at the crucifixion, they failed to follow Joseph to the tomb as reported? There is no doubt they would have wanted to anoint Jesus' body and would not have made a mistake about the tomb's location. In addition, we have the same problems as before that the Jews would only have been too happy to point out the correct tomb

---

[6] Gary R. Habermas, "The Late Twentieth-Century Resurgence of Naturalistic Responses to Jesus' Resurrection," *Trinity Journal* 22 (2001), 5. http://www.garyhabermas.com/articles/trinityjournal_latetwentieth/trinityjournal_latetwentieth.htm.

with Jesus' body still it. But there is no hint of such a suggestion, a fact corroborated by the concoction of the story about the disciples stealing the body.

Another fringe theory suggests that a twin brother or another person who looked like Jesus represented him after the crucifixion. Some have said James, the brother of Jesus, played that role. But it is hard to take this seriously. Again, are we supposed to believe that a group of close disciples who spent years with Jesus could not tell him apart from his brother James, who they would have known, or someone else who reminded them of Jesus? Highly unlikely does not begin to describe this scenario. The twin idea fares no better. We have no evidence from any tradition that Jesus was born a twin. Thus, this theory hasn't had many followers other than a fringe element of popular thinkers.

Deficient Sources?

Some critics argue that the Gospels are deficient sources that prevent historians from discovering what actually happened to Jesus. As support, they contend that the Gospels weren't written by eyewitnesses, were late since they were written thirty-five to sixty-five years after Jesus' death, and have material that was altered during the various stages of transmission.[7] Further, they contend, no source outside the New Testament mentions Jesus until about eighty years after his death.

We should note several objections to this line of reasoning. First, we have seen ample evidence that the Gospels contain clear stamps of eyewitness testimony, including firsthand reports from Peter and then other traditions that in all likelihood have eyewitness authority behind them. Cleopas, the women, and very probably some of the miracles have witnesses that stand behind the traditions. Further, there is strong evidence that John's personal recollections stand behind both his Gospel and first letter. With the cumulative weight of the data, the idea that eyewitness testimony does not stand behind the foundational events is historically unsound.

---

[7] Licona, *The Resurrection of Jesus*, 588ff.

Second, Michael Licona notes that even if the Gospels weren't written by eyewitnesses, it would not be a challenge unique to the New Testament. No surviving account of Alexander the Great was written by an eyewitness. Tacitus and Suetonius weren't eyewitnesses to the majority of what they reported. Yet historians are confident they're able to recover the past without knowing who the sources were. Third, the objection that the Gospels weren't written until thirty-five to sixty-five years after Jesus' death and that we find no reference to Jesus outside the New Testament until eighty years after his death is misleading. Josephus mentions Jesus within sixty-five years. Moreover, compared to written sources of other historical figures and events, thirty-five to sixty-five years is short.

Augustus is generally regarded as the greatest emperor of Rome, and we have nine sources used for his history. Three of them are contemporary with Augustus, and a fourth is written from fifty to one hundred years after Augustus' death, with the final four from one hundred to two hundred years after his death. Comparing the two cases (Augustus and Jesus), Licona notes that "it is remarkable that four biographies of Jesus were written within 35-65 years of his death."[8] Just as important, though, is the fact that we have multiple independent oral traditions throughout the New Testament, which include formulae, hymns, creeds, and early sermons Luke records in Acts. We demonstrated in a previous chapter that many of these must be dated to within just a few years of Jesus' crucifixion. The sheer amount of early evidence for the major events surrounding Jesus' death and resurrection is impressive by any historical standard.

What about the supposed lack of non-Christian references to Jesus? This complaint is also misleading. The Roman emperor Tiberius was a contemporary of Jesus, but the number of non-Christian sources that mention Tiberius within 150 years of his life is the same as the number of non-Christian sources that mention Jesus within the same time period. Licona notes, "If we add Christian sources, the Jesus: Tiberius ratio goes from 9:9 to at least 42:10." Fourth, the claim that the stories of Jesus were altered during the transmission process is a red herring, the reasons for which I'll explain momentarily.

---

[8] Licona, *The Resurrection of Jesus*, 589–90.

First, though, here are a few of the examples given as evidence of the claim. Concerning the resurrection, did Mary go alone or were other women with her, and what did they see when they got to the tomb? A man (Mark), two men (Luke), or an angel (Matthew)?

Let's take a closer look at the apparent conflicts. Matthew, Mark, and Luke report that a small group of women went to the tomb, while John focuses on Mary, who seems to speak for the others. In John, Mary is the one who visits the tomb, but in the following verse she announces to the disciples, "and *we* do not know where they have laid Him" (20:1–2). It is unlikely John uses a literary plural, and he is probably referring to the other women who were with Mary. This is similar to Luke's account of Peter running to the tomb after hearing the women's report (Luke 24:12); in that he isn't excluding the others who may have gone with Peter to the tomb, since only a few verses later he reports that more than one disciple went (24:24). In other words, in both cases John and Luke focus on a single individual even though more were probably present. This wasn't uncommon among ancient authors.

What about what they saw when they arrived at the tomb? The apparent difference can be resolved with the understanding that an angel was sometimes referred to as a man, which we see particularly in Luke. First he refers to the two men at the empty tomb and then eleven verses later calls them angels. Whether there were one or two angels can be explained by the fact that the focus of the Gospel writers (as in the case of Mary and Peter above) is on the one speaking at the moment.

But besides the plausible resolution of such conflicts, it is more important to point out that discrepancies in the accounts concern the periphery details and not the core of the story. We have already seen in our discussion about memory that it is normal to find variation in noncentral details of eyewitness accounts, but by itself, that does not justify wholesale skepticism about the core event. Remember that the *Titanic* survivors offered conflicting testimonies about whether it went down intact or broke apart before sinking. Despite this there is no reason to question the core story that it actually sank. Thucydides knew of different reports about the Peloponnesian War, but since he'd been in the war himself, he would have never doubted it took place. Same with the burning of Rome. No matter what story one believes about who or what caused the fire, no one doubts that Rome burned. We could say the same with our extant accounts of Socrates. Despite conflicting details from his own students, historians still feel confident about the broad details of his life. Citing Craig, Licona makes an important point:

> Compared to the sources for Greco-Roman history, the Gospels stand head and shoulders above what Greco-Roman historians have to work with, which are usually hundreds of years after the events they record, usually involve very few eyewitnesses, and are usually told by people that are completely biased. And yet Greco-Roman historians reconstruct the course of history of the ancient world.[9]

The irony in these objections is that virtually every scholar (critics included) accepts our historical bedrock, so the argument about the supposed unreliability of the Gospels is simply a red herring. Either way, the historical bedrock—which is all our case depends on—is enough to establish a probable case for the historicity of Jesus' resurrection from the dead.

Hallucination Theory

One of the most popular counter-theories for the past one hundred years is a variation of the hallucination theory. Hallucinations are false sensory perceptions that have the sense of reality despite the absence of external stimuli. Or more simply, they're subjective experiences of something that does not exist outside the person experiencing the vision. It postulates that the disciples were inflicted with various psychological conditions that brought about experiences of the risen Jesus. Second-century critic Celsus was the first to propose that the resurrection of Jesus was the "cock and bull story" of a "hysterical female" who "through wishful thinking had a hallucination due to some mistaken notion."[10]

---

[9] Licona, *The Resurrection of Jesus*, 597–99.

[10] Joseph W. Bergeron and Gary Habermas, "The Resurrection of Jesus: A Clinical Review of Psychiatric Hypotheses for the Biblical Story of

Today, hallucination theories usually begin with Peter and suggest that he experienced a hallucination of Jesus because of his sorrow and guilt. Unable to cope, his unconscious mind created a hallucinatory experience of the risen Jesus to ease his intense anguish.[11] Peter shared his experience with the other disciples, who then had similar experiences in groups of various sizes. These constituted shared hallucinatory fantasies that assured them forgiveness for their desertion of Jesus at his time of need. However, in reality they were victims of self-deception.

But what about Paul? Certainly we can't claim that his experience resulted from the same guilt over abandoning Jesus. Adherents to the theory have entertained the idea that Paul was secretly harboring doubts about Christianity and had a growing distaste for Judaism. Given his later references to the law as "yoke" that places one in "spiritual bondage," it is argued that he felt bondage to the strict form of Pharisaism he was aligned with. His vehement response to Christians reflects the fact that it had a powerful effect that unconsciously attracted him to the movement. Railing against his subconscious, he projected his inner struggle against the early believers all the more savagely. These factors led him to flee from his painful situation, and he experienced a hallucination of the risen Jesus on the road to Damascus. Like Peter and the others, Paul was a victim of self-deception. Fortuitously, he was also able to capitalize on the situation by assuming the exalted position of apostle to the Gentiles, something that fulfilled his tendency to be a competitive overachiever.

As the theory proceeds, it argues that thirty to seventy years later there were tensions within Christian groups about what else may have happened. As speculations grew, people started to fill in the gaps, leading eventually to myths such as a prominent person burying Jesus, an empty tomb, and then physical resurrection appearances to his disciples (resulting from their Jewish belief in a physical

---

Easter," *Irish Theological Quarterly* 80/2 (2015), 4. Available online at http://www.garyhabermas.com/articles/irish-theological-quarterly/Habermas_Resurrection%20of%20Jesus.pdf.

[11] Licona, *The Resurrection of Jesus*, 479–82, 496–505.

resurrection). In reality Jesus' tomb contained a decomposing body. Paul's reference to Jesus' appearance to more than five hundred is assumed to be an instance of mass ecstasy stimulated by one or a few of the others. Adherents of the theory argue that modern communal delusions such as sightings of Mary, Bigfoot, and UFOs give plausibility to the group experiences of the disciples. Bottom line is that all of the appearances were visionary in nature and induced some sort of individual and group hallucinations. On this view we could only conclude that they were no more than a fantasy of the disciples' minds, making early Christianity a history of self-deception.

Possible Causes for Hallucinations

Before we discuss potential problems with the theory, let's first ask what the research says about the causes for hallucinations. In their detailed study, Bergeron and Habermas point out that hallucinations are symptoms of an underlying medical pathology. Causes can vary, but three stand out. The first is structural injury to the brain such as tumors, midbrain strokes, or localized dysfunction of brain structures.[12] Seizures causing the irritation of visual regions of the cortex and lesions causing the loss of input to visual cortices can be associated with hallucinations. Also, some progressive neurologic diseases such as dementia with Lewy bodies and Parkinson's can be associated with hallucinations.

Second, biochemical derangement that includes things like toxicity, drugs effects, withdrawal, and infections can cause hallucinations. These usually occur in delirium and are often unpleasant. A third cause of hallucinations is mental illness, such as conditions like schizophrenia. At times, symptoms of psychosis can include religious thoughts and hallucinations. While auditory hallucinations are more common, visual hallucinations can occur and are associated with more severely affected patients. Bottom line is that those who suffer hallucinations are sick and require medical and psychosocial help.

---

[12] Bergeron and Habermas, "The Resurrection of Jesus," 7–8.

Critical Review

While hallucination theories claim to account for the disciples' simultaneous encounters with the risen Jesus, there are several problems attending the proposals. First and foremost is that by their very nature, hallucinations are individual, private experiences. Given that obvious fact, Bergerson and Habermas ask, "What are the odds that separate individuals in a group could experience simultaneous and identical psychological phenomena mixed with hallucinations?"[13] It would require a mind-boggling number of coincidences. Despite the fact that hallucinations are experienced by roughly 15 percent of the general population, an incredible 100 percent of the Twelve would have to have simultaneously experienced the exact same phenomena around the risen Jesus. As Licona states, "It would be an understatement to claim that such a proposal has only a meager possibility of reflecting what actually occurred. Embracing it would require an extraordinary amount of faith."[14]

It is important to point out that hallucination proposals for the appearances are far outside mainstream clinical thought. The concept of collective hallucination isn't found in peer-reviewed medical or psychological literature—and there is no mention of such phenomena in the *Diagnostic and Statistical Manual of Mental Disorders*. It is simply not part of current psychiatric understanding or accepted pathognomy. "This is noteworthy since these hypotheses propose hallucinatory symptoms which imply an underlying medical condition."[15] So where do the theories come from if not from the medical literature? The answer is primarily from New Testament scholars who lack the appropriate medical background.

That is not to say that on rare occasions collective hallucinations don't occur, but the things characterizing such events don't explain the disciples' encounters with the risen Jesus. Here is why. Experts tell us that in these rare cases, we find a group sense of "expectation" and "emotional excitement." However, not everyone in the group

---

[13] Bergeron and Habermas, "The Resurrection of Jesus," 3, 8–10.

[14] Licona, *The Resurrection of Jesus*, 479–82, 485–86.

[15] Bergeron and Habermas, "The Resurrection of Jesus," 3, 10.

experiences a hallucination, and those who do see something have different hallucinations from one another. In this sense, they're a lot like dreams—a person can't share in the dream of another. Also important is that apparitions in hallucinations don't carry on conversations. But none of these facts are consistent with the biblical accounts of Jesus' appearances.

We have demonstrated throughout this book that the disciples were far from expecting Jesus' resurrection. Scholars agree that they were demoralized and feared for their lives. We have also shown that they doggedly interpreted Jesus within the construct of their first-century Jewish beliefs and could not make the necessary connections for them to expect his imminent resurrection. Their behavior is exactly what we'd expect of people who had someone they're close to die a brutal death. Their long-held schemas were in full force during the crucifixion and the days following. Because they already understood the category of being translated directly to heaven on the model of Enoch and Elijah (Gen. 5:24; 2 Kings 2:11–18), even if they had hallucinations, it is highly unlikely they would have concluded Jesus rose from the dead—a notion that contradicted their Jewish belief in the resurrection.[16] Rather they would have likely concluded that God had translated him to heaven. Yet the fact that the disciples proclaimed not the translation of Jesus but contrary to their Jewish thinking, the physical resurrection from the dead, strongly suggests that the origin of the disciples' belief can't be accounted for by visions or hallucinations. No experiences consistent with hallucinations were present, and neither were they psychologically able to experience such an event.

But what about the contention that their sorrow and guilt led to a wish fulfillment in Jesus' appearance? Implicitly smuggled in this idea is the unstated assumption that the disciples *expected* Jesus to rise from the dead before the end time. Implicit also is the assumption that they could have connected the ideas of crucifixion and Messiah and Messiah and YHWH. However, as we have already demonstrated, nothing supports this either from our general knowledge of the period or from what we know about the disciples

---

[16] Craig, *Assessing the New Testament Evidence*, 414, 417.

themselves. In other words, to avoid the most plausible explanation that Jesus rose from the dead, hallucination theories have to propose ideas flatly contradicted by the bedrock facts accepted by the vast majority of scholars.

Some writers add the seemingly plausible claim that the disciples displayed the same bereavement phenomena we see at times with widows who were married for a long time. Evidence used for this is found in a 1971 study in which 293 subjects were surveyed after the death of a spouse. It was discovered that 46 percent of the participants reported bereavement experiences, the most common of which was "feeling the presence" of the deceased spouse,[17] and of those, 14 percent reported visual experiences, 11 percent reported speaking with the spouse, and 2 percent reported experiencing some sort of disturbing contact. Visual experiences were more common in those over forty, and speaking with the apparition was more common among those over sixty. However, if the grieving spouse tried to speak with the apparition, the vision would dissipate. An important finding was that even when visual apparitions occur, they're recognized as not real. Further, 72 percent of the subjects did not disclose their bereavement experiences to others until their participation in the study.

Even if some of Jesus' disciples had bereavement experiences, it is certain that not all of them would have. Moreover, bereavement visions would not have been considered as actual encounters with a physically living Jesus.

> It is also unlikely that the disciples would have disclosed their bereavement experiences to others, let alone launch a campaign of widespread public proclamation of Jesus' resurrection based on such illusions of bereavement.... The premise that bereavement experiences formed the basis for the disciples' belief in Jesus' resurrection is indefensible.[18]

Last, it should be noted that bereavement experiences convince people that the individual is dead, which means they don't go

---

[17] Bergeron and Habermas, "The Resurrection of Jesus," 19–21.

[18] Bergeron and Habermas, "The Resurrection of Jesus," 22–24.

looking elsewhere for the deceased spouse. Jesus' appearances, on the other hand, convinced everyone who saw him that he was very much still alive.

This is all on top of the problem facing those trying to psychoanalyze people long-since dead. We noted previously in the case of St. Paul how speculative and shaky such proposals are. Some scholars have gone so far as to speculate that Paul had a childhood friend who was a Gentile and who unconsciously contributed to his call to the Gentiles. Or that he had secret doubts about Judaism and was unconsciously attracted to Christianity, consumed as he was by a need to be important and accepted.[19] A lack of evidence hasn't slowed down the story-making machinery of many proposals no matter how conspiratorial they sound. Despite the absence of data, it is possible that what has made hallucination theories appear plausible is their mere repetition—a phenomenon we mentioned earlier that makes implausible ideas believable.

Beyond the problem with armchair psychoanalysis, the suggestion that Paul subconsciously desired a leadership position in the early church is untenable. Not only is there no hint of the idea, but considering his lofty stature as a Pharisaic Jew at the time of his conversion, this makes no sense. He already had a leading position and was on his way to being notable among his contemporaries. The only thing to be won by converting to this despised little movement was persecution and the threat of death. This was certainly no way to advance his career. It would have been a huge step in the wrong direction.

Further, the claim that the physical resurrection of Jesus was a late invention by subsequent believers is refuted by the fact that it is found in our earliest resurrection formulae. We have seen that the pre-Pauline formula in 1 Corinthians 15:3–8 is universally recognized as being extremely early, to be dated no later than one to three years after Jesus' crucifixion—way too early to bear the stamp of pure myth. We also documented other early formulae that corroborate the early Christian claims of the physical appearances of Jesus.

---

[19] Licona, *The Resurrection of Jesus*, 507.

Last, how about the comparison of apparitions of Mary and sightings of Bigfoot and UFOs? I don't believe the analogies are valid for several reasons. Licona points out the obvious but important fact that people who claim to have seen Bigfoot actually *saw* a physical being and large footprints in the mud.[20] They weren't experiencing hallucinations. They were deceived, yes, but there is no evidence any of them were hallucinating. Weather balloons and hoaxes have been often mistaken as UFOs. In both of these people saw something they mistook for something else. Either way, they weren't hallucinatory or communal and stand in no relation to the appearances of Jesus.

Apparitions of Mary, on the other hand, can often be accounted for as hallucinations or optical illusions. Yet the details around them are so different than the resurrection appearances that they're useless for comparison. Those sitting next to recipients of the apparitions can't see a thing. The appearances, however, were empirical events in time and space and occurred individually and in group settings, involving back-and-forth dialogue between Jesus and the disciples, physical proof that it was the same Jesus who'd been crucified, and eating and drinking. And all of them described the same core elements. At the heart of the difference is the thoroughly empirical nature of the appearances versus the inherently subjective nature of the apparitions of Mary.

Conclusion

Despite the varying objections to Jesus' resurrection, one often gets the sense that the real issue is the critic's underlying commitment to naturalism. This isn't really a valid argument, however, against the historicity of the appearances as much as it is a signal of the author's unstated presuppositions. You might recall Licona referring to these as a person's horizons, and they're often the driving force behind rejection of the early Christian accounts. As we have shown in this chapter, naturalism comes up wanting as a worldview because it automatically forecloses certain theories under the guise of science, but science has progressed and achieved success by eschewing limiting

---

[20] Licona, *The Resurrection of Jesus*, 489–91.

presuppositions. None of us are in a position to say with certainty what is possible and what is not, and periods in the history of science where we find such attitudes have always impeded knowledge of the universe. As Craig notes, once we give the presupposition up that dead men can't rise, then we are forced to accept the resurrection as the simplest explanation of the facts.[21]

We have also seen that the counter-theories involve too many ad hoc proposals that make light of the bedrock facts, as well as other well-attested facts that the majority of scholars accept. We have noted many throughout this book. While there are a few fringe ideas in popular literature that have the feel of conspiracy theories, none of them have gained much acceptance for obvious reasons. The most widely proposed counter-theory is the mass-hallucination theory, but a closer examination of what would have been required for this is mind-boggling and highly improbable. Hallucination proposals are better relegated to the trash bin. Bergerson and Habermas rightly conclude:

> Those suffering illnesses characterized by hallucinations are sick. They require medical and psychosocial support, a structured environment, pharmacological support, and behavioural treatment. Persons suffering from psychosis in Jesus' time, not having benefit of modern medical treatment, might be considered lunatics or demon possessed . . . They would be unlikely candidates to organize as a group and implement the rapid and historic widespread expansion of the Christian religion during the first century.[22]

In the end, the theory with the most plausibility, simplicity, and explanatory power is the actual resurrection of Jesus. Considering all the other generally accepted facts we have looked at, it alone best brings all of the data into a coherent explanation of what happened on that first Easter morning. Biases against the idea of miracles notwithstanding, the resurrection fits the facts like a key does a lock.

---

[21] Craig, *Assessing the New Testament Evidence*, 378.
[22] Bergeron and Habermas, "The Resurrection of Jesus," 11–12.

Conclusion

Throughout this book I have made the case that Jesus' physical resurrection from the dead is the most probable explanation for his appearances to the disciples and Paul. To avoid controversial assumptions, we used the minimal facts approach of Habermas and Licona, which takes a core group of facts virtually every scholar accepts (no matter what their religious leanings) and argues that the resurrection best accounts for the Easter event. Staying clear of possibility thinking was important as we navigated the emotionally charged subject of God's existence, a purported miracle, and the meaning of life. Taking our cues from the data, I have suggested that the disciples—as well as Paul—were in no position to fantasize events that never occurred. In fact, appearances of the risen Jesus were the last thing any of them expected.

I have argued that in light of a small group of bedrock facts, the probabilities heavily favor the disciples' own account for their claims. As a quick review, here are the facts: (1) Jesus died by crucifixion. (2) Shortly after Jesus' death, the disciples claimed he'd returned to life and appeared in both individual and group settings. (3) Paul, known early on as Saul of Tarsus, zealously persecuted early Christians and then claimed that the risen Jesus appeared to him on the road to Damascus. (4) The resurrection formulae, particularly 1 Corinthians 15:3–8, are extremely early and show that belief in Jesus' resurrection erupted suddenly and seemingly out of nowhere. We find no evidence of any evolutionary development—only a big bang explosion. (5) The belief that Jesus is YHWH—the God of Israel—erupted along with the belief in the resurrection, and again we find no traces of evolutionary development.

It bears repeating that because these core facts are accepted by scholars of all stripes, any theory attempting to explain the appearances must account for *at least* these in a way that does justice to their individual and combined force. In my opinion, the keystone idea that best explains all the relevant data is the historic resurrection of Jesus. Accounting for more evidence than other theories, and involving fewer assumptions, the resurrection has greater explanatory power and makes better sense of the other evidence we can deduce from the bedrock facts.

We have seen several things in support of this. For starters, no one made the connection between crucifixion and Messiah, Messiah and one man's resurrection before the end of time, and resurrected Messiah and YHWH. The Messiah was supposed to come with sword in hand and achieve a sociopolitical victory for Israel and deliver it from pagan oppression. No one conceived of a crucified and dying Messiah. Crucifixion was the most degraded form of punishment and was associated with criminality and treason. Making a Messiah out of a man who'd been justly condemned by the state would have been unthinkable—not only because of the manner of his death but also because no one thought of resurrection outside of the resurrection of all at the end of time. The simple fact is that Jesus did not fit any Messianic picture of the period.

At his arrest, the disciples behaved just as one would expect. They ran and hid. In no way were they psychologically capable of perpetuating an elaborate hoax that Jesus had been raised from the dead. Not only was a Roman guard stationed at the tomb, but the evidence shows a terrified group that was trying to come to terms with its shattered hopes at the sudden execution of their Master. Cleopas and his companion on the Emmaus road lamented how they had hoped Jesus was the one to deliver Israel. But they were wrong, and the only thing left was to recover from disappointed expectations and remain inconspicuous. To say they continued steadfast in their long-held Jewish schemas is an understatement. The data shows that they interpreted Jesus through a typical first-century prism all along, betraying an inability time and again to process Jesus' predictions of his impending death and resurrection. We have seen ample research on how status quo beliefs tend to reign supreme and why dramatic change is so rare. I have argued that the only adequate

CONCLUSION

explanation of their sudden about-face from terror and dejection to fearless proclaimers of Jesus' resurrection is the historicity of the Easter event.

It is the only thing explaining the big bang explosion of the centrality of Jesus' resurrection—against every religious and social norm—as well as the spontaneous belief that Jesus is YHWH, Israel's God. We noted that early Christians had a fully developed view of Jesus as *kyrios* (YHWH) by the time Paul started writing his letters in the 50s. Working backward, it is highly likely the belief originated in Jerusalem simultaneously with the appearances. As is the case with the resurrection itself, we find no trace of any evolutionary development in the belief, which would be inconceivable had it gone through multiple iterations until landing on a fully resurrected and divine Jesus. We saw evidence of this in liturgical and confessional formulae and the earliest hymns that were already fixed in dispersed geographical areas. All in all, we can conclude that the belief in a fully divine and resurrected Jesus must be dated to within just a few years of the crucifixion—which is much too soon for a wholesale replacement of history with myth.

Concerning the integrity of our sources, we found not only that the New Testament textual tradition is remarkably stable but also that the earliest oral traditions guarded against corruption, to the notable extent that oral traditions of one or two generations beyond the eldest living member in a community suffer only small damage, if any. In the case of the Jesus tradition, we can be confident that a substantial portion would have been memorized verbatim (such as 1 Cor. 15:3–8), with narratives being memorized as a structure. Because Jesus made an enormous impact and would doubtless have been considered a great prophet, we know that Jesus tradition would have been fixed in memory (along the lines of the rabbis) at the *very same time* he said or acted. As for memory accuracy, the appearances have all the qualities that solidify reliable recall. They were emotionally significant, unique, life-altering, and frequently rehearsed, as was customary in this oral period. On top of this, scholars now recognize that the Gospels are Graeco-Roman biography, meaning that readers would have expected them to contain relatively accurate accounts. If the early church hadn't been interested in preserving the past *as past*, they would not have written biography.

These facts corroborate evidence that the Gospels and early letters have eyewitness testimony behind them. We observed various places where the eyewitness testimony of Peter, John, the women, Cleopas, and recipients of some of the miracles emerge as the probable source. Autopsy reports were considered the most reliable of the period, so it is not surprising that "What we have heard, what we have seen with our eyes, what we have looked at and touched with our hands" was the constant refrain of the earliest witnesses. In fact, firsthand testimony was so critical that second-generation Christians sought out those who'd personally heard one of the disciples. Further, we have considerable evidence from this later generation corroborating the eyewitness testimony behind the Gospels. On these bases, we can conclude with a high degree of probability that the reports came directly from those who personally witnessed the Jesus events and continued to stand behind them throughout their lives.

Looking at Paul's trajectory, we observed a stark contrast to the disciples in that he was no Jesus sympathizer. We know he was zealous in the traditions of his fathers and a Pharisee by training. Not only was he well known as a persecutor of the early church, but he was also complicit in the stoning of Stephen, and probably others. As he rode to Damascus, he was breathing threats against believers and thus in no psychological condition for radical change. Given his abrupt transformation from persecutor to defender of Christianity, I have argued that the actual appearance of the risen Jesus best accounts for his sudden about-face. Not to be underestimated, his conversion was a wholesale reversal of his earlier beliefs. Everything he'd been taught from childhood, including his understanding of God, the law, works, and the Temple, was radically transformed in that Damascus moment. Moreover, he endured countless hardships for his confession of the risen Jesus and was thrust into an unpleasant spotlight with his contemporaries, who now pursued him as an enemy. In combination with the appearances to the disciples, Paul's conversion tilts the probabilities heavily in favor of the physical resurrection of Jesus.

None of the alternative theories we examined explain the bedrock facts sufficiently or account for the other well-established data we have examined. The most popular of the alternatives, hallucination theories, fall flat on multiple levels and are not supported in any medical or psychological peer-reviewed literature. One suspects that the real objection behind such theories is an unstated commitment to naturalism, but as we have seen, it is neither scientific nor self-authenticating. Merely asserting that dead men don't rise and then concluding on that basis that Jesus did not either isn't an argument. It does not matter if no one else has risen from the dead. What matters is determining whether the specific claims of the disciples and Paul warrant belief. In other words, we have to look at the evidence and base our judgments on that, not prior assumptions. Science was hindered for centuries because of unwarranted presuppositions.

Finally, we started the book by referencing the importance of thinking in probabilities, by thinking in bets based on where the data leads. In the end, the theory with the most plausibility, simplicity, and explanatory power is the actual resurrection of Jesus. Considering all the other generally accepted facts we have looked at, it alone brings all of the data into a coherent explanation of what happened on that first Easter morning. Biases against the idea of miracles notwithstanding, the resurrection fits the facts like a key does a lock.

Postscript

On Happiness

Modern culture is obsessed with happiness—so much so that marriages are ended, families uprooted, and careers abandoned if they don't deliver enough. We have seen the rise of an entire literary category telling us how to eliminate worry, anxiety, and sadness; and with it, feelings not associated with positive emotion have been expelled, as though above all else human beings have the right to *feel* happy. Yet despite the fact that every objective indicator of well-being—purchasing power, amount of education, availability of music, and nutrition—has increased, depression is sharply on the rise. Research shows that it is now *ten times* as prevalent as it was in 1960. Further, while the mean age of a person's first depressive episode forty years ago was twenty-nine, today it is only fourteen.[1] Clearly there is a disconnect. If obsessing over feeling happy works, why the corresponding increase in depression rates?

Whatever the answer, the fact remains that we often make life-changing choices based on what we think will make us happy. But how often do we consider what happiness is and what issues need to be resolved to achieve it? In this postscript, I intend to examine just that. We will see that happiness is a vague concept about which even the greatest thinkers have failed to come to agreement. But we will also encounter some interesting advances made by the relatively

---

[1] Martin E. P. Seligman, *Authentic Happiness* (New York: 2002), 117–18.

new field of positive psychology that help us understand more about happiness and its effects on emotional and physical health.

Notwithstanding its progress, we will explore some important shortcomings. Despite its best efforts, it fails to deal with our core problem as human beings. Whatever happiness is, it has to begin with our relation to God, sin, and death; it must deal with the facts—very often brutal—of our existence. Failure to do so eliminates any sure foundation upon which happiness can rest. What we will see is that Christianity offers uniquely potent answers to questions that have eluded classical thinkers and their modern counterparts alike.

Happiness Through History

The question of happiness has plagued, and more often eluded, the greatest of the world's thinkers. Some said it is simply getting what you want. To achieve happiness, we need to satisfy our desires as much as possible. But clearly some desires conflict with others, as for example my desire to smoke conflicting with my desire to be healthy. Given this, would we want to satisfy just any desire? There are some that are unhealthy (emotionally and physically) and some that might be shameful. Others might create happiness in the short term and end up harmful in the long term (drug use, for example). And even if a desire is good in the long term, it may not be in the short term (marriage at eighteen might be an example). Not knowing how to fit our desires together or how they're all compatible, we ask what it is to be happy. The question arises because of the conflict among our aims: they can't all be fulfilled in the time we have. Thus we want a guiding principle that answers which ones we should pursue, and to what extent.

> Compare such a person to someone who has a lot of puzzle pieces but does not know what picture they're supposed to make up when they're put together, or even which of them actually belong to the puzzle. He thinks that if he knew the picture he'd be able to determine which pieces belong and how they fit together. The picture will guide him, he thinks, in assembling the pieces.[2]

---

[2] Nicholas White, *A Brief History of Happiness* (New York: 2006), 3, 162.

History's replete with proposed principles that allow us to put the pieces together in the right way. Going in one direction, some said it should be pleasure. Plato argued differently, suggesting the best results come from harmonizing our various aims. In another direction, Hobbes and Kant denied that there is such a principle, with Nietzsche going so far as to say that we are better off not having one. Kant rejected the quest on the grounds that though we desire one thing, we can't be certain what will happen if we get it. In other words, we can't be certain what effect the fulfillment of one desire will have on another. If you satisfy your desire for a long life, that may lead to the frustration of another desire, namely the desire not to live a disabled life.[3] Against all this, Aristotle says that contemplation and politics should be the aim of a happy life—although practically only one should occupy our attention, meaning that one is sacrificed for the other.

Despite the musings of philosophers, in practice we don't start with a picture of what the puzzle should be and then tailor our aims accordingly. Rather we have particular aims, some of which are specific and some more general. For the most part, we build an idea of what happiness would be out of the aims we have. But we don't try for a completely articulated concept of happiness, or even suppose that there must be such a thing. "If that is right," concludes Nicholas White, "then in an important sense the history of the concept of happiness has been a search for something that is unattainable."[4]

Positive Psychology

Perhaps no other field in the last century has studied happiness with more rigor than positive psychology. Often described as the field's father, Martin Seligman argues that traditional psychology has gone only halfway in treating patients. Most psychologists work on the disease model and concentrate on therapy once problems become unbearable. His point is that equal focus should be on prevention, when the individual is doing well. Cure is uncertain, but prevention

---

[3] White, *A Brief History*, 164–68.

[4] White, *A Brief History*, 173.

is massively effective. Having midwives wash their hands ended childbed fever, and immunizations ended polio. The traditional view since Freud has been that mental health consists in the absence (or minimization) of mental illness, but Seligman finds that even when the illness is cured, you still have an empty patient with little increase in happiness.

Fortunately, much has been learned since the time of Freud. It is now known that progress in preventing mental illness can come from nurturing a set of strengths and virtues, such as future-mindedness, hope, interpersonal skills, courage, the capacity for flow, faith, and a strong work ethic. "The exercise of these strengths then buffers against the tribulations that put people at risk for mental illness."[5] Seligman suggests that positive psychology should aim broadly at what he calls well-being, which addresses roughly five areas. These consist of positive emotion, engagement, meaning, positive relationships, and accomplishment.

Let's take them one by one. Positive emotion is a sign of life satisfaction, and like it, engagement signals whether a person is completely absorbed by a task (somewhat similar to Mihaly Csikszentmihalyi's notion of flow). Each of these can only be measured subjectively. Meaning might have both a subjective and objective measure in that we may feel a certain event had meaning and on later reflection realize it did not. Abraham Lincoln was a profound melancholic and may have at times judged his life to be meaningless, but we judge it differently. Seligman's fourth criterion suggests that very little we consider positive is solitary; most positive experiences take place around other people—whether laughter, joy, or sensing meaning in life. Other people are the best antidote to life's down times. Last, people pursue accomplishment for its own sake—and it needn't be pursued merely in the service of pleasure or meaning (for example, one could play a game just to win without the game being about anything larger than itself). In fact, people often pursue accomplishment even when it brings no positive emotion, no meaning, and nothing in the way of positive relationships. No one element defines well-being, but each contributes to it.

---

[5] Seligman, *Authentic Happiness*, 8, 13, 11–7.

Before talking about why all this may matter, we need to note one caveat. Experts believe that there is a personality trait of good cheer (called positive affectivity) that is highly heritable. Some people have a lot of positive affect that stays fixed over a lifetime, and they *feel* great a lot of the time. However, just as many have little of it. Most of us are somewhere in between. There appear to be strong biological underpinnings predisposing some of us to sadness, anxiety, and anger. Therapy can modify these but only within our biological limits, meaning they can be helped but not eliminated. Thus the best the clinician can do is get patients to live in the best part of their set range of those personality traits. Abraham Lincoln and Winston Churchill both suffered from depression but nevertheless learned to function in spite of it. Seligman argues that clinical psychology needs to develop a method of "dealing with it"—in other words, an approach that helps people realize there will be days when they wake up feeling blue and hopeless. The job of the therapist should be to encourage them to fight the feelings and live heroically—to function well even when sad.[6] The takeaway is that a person can be happy even if he or she does not have much in the way of positive emotion.

Why Happiness May Matter

Studies show that a positive mood jolts us into a different way of thinking than when we are negative. A negative mood activates a battle-stations way of thinking in which we focus on what is wrong to eliminate it. In contrast, a positive mood places us into a creative, tolerant, constructive, generous, and undefensive way of thinking. In an interesting study, forty-four medical internists were randomly separated into three groups: one was given a small package of candy, another read aloud humanistic statements about medicine, with the final third being the control group. All the physicians were then presented with a difficult-to-diagnose case of liver disease and asked to think aloud as they made their diagnosis. The candied group did best and considered liver disease earliest and most efficiently. They also

---

[6] Seligman, *Authentic Happiness*, 32–5. See also Seligman, *Flourish* (New York: 2011), 52–53.

resisted premature closure and other forms of superficial intellectual processing.

Daniel Goleman points out that even mild mood changes can affect a person's thinking. People in good moods tend to have a perceptual bias that leads them to be more expansive and positive in their thinking.

> This is partly because memory is state-specific, so that while in a good mood we remember more positive events; as we think over the pros and cons of a course of action while feeling pleasant, memory biases our weighing of evidence in a positive direction, making us more likely to do something slightly adventurous or risky, for example.[7]

Evidence also suggests that positive emotion predicts health and longevity. In the most remarkable study ever done on happiness and longevity, a group of nuns was followed to see what conditions shorten and lengthen life. Though the group ate roughly the same diet, did not smoke or drink, and had access to the same medical care, they fared quite differently. In the study, the nuns were asked to write a short sketch of their lives on the momentous occasion of taking their final vows. Seligman cites two notable sketches. The first is by Cecilia O'Payne, who wrote the following in 1932:

> God started my life off well by bestowing upon me grace of inestimable value. . . . The past year which I spent as a candidate studying at Notre Dame has been a very happy one. Now I look forward with eager joy to receiving the Holy Habit of Our Lady and to a life of union with Love Divine.

In the same year, in the same city, and taking the same vows, Marguerite Donnelly wrote this:

> I was born on September 26, 1909, the eldest of seven children, five girls and two boys. . . . My candidate year was spent in the motherhouse, teaching chemistry and second year Latin at Notre Dame

---

[7] Daniel Goleman, *Emotional Intelligence* (New York: 1994), 85.

Institute. With God's grace, I intend to do my best for our Order, for the spread of religion and for my personal sanctification.

As of 2002, Celia was still alive at age ninety-eight and had never been sick a day in her life. Contrast Marguerite, who had a stroke at age fifty-nine and died soon thereafter. The study showed that the difference in disposition was no coincidence in how long they lived. Cecilia used words "very happy" and "eager joy," betraying her general good cheer. Marguerite, on the other hand, does not even hint at positive emotion. But the most interesting thing about the study goes beyond these two nuns. After researchers quantified the amount of positive feeling of the participants, it was discovered that 90 percent of the most-cheerful quarter was alive at age eighty-five versus only 34 percent of the least-cheerful quarter. Similarly, 54 percent of the most-cheerful quarter was alive at age ninety-four, in contrast to 11 percent of the least-cheerful quarter.[8]

In addition to this study, thousands of Mexican Americans from the southwest United States sixty-five years or older were given a battery of tests, demographic and emotional, and tracked for two years. Positive emotion strongly predicted who lived and who died, as well as predicting disability. In fact, researchers found that happy people were half as likely to die, and half as likely to become disabled. Positive emotion also protects against the ravages of aging, and happy people have better health habits, lower blood pressure, and better immune systems than unhappy people.

Not surprisingly, it also turns out that happier people are more satisfied with their jobs. In one study, employees were measured on the amount of positive emotion they had and were tracked on their job performance over eighteen months. Happier people received better evaluations from their supervisors and higher pay. In yet another study, children and adults who were made happy displayed more empathy and were more willing to donate money to those in need. When we are happy, we are less self-focused, we like others more, and we want to share our good fortune. On the other hand, when we are down, we become distrustful, turn inward, and focus on our

---

[8] Seligman, *Authentic Happiness*, 3–4.

own needs. Looking out for ourselves, then, is more characteristic of sadness than of well-being.[9]

Optimism and Pessimism

One of the centerpieces of Seligman's work is his analysis of optimism and pessimism, which he says dramatically affects happiness and health. He shows that pessimists have a pernicious way of construing setbacks and frustrations, in that they believe the cause is permanent, pervasive, and personal. Whenever something bad happens—a tax audit, marital squabble, a frown from a boss—they imagine the worst: bankruptcy, divorce, and dismissal. They're more prone to depression, they have long bouts of listlessness, and their health suffers. Optimists, on the other hand, have a strength that allows them to interpret setbacks as surmountable, particular to a single problem, and a result of temporary circumstances. Whenever bad events happen, they see them in the least-threatening light; they're temporary and surmountable, challenges to be overcome. Their health is excellent, and they come back from setbacks quickly, soon regaining energy.[10]

Interestingly, pessimists are up to eight times more likely to become depressed when bad events occur; they do worse at school, sports, and jobs; and they have worse physical health and shorter lives, and they have rockier interpersonal relationships. They seem to lose sight of the fact that most of what happens has multiple causes, yet they tend to latch onto the worst of them—the most permanent and pervasive one. People who have the most pessimistic explanatory style are likely, once they fail, to have symptoms of learned helplessness for a sustained period and across many endeavors, which can result in depression. On the other hand, people with an optimistic explanatory style tend to resist depression.

One helpful mechanism for breaking the pessimistic tendency is through another relatively new field (1980s) known as cognitive therapy, which teaches patients to dispute destructive beliefs. Patients

---

[9] Seligman, *Authentic Happiness*, 38–43.

[10] Seligman, *Learned Optimism* (New York: 1990), 4, 77.

are taught to generate alternative ideas and not leave the mind free to roam among the worst of them.[11] It is a well-documented method for building optimism that consists in first recognizing and then disputing pessimistic thoughts. Unfortunately, when we say groundless things to ourselves, we believe them because the source is ourselves, which we think is more credible than others. Trouble is that we can distort reality as much as if we were under the influence of a strong drug.

Studies show that the more therapy a person receives, the more thorough the change to optimism—and in turn, the greater the relief from depression. It is proven to prevent symptoms more permanently than drugs because patients acquire a skill they can use again without relying on medicine or doctors.

> I conclude from these studies that among people who are not now depressed, pessimistic explanatory style predicts who is going to get depressed. It also predicts who will stay depressed, and it predicts who will relapse after therapy. Changing explanatory style from pessimism to optimism relieves depression markedly.[12]

Optimism and Cardiovascular Disease

Findings on physical health have interesting implications as they relate to optimistic and pessimistic styles.[13] Men with the most optimistic styles had 25 percent less cardiovascular disease than average, and men with the least had 25 percent more than average. Because the trends have been strong, it indicates that greater optimism protects men where less optimism weakens them.

To illustrate, more than 20,000 healthy British adults were followed from 1996–2002, during which 994 died and 365 from cardiovascular disease. What is interesting is that many physical and psychological variables were measured. One of those was a sense of

---

[11] Seligman, *Authentic Happiness*, 24, 93, 96.

[12] Seligman, *Learned Optimism*, 81, 87, 89–91.

[13] Seligman, *Flourish*, 191–193. Other studies have shown similar results with the cold and flu viruses.

mastery. Mastery can be viewed as being the opposite of helplessness: people become helpless when they feel nothing they do affects their situation. With mastery, people feel their actions matter and have an effect on their situations.

In the study, the people high in mastery had 20 percent fewer deaths caused by cardiovascular disease than those with an average mastery, while people high in a sense of helplessness had 20 percent more deaths caused by cardiovascular disease than average. This held true of deaths to all causes. Similarly, in the largest study of the relationship between optimism and cardiovascular disease to date, ninety-seven thousand women (healthy at the outset beginning in 1994) were followed for eight years. The optimists had 30 percent fewer coronary deaths than pessimists: "The trend of fewer deaths, both cardiac and deaths from all causes, held across the entire distribution of optimism, indicating again that optimism protected women and pessimism hurt them relative to the average."[14]

Study after study shows similar results. Pessimism is strongly associated with mortality rates while optimism is associated with fewer deaths. Seligman provides three reasons why an optimistic style might make people less vulnerable to cardiovascular disease. First, they tend to take action and have healthier lifestyles, which makes sense given earlier findings that they believe their actions matter, whereas pessimists believe they're helpless and that theirs don't. Also, those with higher life satisfaction are more likely to diet, not smoke, and exercise regularly than those with lower satisfaction. Happy people have also been shown to sleep better than unhappy people.

Second, the more love and friends you have, the less illness you experience. People who have one person they were comfortable calling at three in the morning were healthier, while lonely people were much less healthy than sociable people. Happier people have richer social networks, and social connectedness contributes to a lack of disability as we age. "Misery may love company, but company does not love misery, and the ensuing loneliness of pessimists may be a

---

[14] Seligman, *Flourish*, 193.

path to illness."¹⁵ Third, there may be a biological mechanism at work in optimists not present to the same extent in pessimists. In a 1991 study, blood was taken from elderly optimists and pessimists and tested for immune response. The blood of the optimists had a feistier response to threat than the pessimists. One other biological possibility is a pathological circulatory response to repeated stress. As has been shown, pessimists give up and experience more stress, whereas optimists cope better with stress.

> Repeated episodes of stress, particularly when one is helpless, likely mobilize the stress hormone cortisol and other circulatory responses that induce or exacerbate damage to the walls of blood vessels and promote atherosclerosis. Sheldon Cohen . . . found that sad people secrete more of the inflammatory substance interleukin-6, and that this results in more colds. Repeated episodes of stress and helplessness might set off a cascade of processes involving higher cortisol and lower levels of the neurotransmitters known as catecholamines, leading to long-lasting inflammation. Greater inflammation is implicated in atherosclerosis, and women who score low in feelings of mastery and high in depression have been shown to have worse calcification of the major artery, the trunk-like aorta.¹⁶

Seligman says there are two things we can do to maximize our chances of living longer. The first is to be future-oriented—namely, to be drawn into the future as opposed to dwelling in the past. This means working not just for your personal future but also for the future of your family, nation, and ideals. His second item should come as no surprise: exercise.

Pessimism and Optimism at Work

There is an interesting flipside to what we have said so far. Evidence suggests that depressed people, while sadder, are actually wiser.¹⁷ In

---

[15] Seligman, *Flourish*, 206.

[16] Seligman, *Flourish*, 205–07, 213.

[17] Elster, *Alchemies of the Mind*, 300; Seligman, *Learned Optimism*, 109–12.

experiments that gauged how much control participants thought they had over events, depressed people were more accurate on when they did and did not have control. The nondepressed people were accurate when they had control, but when they were helpless, they were undeterred and still judged they had a great deal of control. Depressed people—mostly pessimists—accurately judge how much control they have, while nondepressed people—mostly optimists—believe they have much more control than they actually do—particularly when they are helpless and have no control at all.

Similar findings are found in experiments on how people judge their own skills. In one, depressed and nondepressed participants were put in a panel discussion and later asked to judge how well they did, which was then measured against the independent panel. The panel of observers judged that the depressed patients weren't very persuasive or likable; they had poor social skills, which is a symptom of depression. Depressed participants judged their lack of skill accurately. The nondepressed group, however, blatantly overestimated their skill and judged themselves as more persuasive and appealing than they actually were. In summary, there is clear evidence that nondepressed people distort reality in a self-serving way, with depressed people tending to see reality more accurately. "The pessimist seems to be at the mercy of reality, whereas the optimist has a massive defense against reality that maintains good cheer in the face of a relentlessly indifferent universe."[18]

But given the two tendencies, it seems there might be an important role for pessimism in some contexts. One of those could be in larger organizations, like a company, in which we'd want someone giving an accurate picture of reality. Within such an environment there exists a variety of personalities, *all of which* seem necessary to its optimal state. There are the optimists who tend to be the visionaries, dreaming things that don't yet exist. But Seligman asks us to imagine a company consisting only of optimists, all of which are fixed on the exciting possibilities ahead. It would be a disaster, which means the company also needs its pessimists, the people who have accurate knowledge of present realities. "They must make sure

---

[18] Seligman, *Learned Optimism*, 112.

grim reality continually intrudes upon the optimists. The treasurer, the CPAs, the financial vice-president, the business administrators, the safety engineers—all these need an accurate sense of how much the company can afford, and warn of danger. Their role is to caution, their banner is the yellow flag."[19]

The pessimists may be otherwise cheery except for their caution at the desk. Some may be prudent and measured people who've nurtured their pessimistic side in the company's service. "So the successful corporation," concludes Seligman, "has its optimists, dreamers, salesmen, and creators. But the corporation is a form of modern life that also needs its pessimists, the realists whose job it is to counsel caution. I want to underline, however, the fact that at the head of the corporation must be a CEO, sage enough and flexible enough to balance the optimistic vision of the planners against the jeremiads of the CPAs."[20]

The Balance Sheet: Optimism vs. Pessimism

After what we have said so far, you might think the balance sheet comes out on the side of optimism. However, we have seen that there are occasions when we need a dose of pessimism. The reality is that most of us experience both from time to time. In fact, evidence suggests that fluctuations in explanatory style visit us more at certain times of day or night, and when they do, we can see pessimism's constructive role. In its milder form, it pulls us back from risky optimistic exaggerations, making us think twice and keeping us from making foolhardy decisions. Our optimistic moments are the ones that contain great plans, dreams, and hopes—and in which reality is distorted to give dreams room to flourish. Without these times, we'd never accomplish anything difficult. Mount Everest would remain unscaled and Boeing would never have created the hugely risky 747. It is the dynamic tension between our optimism and pessimism that makes corrections to the excesses of the other. That tension allows us

---

[19] Seligman, *Learned Optimism*, 113.

[20] Seligman, *Learned Optimism*, 114.

to venture and retrench without danger, and as we move toward an extreme, the tension pulls us back.

Like the successful company, we each have an executive who balances the counsels of daring against the counsels of doom. When optimism prompts us to take a chance and pessimism tells us to recoil, a part of us heeds both. Seligman says the executive is sapience.

> It is the entity to whom is addressed the most basic point of this book: By understanding the single virtue of pessimism along with its pervasive, crippling consequences, we can learn to resist pessimism's constant calling, as deep-seated in brain or in habit as they may be. We can learn to choose optimism for the most part, but also to heed pessimism when it is warranted.[21]

In his best-selling business book *Good To Great*, Jim Collins refers to the same tension from a different viewpoint. In all of the visionary companies he examines—which generated cumulative stock returns that beat the general stock market by an average of seven times in fifteen years—pessimism is actually encouraged to run wild as long as it is kept within limits and held next to an "unwavering faith amid the brutal facts" (i.e., optimism). Thus the good-to-great companies *institutionalized* both characteristics and placed them side by side.

> The good-to-great leaders were able to strip away so much noise and clutter and just focus on the few things that would have the greatest impact. They were able to do so in large part because they operated from both sides of the Stockdale Paradox [understanding the brutal reality *and* having an unwavering faith that they would prevail], never letting one side overshadow the other.[22]

Instead of a compromise, Collins highlights a counterintuitive approach and shows how some organizations embed the dynamic tension between the two in corporate culture. Understanding the

---

[21] Seligman, *Learned Optimism*, 112–15.
[22] Collins, *Good To Great*, 85, 87.

brutal facts allows us to see the way things actually are. We saw this ability in George Washington. It is a recognition of where we sit in the big picture, which in turn provides us with crucial information about how to move forward. An unwavering faith is its necessary corollary, without which the fight could not be won or waged at all.

The Achievement of Christianity

It is clear that pessimism and optimism have implications for happiness. Based on the data, there is little doubt that explanatory styles have consequences on emotional and physical well-being. Nevertheless, we are missing something that grounds happiness beyond ourselves—or beyond man. Because I believe it has to have a firmer foundation, I want to conclude our discussion with the unique achievements of Christianity.

To do so, let's look at an alternative view of pessimism and optimism. G. K. Chesterton argued that both have significant downsides we need to recognize. The evil of the pessimist is that he does not have loyalty or love for what he criticizes; he looks at the colossal evil of the world and feels despair. He uses the freedom life gives to lure people away from its flag. The evil of the optimist is that he defends the indefensible and is less inclined to reform things and more inclined to give a front-bench official answer to all attacks, soothing everyone with assurances. The optimist won't wash the world so much as whitewash the world.[23] Chesterton argues that our attitude toward life could be better expressed as a sort of military loyalty than of criticism and approval. Thus, our acceptance of the world shouldn't be optimism but rather a cosmic patriotism, or primary loyalty:

> The world is not a lodging-house at Brighton, which we are to leave because it is miserable. It is the fortress of our family, with the flag flying on the turret, and the more miserable it is the less we should leave it. The point is not that this world is too sad to love or too glad not to love; the point is that when you do love a thing, its gladness

---

[23] G. K. Chesterton, *Orthodoxy* (San Francisco: 1995), 74–75, 77.

is a reason for loving it, and its sadness a reason for loving it more. All optimistic thoughts about England and all pessimistic thoughts about her are alike reasons for the English patriot. Similarly, optimism and pessimism are alike arguments for the cosmic patriot.[24]

What we *don't* want is a compromise between optimism and pessimism, just as we would not want joy and anger neutralizing each other to produce an unpleasant contentment. Being a mixture of two things, it weakens both, with neither present in its full strength or contributing its full color. What we want is a fiercer delight and a fiercer discontent. We want the two side by side in all their ferocity and at the top of their energy. The enemy is an amalgam or compromise of the two. He asks, can we be at once not only a pessimist and an optimist but a fanatical pessimist and a fanatical optimist?

To answer, Chesterton suggests that both ideas can be free to roam because each is kept in its place. The optimist can pour out all the praise he likes on the triumphant music of the march, the golden trumpets, and the purple banner going into battle. But he mustn't call the fight needless. The pessimist might draw the picture of the battle's wounds as darkly as he chooses. But he must not call the fight hopeless.[25] His point is that, taken separately, the optimists and the pessimists are not quite right enough to run the world. Having both coexist in all of their energy keeps black from evolving into a dirty gray. This strange equilibrium, argues Chesterton, is precisely the achievement of Christianity: "Christianity got over the difficulty of combining furious opposites, by keeping them both, and keeping them both furious. The Church was positive on both points. One can hardly think too little of one's self. One can hardly think too much of one's soul."[26]

---

[24] Chesterton, *Orthodoxy*, 72.

[25] Chesterton, *Orthodoxy*, 102–03.

[26] Chesterton, *Orthodoxy*, 100–01.

Confronting What Ails Us

With a both/and framework in place, we are now in a position to ask some tougher questions around how the presence of anxiety, guilt, and death impact a person's happiness. It is important because, sadly, our culture has managed to minimize or deny the one thing that seems undeniable: the abundance of evil in the world and ourselves. In the last century alone, tens of millions were executed in the most inhumane way by the totalitarianism of the Nazis, Stalinists, and Maoists. But suffering and evil aren't just a communist or fascist problem; they afflict human beings across culture, time, and space. With his typical poignance, Jordan Peterson notes our own capacity to act like a Nazi prison guard or a gulag archipelago (which is corroborated by several well-known experiments). We have an immense capacity for voluntary evil.[27] It is easy to forget that even the worst of the concentration camp guards were all too human. Only man can conceive of such things as at the rack or the iron maiden; only man inflicts suffering for the sake of suffering; and only man knows what it means to be exploited and how to exploit others.

> And with this realization we have well-nigh full legitimization of the idea, very unpopular in modern intellectual circles, of Original Sin... And who can deny the sense of existential guilt that pervades human experience? And who could avoid noting that without that guilt—that sense of inbuilt corruption and capacity for wrongdoing—a man is one step from psychopathy?[28]

To alleviate his guilt and anxiety, Jürgen Moltmann adds that man develops neurotic patterns and obsessions. He does so to repress his dread of having to face his grief, but where anxiety and guilt are suppressed, the result is apathy, insensitivity, and a life of obsessive repetitions. "He cannot accept the particular experiences of the anxiety of guilt, and so he builds up defense systems in which he encloses himself and which increasingly constrict his psyche."[29] Delivering only

---

[27] Peterson, *12 Rules*, 54–55, 179, 196–98.

[28] Peterson, *12 Rules*, 54–55.

[29] Moltmann, *The Crucified God*, 300–01.

temporary relief, these defenses end up strengthening the anxiety of guilt, making anxiety ever-present. The result is increasing apathy toward others because his energy is focused on repulsing the threat against him. In this sense his defenses become idols.

Given the harsh realities, I can't see how it is possible to address happiness absent something as fundamental as sin, which destroys man's emotional, physical, and spiritual well-being. This means that an answer to the happiness question must involve an answer to evil, especially the individual human capacity for evil. Interestingly, Peterson hints at a way forward. Citing Carl Jung, he says, "No tree can grow to Heaven unless its roots reach down to Hell,"[30] meaning that upward movement isn't possible without a corresponding move down. "Who is willing to do that?" Peterson asks, "Do you really want to meet who's in charge, at the very bottom of the most wicked thoughts?" The brutal truth lying in each of us, he argues, is why enlightenment is so rare. Understood this way, Jung is right. Avoiding what is beneath is like trying to cure disease by treating symptoms.

More consequential than he himself is willing to accept, Peterson says that this is where the idea of Christ's taking on the sins of humankind as if they were his own becomes key. "It means that Christ *is forever He who determines to take personal responsibility for the full depth of human depravity.*"[31] While Peterson seems to take this mythically (yet meaningfully), I have given sufficient reasons for regarding it as literally and historically true. At any rate, Moltmann hits the mark when he says that in humbling himself and becoming flesh, Jesus takes up suffering, anxious man into his situation. "In becoming weak, impotent, vulnerable and mortal, he frees man from the quest for powerful idols and protective compulsions and makes him ready to accept his humanity, his freedom and his mortality."[32] If man sees and believes God in the suffering and dying Jesus, he is set free from the concern to be his own god. Man in his corruption is in reality inhuman in the sense that he is not as God intended; and that is because he is under the compulsion of self-justification

---

[30] Peterson, *12 Rules*, 180.

[31] Peterson, *12 Rules*, 180.

[32] Moltmann, *The Crucified God*, 303.

and illusory self-deification. Unable to let God be God, he makes himself the unhappy god of his own self. But the cross liberates dehumanized man from his fatal obsession with being a god himself. "It sets him free from his inhuman hubris, to restore his true human nature. It makes the *homo incurvatus in se* [the man turned in on himself] once again open to God and his neighbor and gives Narcissus the power to love someone else."[33]

Thus we can see that happiness is conditioned on the resolution of sin and guilt, and man's capacity for voluntary evil. In one way or another, we all know this about ourselves, which is why we build defenses as protection from the constant threat posed by our own depravity. To speak of happiness without addressing such fundamental issues is superficial, and that is where Seligman misses the mark.

Conclusion

Despite the fact that people create havoc in their lives to attain it, we have seen how elusive happiness is—so much so that the greatest thinkers disagreed about what it is and how it should be sought. Seligman and his colleagues have done much to help, however. For the first time, we are able to look at raw data and see the emotional and physical effects of different thinking patterns—effects that shouldn't be ignored. How we think and our resulting explanatory styles matter a great deal. There is much to be said for developing a more optimistic style and minimizing the often-devastating effects of pessimism. At the same time, we have seen the downsides of all approaches, ancient and modern.

Man's capacity for evil and his sense of dread, anxiety, and guilt have to be dealt with if happiness is going to mean anything. Facing the brutal facts without trying to whitewash them is the key to moving toward a solution. Sin and evil must have a resolution for man's happiness to be realized. We have suggested that there is only one solution to man's problem of being alienated from himself and his compulsive desire to be his own sad little god: to see and believe God in the suffering and dying Jesus, who took up man's sin, guilt,

---

[33] Moltmann, *The Crucified God*, 69–72.

and anxiety and set him free from his self-protective compulsions. As St. Paul says, "God demonstrates His own love toward us, in that while we were yet sinners, Christ died for us." In this way he frees us from our self-love, from the Narcissus in all of us, and gives us the ability to love others. With the both/and framework suggested here, we can accept *both* the brutal reality of our own sin and guilt, *and* our unmerited forgiveness through the crucifixion of Jesus, who rose from the dead as the firstfruits of those who follow. Having the anxiety of guilt and sin taken up by Jesus and nailed to his cross, we are free to roam lavishly under his protection instead of our own pathetic idols. I can't imagine a more secure basis for human happiness.

With this said, Seligman's work on explanatory style is even more significant. Of all people, Christians have the surest justification for an optimistic explanatory style. God in Christ has had mercy on us and has forgiven our sins, guilt, and anxiety: all setbacks in life should be viewed as temporary and surmountable. Death itself has been defeated, and we too will be raised from the dead. Optimism has its place within Christianity to run wild. If this isn't the ultimate ground for happiness, I don't know what would be. But Christianity leaves pessimism with its role as well, in that we still need the brutal truth of our own continuing depravity, of our own capacity for voluntary evil, which will cling to us as long as we live this mortal life. The sixteenth-century Reformers put this within the framework of law and Gospel—the law condemning sin and evil and the Gospel offering the sweet words of forgiveness and absolution. As before in our both/and scenario, each must be maintained in all its ferocity for man's happiness to be possible. The law, in showing us our sin, drives us to the foot of the cross, where we hear absolution in those sweetest of words, "Given and shed for you for the forgiveness of your sins."

Finally, we saw research that when happy, we are less self-focused, we like others more, and we want to share our good fortune. When we are down, we become distrustful, turn inward, and focus on our own needs—which makes looking out for ourselves more characteristic of sadness than well-being. Being liberated from our own alienation and sin by the crucified God frees us to love others in a deeply meaningful way. It seems built into the universe that obsession with self closes us off from others, with liberation from our curvature inward the only cure. That is uniquely the answer of the cross.

Bibliography

Aland, Kurt and Barbara. *The Text of the New Testament: An Introduction to the Critical Editions and to the Theory and Practice of Modern Textual Criticism*. trans. Erroll F. Rhodes. Grand Rapids, MI: William B. Eerdmans Publishing Company, 1995.

Anthony, Scott D. "Kodak's Downfall Wasn't About Technology." *Harvard Business Review* (July 15, 2016).

Ashton, Kevin. *How To Fly A Horse*. New York: Doubleday, 2015.

Bauckham, Richard. *Jesus and the Eyewitnesses: The Gospels as Eyewitness Testimony*. Grand Rapids, MI: William B. Eerdmans Publishing Company, 2006.

———. *Jesus and the God of Israel: God Crucified and Other Studies on the New Testament's Christology of Divine Identity*. Grand Rapids, MI: William B. Eerdmans Publishing Company, 2008.

Bergeron, Joseph W., and Gary Habermas. "The Resurrection of Jesus: A Clinical Review of Psychiatric Hypotheses for the Biblical Story of Easter." *Irish Theological Quarterly* 80/2 (2015): 157–72.

Brown, Brené. *Rising Strong: How the Ability to Reset Transforms the Way We Live, Love, Parent, and Lead*. New York: Random House, 2017.

Brown, Raymond E. *The Death of the Messiah: From Gethsemane to the Grave, 2 vols*. New York: Doubleday, 1994.

Bruce, F.F. *The New Testament Documents: Are They Reliable?* 5th edition. Grand Rapids, MI: William B. Eerdmans Publishing Company, 1988.

Burridge, Richard A. *What Are the Gospels? A Comparison with Graeco-Roman Biography*. Grand Rapids, MI: William B. Eerdmans Publishing Company, 2004.

Burton, R. A. *On Being Certain: Believing You Are Right Even When You're Not*. New York: St. Martin's Press, 2008.

———. *Story as History—History as Story: The Gospel Tradition in the Context of Ancient Oral History*. Boston: Brill Academic Publishers, 2002.

Chesterton, G. K. *Orthodoxy*. San Francisco, CA: Ignatius Press, 1995.

Cohen, Geoffrey L. "Party Over Policy: The Dominating Impact of Group Influence on Political Beliefs." *Journal of Personality and Social Psychology* 85/5 (2003): 808–22.

Collins, Jim. *Good to Great: Why Some Companies Make the Leap . . . and Others Don't*. New York: Harper Business, 2001.

Craig, William Lane. *Assessing the New Testament Evidence for the Historicity of the Resurrection of Jesus*. New York: Edwin Mellen Press, 1989.

Craig, William Lane, and Bart D. Ehrman. "Is There Historical Evidence for the Resurrection of Jesus? A Debate Between William Lane Craig and Bart D. Ehrman" (2006). www.holycross.edu/assets/pdfs/resurrection_debate.pdf.

Dalio, Ray. *Principles*. New York: Simon & Schuster, 2017.

Damasio, Antonio. *Descartes' Error: Emotion, Reason, and the Human Brain*. New York: Penguin Books, 1994.

Downes, Larry, and Paul Nunes. "Blockbuster Becomes a Casualty of Big Bang Disruption." *Harvard Business Review* (November 7, 2013).

Duke, Annie. *Thinking in Bets: Making Smarter Decisions When You Don't Have All the Facts*. New York: Portfolio/Penguin, 2018.

Dunn, James D. G. *Jesus Remembered*. Grand Rapids, MI: William B. Eerdmans Publishing Company, 2003.

Elster, Jon. *Alchemies of the Mind: Rationality and the Emotions*. New York: Cambridge University Press, 1999.

Freeman, Joanne B. *The Field of Blood: Violence in Congress and The Road to Civil War*. New York: Macmillan, 2018.

Gavetti, Giovanni, Rebecca Henderson, and Simona Giorgi, "Kodak and the Digital Revolution (A)." *Harvard Business School* (Nov. 2, 2005).

Gerhardsson, Birger. *Memory and Manuscript: Oral Tradition and Written Transmission in Rabbinic Judaism and Early Christianity with Tradition and Transmission in Early Christianity.* Grand Rapids, MI: William B. Eerdmans Publishing Company, 1998.

Gilbert, Roberta. *The Eight Concepts of Bowen Theory: A New Way of Thinking about the Individual and the Group* (Lake Frederick, VA, 2004).

Goleman, Daniel. *Emotional Intelligence.* New York: Bantam Books, 1994.

Goodwin, Doris Kearns. *Leadership In Turbulent Times.* New York: Simon & Schuster, 2018.

Habermas, Gary. "Jesus' Resurrection and Contemporary Criticism: An Apologetic." *Criswell Theological Review*, Part 1, 4/1 (Fall 1989): 159–74.

———. "Jesus' Resurrection and Contemporary Criticism: An Apologetic." *Criswell Theological Review*, Part 2, 4/ 2 (Winter 1990): 373–85.

———. "The Late Twentieth-Century Resurgence of Naturalistic Responses to Jesus' Resurrection." *Trinity Journal*, 22 (2001): 179-196.

——— and Robert B. Steward, Eds. *Memories of Jesus: A Critical Appraisal of James D. G. Dunn's Jesus Remembered.* Nashville, TN: B & H Academic, 2010.

———. "The Minimal Facts Approach to the Resurrection of Jesus: The Role of Methodology as a Crucial Component in Establishing Historicity." *Southeastern Theological Review* 3/1 (Summer 2012): 15–26.

Hengel, Martin. *Crucifixion.* Philadelphia, PA: Fortress Press, 1977.

———. *Studies in Early Christology.* London: T & T Clark International, 2004.

———. *The Pre-Christian Paul.* London: SCM Press, 1991.

Hospers, John. *An Introduction to Philosophical Analysis.* Upper Saddle River, NJ: Prentice Hall, 1988.

Hurtado, Larry W. *Lord Jesus Christ: Devotion to Jesus in Earliest Christianity.* Grand Rapids, MI: William B. Eerdmans Publishing Company, 2003.

Kahneman, Daniel. *Thinking Fast and Slow.* New York: Farrar, Straus and Giroux, 2011.

Keener, Craig S. *The Historical Jesus of the Gospels.* Grand Rapids, MI: William B. Eerdmans Publishing Company, 2003.

LeDoux, Joseph. *The Emotional Brain: The Mysterious Underpinnings of Emotional Life*. New York: Simon & Schuster, 1996.

Lewis, C. S. *Miracles: How God Intervenes in Nature and Human Affairs*. New York: Collier Books, 1960.

Licona, Michael R. *The Resurrection of Jesus: A New Historiographical Approach*. Downers Grove, IL: IVP Academic, 2010.

McGrath, Alister. *A Scientific Theology: Volume 1—Nature*. Grand Rapids, MI: William B. Eerdmans Publishing Company, 2001.

———. *A Scientific Theology: Volume 2—Reality*. Grand Rapids, MI: William B. Eerdmans Publishing Company, 2002.

Metzger, Bruce M. *The Text of the New Testament: Its Transmission, Corruption, and Restoration*. 2nd edition. New York: Oxford University Press, 1968.

Moltmann, Jürgen. *The Crucified God: The Cross of Christ as the Foundation and Criticism of Christian Theology*. Minneapolis, MN: Fortress Press, 1993.

Montgomery, John Warwick. *The Suicide of Christian Theology*. Irvine, CA: NRP Books, 2015.

———. *Where Is History Going? A Christian Response to Secular Philosophies of History*. Minneapolis, MN: Bethany Fellowship, Inc., 1969.

Moreland, J. P. *Scaling the Secular City: A Defense of Christianity*. Grand Rapids, MI: Baker Book House, 1987.

Pannenberg, Wolfhart. *Systematic Theology*, vol. 2, trans. by Geoffrey W. Bromiley. Grand Rapids, MI: William B. Eerdmans Publishing Company, 1994.

Peterson, Jordan B. *12 Rules for Life: An Antidote to Chaos*. New York: Random House, 2018.

Richardson, Ronald W. *Family Ties That Bind: A Self-Help Guide to Change Through Family of Origin Therapy*. Vancouver: Self-Counsel Press, 2002.

Rosenzweig, Phil. *The Halo Effect . . . and the Eight Other Business Delusions That Deceive Managers*. New York: Free Press, 2007.

Rubin, David C., ed. *Autobiographical Memory*. New York: Cambridge University Press, 1986.

———. ed. *Remembering Our Past: Studies in Autobiographical Memory*. New York: Cambridge University Press, 1995.

Satell, Greg. "A Look Back at Why Blockbuster Really Failed And Why It Did not Have To" (2014). https://www.forbes.com/sites/gregsatell/2014/09/05/a-look-back-at-why-blockbuster-really-failed-and-why-it-didnt-have-to/#605b35a1d64a.

Seligman, Martin E. P. *Authentic Happiness*. New York: Atria, 2002.

———. *Flourish*. New York: Atria, 2011.

———. *Learned Optimism*. New York: Vintage Books, 1990.

Tobore, Onojighofia. "On Energy Efficiency and the Brain's Resistance to Change: The Neurological Evolution of Dogmatism and Close-Mindedness" (2018). https://journals.sagepub.com/doi/abs/10.1177/0033294118792670?journalCode=prxa.

Vansina, Jan. *Oral Tradition as History*. New York: James Currey, 1997.

White, Nicholas. *A Brief History of Happiness*. Oxford: Blackwell Publishing, 2006.

Wright, N. T. *Paul: A Biography*. New York: Harper One, 2018.

———. *The Resurrection of the Son of God*. Minneapolis, MN: Fortress Press, 2003.

Zaltman, Gerald. *How Customers Think: Essential Insights into the Mind of the Market*. Boston: Harvard Business School Press, 2003.

www.ingramcontent.com/pod-product-compliance
Lightning Source LLC
LaVergne TN
LVHW041332080426
835512LV00006B/410